Mystical Murders

John Dunning has had a varied and adventurous career, including service in the US Navy and the Shanghai Municipal Police. He spent four years in a Japanese POW camp during the Second World War and then worked in American intelligence. He subsequently became a journalist, travelling to China and Europe. Now a full-time writer, he lives in Luxembourg. He is the top-selling author of murder stories for *True Detective* magazines and has written over a thousand accounts of true crime.

Also in Arrow by John Dunning

MYSTICAL MURDERS

John Dunning

ARROW BOOKS

Arrow Books Limited
20 Vauxhall Bridge Road, London SW1V 2SA

An imprint of Random Century Group

London Melbourne Sydney Auckland
Johannesburg and agencies throughout
the world

First published in 1989

Photypeset by Input Typesetting Ltd, London

Printed and bound in Great Britain by
Courier International Ltd, Tiptree, Essex

ISBN 0 09 963530 5

CONTENTS

INTRODUCTION

Of motives for murder, the occult is one of the more rare. Few people today are burned by their neighbours as witches. Only occasionally is the black mass celebrated with a human sacrifice.

This is not due to lack of interest in the so-called supernatural – an illogical term as anything that exists is, by necessity, natural. Probably a higher proportion of people in the world today believe in some form of the supernatural than during the Middle Ages.

Part of this is due to modern methods of merchandizing. Many magazines carry full-page advertisements for good luck charms, amulets, love potions, correspondence courses in sorcery or introductions into the theory and practice of devil worship. Such advertising is expensive and, as it continues to appear, it may be assumed that business is brisk.

Belief in either the occult or more conventional religions generally reflects a search for immortality. Regarded dispassionately, there is some justification for the conclusion that evil is the stronger power. The basic principles of life on earth are not conducive to faith in the existence of a compassionate deity.

A central principle is the food chain, in which all sentient beings kill and devour the weaker, often with appalling cruelty, and are, in turn, killed and devoured by the stronger.

At the top of the chain, humans kill and sometimes devour all of the rest and each other as well.

Reassurances by propagandists to the contrary, war

has not been banished. Only the Americans and the Europeans have temporarily stopped killing each other. Elsewhere, war casualties since the Second World War have been higher than during it.

At the same time, any sense of permanence in the world has been eroded by technology. Vast oceans of information wash over the heads of a populace neither technically qualified nor intellectually inclined to understand it.

Events and developments, some real, some media inventions, arise and vanish with bewildering speed for obscure reasons and in obscure parts of the world.

In this restless universe of relentless permutation, the individual struggles to retain faith in an immortal soul which may, perhaps, one day relive the sunny, unending summers of childhood, the ecstasy of first love, the comfort of old friendship, the scent of flowers, the colours of sunset, the taste of food.

Belief in God or the devil supposes faith, and faith is the most lethal of human qualities. It was faith that fuelled the Inquisition, the Crusades, the Cultural Revolution in China, the Cambodian genocide and other great butcheries, past and present. It was faith too that resulted in the immolation of one little girl in Belgium. Her murderers were desperate. Their personal immortality was at stake.

People who sacrifice children to Satan do not necessarily dislike children. Nor do I, although it is comforting to think that they will eventually grow out of the condition.

Assuming, of course, that they survive – but here I shall, for once, refrain from my usual appeal for an end to the torturing and murdering of children.

For over ten years now I have been making such appeals and, during this time, the number of martyred children has never ceased to increase.

Nor will I ask people to discontinue to vote into office politicians who advocate the rehabilitation and release of those convicted of crimes against children.

The result will be the same.

Fortunately, not everyone interested in the occult finds it desirable to sacrifice children. For many, it represents merely an opportunity to dance around campfires with nude members of the opposite sex, an activity involving healthful light exercise and no greater risk than the possibility of a head cold – disregarding AIDS and the off chance that other members of the coven may be as mad as born-again maoists. Confusion over the difference between sex and sadism can be fatal.

Otherwise, the occult usually enters into murder only peripherally. Clairvoyants in many countries have had astounding success in locating the bodies of victims. Haunted castles have turned out to have remarkably solid ghosts. People have become convinced that they were vampires or werewolves and have acted accordingly. A fifty-year-old tailor was magically transformed into a transvestite prostitute. Fairly routine stuff.

Many occult phenomena noted here and elsewhere are real and not readily explained by traditional science. Indeed, science has been investigating for some time now such paranormal manifestations as clairvoyance, telepathy, telekinesis and out-of-the-body experiences.

It is gratifying to learn that such phenomena apparently do exist, for they indicate an aspect of living things that is not material and which could, therefore, survive the dissolution of the body.

We are, it seems, getting back to the idea of a soul, which would be a comforting thing.

For if there is a soul, it may be immortal.

And immortality, if you do not think too much about what that implies, is an attractive prospect.

AMATEUR EXORCIST

There was something about this visitor that Wednesday morning of 22 April 1987 that Pastor Herbert Jaeger did not like. The man made him nervous.

Not that there was anything very remarkable about his appearance. He was clean, neatly dressed and, if his wavy dark hair was down to his shoulders, it was, at least, carefully combed and trimmed as was the tiny black wisp of a goatee beneath his lower lip and the thin pointed moustache above.

Perhaps it was the eyes – too dark, too liquid, filled with quick gleams and movements, almost as if something alien was lurking in their depths.

'Driving a stake through a person's heart is not exorcism,' said the pastor a little unsteadily. 'Not even in the Catholic church.'

'But it will prevent the devil from taking possession?' asked the man, looking earnestly into the pastor's face.

The pastor recoiled slightly, his bluff red features troubled. He was a big man himself, in good condition despite his fifty years, but this strange visitor was bigger and younger. Was he dangerous?

It was a question that he had had to ask himself more than once in the past. A pastor of a parish church in a city of three-quarters of a million inhabitants such as Essen, West Germany, naturally received some strange and even dangerous visits. It was a part of the job.

This one was stranger than most. He had turned up at just after nine o'clock, mumbling that his name was

Frank Something-or-Other and that he wanted to confess.

Jaeger had pointed out that there was no confession in the Lutheran Church, but had said he was willing to listen if it would help.

The man had promptly gone into a description of what he apparently thought was an encounter with the devil.

'He appeared at the window,' said the man in a low awe-filled voice. 'He had a trident in his hand and, on his brow, a great ruby burned like fire. I aimed my right index finger at him and I shot away the trident. He became a cloud hanging over my friend. When it disappeared, I knew that he had entered into possession of Rudi. I had to do it. He would have come again.'

'Do what?' the pastor asked uncomfortably.

'Hammer the stake through his heart,' said the man.

The pastor swallowed, collected himself briefly and sought for the right words. The man was clearly seriously disturbed mentally. The only reasonable course was to send him to a doctor.

'You have had a bad dream,' he said soothingly. 'We all have bad dreams, sometimes even when we are awake. Perhaps you have been reading books or watching films about vampires and zombies. These things do not really exist. A long time ago, people believed that they did and they drove stakes through the hearts of innocent persons because they were afraid that they would come back from the dead. No one can come back from the dead. It was only superstition. We know better now.'

He was uneasily aware that not everyone did know better now. Essen, he often suspected, numbered proportionately more believers in the occult now than ever before. Half the programmes on television dealt with vampires, zombies or the living dead, and the press was full of advertisements for occult trinkets and satanist groups openly soliciting adherents.

'You should go home now and take a rest,' he concluded. 'It would be good for you to see a doctor. He

2

can help you. If you don't know any doctor, I can give you the name of a good one.'

'What can a doctor do against the devil?' the man asked sombrely, but he got up from his chair and left with no further objections, as if he was going to follow the pastor's advice.

The pastor closed the door behind him and went back to his study. It was a fine spring day with a playful little breeze and an astonishing amount of sun. Industrial activity in Essen, in the heart of the iron triangle of the Ruhr, was at such a low level that air pollution had actually been reduced.

It was a cheerful sort of day, but Jaeger felt chilled, shaken, vaguely frightened, as if something evil had touched him in passing. Despite the morning sun pouring in through the windows, the comfortable old rectory seemed full of eerie shadows.

Was it true? Was Satan a real, physical being?

The Bible said he was, and the Bible was Truth.

Pastor Jaeger shuddered.

The Volkwang substation of the Essen Police is not very conspicuous. One of the smaller stations, it lies tucked behind a seven-foot brick wall with only the sign *Polizeiwache* to identify it.

Perhaps for this reason, it receives fewer freak reports than most of the stations within the urban complex.

'This one was a doozy though,' said Otto Weber, the desk sergeant. 'The fellow was totally out of his mind. Said he'd driven a stake though the devil's heart.'

'What did he look like?' asked Sergeant Willi Kronhaeuser, the patrol car dispatcher, who had just come on duty. 'Was that today?'

'Around two o'clock,' said Weber. 'He looked goofy. Sort of fat face with a little goatee and a moustache. Hair down around his shoulders. High on something. LSD, perhaps. They get hallucinations sometimes.'

'And he just walked in and said, "I drove a stake through the devil's heart,"?' said Kronhaeuser, a small, leathery man with a large nose.

3

'Ah no,' said Weber, pushing his heavy body back from the desk so that he could rest his feet on the pulled-out bottom drawer. 'Whole performance about how the devil appeared with his pitchfork and a ruby in his hand. I told him to go to the hospital.'

'Did he?' asked the dispatcher, running his eyes over the big board on the wall to see where his patrol cars were at the moment.

'Don't know,' said the desk sergeant. 'He got out of here, anyway.'

'That was the main thing,' said Kronhaeuser absently.

'That was the main thing,' agreed Weber.

At the Essen General Hospital, Nurse Ilse Bauer had come on duty at five o'clock and was passing through the front entrance hall on the way to her station when she was stopped by the receptionist.

'There's a man here who's either crazy or under the influence of something,' she said. 'Do you think I should call one of the doctors?'

'No,' said Ilse. 'Half Essen is crazy or under the influence of something. Where is he? I'll talk to him.'

The man waiting on the green plastic sofa did not look as if he was crazy or under the influence of something. He was, thought Ilse, rather chic. There were far weirder types in the discotheques where she spent her evenings off.

'What's your problem?' she asked, sitting down on the sofa next to him.

'I drove a stake through my friend's heart because he was possessed by the devil,' said the man, 'but nobody seems to care. I've been to a parson and to the police, but they just tell me to go and lie down. I think Rudi should be buried.'

'So do I,' said Ilse. 'What have you been taking?'

She was a small girl, dark-haired, with the tilted, oval eyes of a fawn, but, like many nurses, astonishingly strong and tough. The man had probably been experimenting with some bizarre combination of drugs, she

4

thought, if she knew what it was, she could decide what action to take.

'I had a beer and a hot wurst in a bun for lunch,' said the man matter-of-factly.

Ilse laid her hand on his cheek and turned his head to look into his eyes.

The pupils were not contracted, but there seemed to be something deep within those eyes that she had never seen before and never wanted to see again. She did not know what it was, but the effect was nearly like an electric shock.

'Where is your friend?' she said, her voice inexplicably hoarse.

'Seventy-three Rheinbaben Strasse,' said the man. 'Our room's on the second floor.'

'You wait here,' said Ilse. 'I'm going to make a telephone call and I'll be right back.'

But she did not make the telephone call. Instead, she asked the receptionist to do it.

'This man is seriously disturbed,' she said. 'Call the emergency police service and tell them that there may be a murder at seventy-three Rheinbaben. They should send someone here to pick this man up.'

She had not wanted to take the time to call herself because she was afraid the man would leave. When she returned to the sofa, however, he was gone.

At police headquarters, the call was processed routinely. As it was a call from the hospital, it was not a crank report, but neither had it been confirmed. The first thing was confirmation, and the dispatcher sent in his nearest patrol car.

Patrol car Dora-Ulrich-Seven with Patrolman First Class Karl Fichter at the wheel and Patrolman Second Class Juergen Krause in the front seat next to him was, at this time, four blocks away and rolling eastwards on Morike Strasse.

Fichter immediately switched on the blue warning lights, made a U-turn and proceeded with prudent speed through heavy traffic to seventy-three Rheinbaben.

'That's government housing,' said Krause. He had grown up in the district and knew it well. 'Temporary centre for DDR refugees.'

Enough people managed to escape from the Deutsche Demokratische Republik – communist East Germany – to make housing arrangements for them necessary in many of the larger cities.

'Probably a fight,' said Fichter. 'The Comrades disagreeing over the hidden significance of the words of Holy St Marx.'

He was bitterly antisocialist, and with reason. He was eleven years old in 1944 and remembered only too well fleeing Prussia with his mother and sisters before the advancing communist hordes. Prosperous landowners, they had lost everything – including his father, who had been killed at Stalingrad.

A man so big that he looked out of place in a normal patrol car, Fichter had one great drawback as a police officer. He could not stand the sight of blood. This explained why, at age forty-four, he was still a patrolman first class. There are few aspects of police work in big cities that do not involve seeing blood.

Krause, who was exactly half his age and nearly as big, was already due for promotion to first class and would, barring accidents, be a sergeant within less than five years.

As the dispatcher had said nothing about stakes driven through hearts or even that there was a possibility of murder, Fichter led the way up to the second floor and began going through the half-dozen flats, one after another.

It was now approaching six o'clock in the evening and someone was at home in all the flats but one.

After ringing the doorbell and hammering vainly on the door panels, Fichter took a look at the lock, got something out of his pocket and expertly opened the door as easily as if he had had the key.

The flat was precisely like all of the others: a small entrance hall with a living room and kitchen opening off

6

to the left, two bedrooms to the right and the bathroom on the end.

The officers advanced into the living room, found the place untidy but unremarkable, moved on to the first bedroom, where the bed had not been slept in, and opened the door to the second bedroom.

Patrolman First Class Fichter looked inside, staggered back a step and fell in a faint on the floor of the hall.

Patrolman Second Class Krause remained rooted in the doorway.

The room contained a wardrobe, a straight-backed chair, two night tables and a bed. Lying on the bed, flat on his back, legs together and arms spread wide to form a cross, was the body of a man. He was wearing pyjamas, but there was no square inch of the material that was not dark reddish-brown with partially dried blood. Around him, sheets, bed cover, pillowcases and the headboard of the bed itself were uniformly stained with the same substance. It seemed impossible that one human body could have contained so much blood.

Standing stiffly up from the man's chest was a three-foot round wooden stake, its length marked with bloody handprints.

'Jesus, Mary and Joseph!' gasped Krause, crossing himself.

He was not Catholic, but, under the circumstances, no other response seemed adequate.

In the hall, Fichter grunted and sat up.

'Tripped,' he mumbled shakily, getting to all fours and then to his feet, but keeping his head turned away from the sight in the bedroom. 'You guard the flat. I'll call headquarters for the homicide people.'

Krause was not sensitive to the sight of blood, but he too had no desire to linger at the scene. He retired to the entrance hall while Fichter went down to the patrol car and radioed in his report to the waiting dispatcher.

It was a very emphatic confirmation of murder and at police headquarters things began to happen.

Detective Inspector Hans Kettenmeyer, who had

taken over the duty in Homicide Three at four o'clock, was hurriedly summoned from the canteen, where he had been having a light supper with his assistant, Sergeant of Detectives Klaus Metternach. Dr Wilhelm Fiedler, the duty medical officer, was called away from his office. The duty technical crew in the police laboratory was alerted and the drivers of the police cars and vans were ordered to the loading entrance. Within half an hour, Homicide Three was on its way, thirty man strong, to the scene of the murder.

'Sticky one according to the desk,' volunteered the sergeant, who was sitting in the front seat next to the driver.

He was a moderately brash young man who dressed trendily and wore his straight yellow hair down to his collar. As he had the flattened nose and rugged face of a boxer, the effect was incongruous.

The inspector, who was sitting with the doctor in the back seat, grunted in recognition that something had been said.

Although a scant ten years older than the sergeant, he looked as if he belonged to another generation altogether. An athletic man with a square-jawed, high-cheekboned face and a thick, drooping, iron-grey moustache, he was inclined to conservative suits, quiet ties and shirts with button-down collars.

The doctor gazed morosely out of the window and said nothing. A weedly, hollow-cheeked man with liquid brown eyes deepset under bushy eyebrows, he was not happy in his work and would have preferred to be in private practice. That, however, required capital – and the doctor had none. In such cases, the classic solution was to marry money, but in this the doctor had so far been unsuccessful.

He was a competent medical officer and, as soon as the photographer had completed the practical record of scene and body as found, he set briskly to work.

'Great number of deep stab wounds,' he called to the inspector, who was standing in the doorway waiting to

8

hear his findings. 'Too many to count here, but over thirty. He's been dead eighteen or nineteen hours.'

'Midnight of last night,' said the inspector, effortlessly counting backwards. 'The stake?'

'It's through where an ignorant person would think the heart would be,' said the doctor. 'Forced in after death, without doubt. It looks as if it may have been driven through the throat and pulled out again. It wasn't used to kill him.'

'Witchcraft,' said the inspector. 'The living dead and all that hogwash.'

'Not entirely hogwash,' said the doctor. 'It had the power to kill this man.'

The inspector snorted.

'Superstition,' he growled. 'That's your estimate of the motive then? Somebody staked a witch?'

'From the appearance of the body, yes,' said the doctor. 'There can be other motives as well, of course.'

'Or this could be a faked motive,' said the inspector.

'That too,' said the doctor. 'It's been done exactly the way you can see it done on television any night in the week.'

'And is that authentic?' said the inspector.

'Fairly,' said the doctor.

His duties at the scene were now completed and he returned to police headquarters to prepare for the autopsy. Knowing Inspector Kettenmeyer, he suspected that he would have to perform the best part of it that night.

He was not mistaken, but the body arrived at the morgue more quickly than he had expected and he was soon finished.

The removal of the stake from the chest of the corpse presented the greatest difficulty as it was wedged between the ribs, and he knew the laboratory would not want him to handle it any more than necessary.

Otherwise, it was largely a matter of counting the wounds. The victim had, apparently, been knocked unconscious with a violent blow to the left temple before the stabbing began, for the skull was fractured and there were no defence cuts on the hands or arms.

All told, there were forty-two stab wounds and one large hole in the throat where the stake had been driven in and pulled out.

The stab wounds had been the cause of death, which had taken place at approximately midnight of the twenty-first.

It was now midnight of the twenty-second and the inspector and sergeant had just returned from the scene of the crime to find the doctor waiting in the office.

'Well?' said the inspector.

The doctor ran quickly over the results of the autopsy.

'No sex. His last meal was bread and cheese and two bottles of beer,' he said. 'He may have been asleep when he was knocked unconscious. He didn't know it was coming. The adrenaline level in the blood was normal.'

'A wonder there was any blood left to test,' said the sergeant. 'I never saw such a mess in – '

'We have a suspect,' the inspector interrupted. 'Victim's roommate. They came over from the DDR together on February second of this year. No indications of whether they knew each other previously or not. The dead man's name is Rudolf Frentrup. He was thirty-one. The suspect is Frank Hedemeier, aged thirty-five. He's a baker by profession, but currently unemployed.'

'The place was full of occult stuff,' said the sergeant. 'Books, magazines, videos. Lot of zombies. I suspect – '

'I've spread the story to the newspapers,' said the inspector. 'It'll run in the morning editions.'

The doctor raised his eyebrows. The German criminal police are normally cautious about releases to the press.

'There's somebody running around out there who believes in witches and the devil,' said the inspector. 'He took his knife with him and I dare say he'll be able to turn up another stake, if he needs one.'

The people of Essen were being given fair warning.

'Do you know what he looks like?' asked the doctor.

'No,' said the inspector. 'We couldn't get a description at the hospital. We don't know what he looks like.'

But Pastor Jaeger did, and no sooner had he opened his morning paper than he realised that he had to call the police, and immediately did so.

'I should have called yesterday,' he apologized. 'I could see that the man was seriously disturbed. It was utterly irresponsible of me . . .'

'It doesn't matter,' said the detective first class who had been sent around to take his statement. 'By the time he turned up here, the victim had already been dead for over twelve hours.'

He left unmentioned the additional time that the murderer had gained before the discovery of the body, and the police fears that there might by now be other victims.

In the Volkwang substation, Sergeant Weber, dropping by to check the duty roster, caught sight of the headlines of the newspaper on the desk and froze.

'*Donnerwetter!*' he exclaimed.

The sergeant's description was added to Pastor Jaeger's. Both corresponded well to the one provided by Nurse Ilse Bauer, who had called shortly after the inspector and the sergeant returned to headquarters to ask if the man had been arrested. She was afraid that he might still be lurking around the hospital. She did not, of course, know that he had murdered anyone.

A red-faced sergeant, who should have realized that the person calling in the report would have a description, went to the hospital, took her statement personally and stationed a patrol car at the hospital entrance.

By eight o'clock in the morning, every police unit in the city had been provided with the man's description and orders to detain by use of all necessary force and, at eight-thirty, the inspector, who had had two hours' sleep in one of the detention cells, reported to the commissioner in charge of the case.

'No sighting of the suspect,' he said, 'and no further homicide reports.'

'Well, that's something,' said the commissioner.

'What's wrong with him, anyway? Is it drugs or is he psychopathic?'

'We don't think he's on drugs,' said the inspector, 'but there's no information on his medical history. He wouldn't be the first psychopath they've sent us from the DDR.'

'Beautiful arrangement,' commented the commissioner. 'They label their criminals and psychopaths dissidents, and we pay them to send them to us. It's a pity we can't find somebody to pay us for ours.'

'Or take them for nothing,' agreed the inspector, 'but I suppose some of them really are dissidents.'

'It doesn't make them any less crazy,' said the commissioner.

The inspector returned to the office, where he found the sergeant drinking black coffee and chain-smoking black-tobacco cigarettes.

The inspector accepted some of both and asked what had happened in his absence.

'Nothing,' said the sergeant. 'We've got all the pastors, all the hospitals and all the police substations staked out. If he's not busy killing somebody, he may try to turn himself in again today.'

The inspector nodded. It was he who had given the orders for the stakeouts, although staking out a police station seemed a strange thing to do.

'You ran a records check of similar cases?' he asked.

The sergeant nodded.

'Nothing like it in twenty years,' he said. 'Some villagers got together and burned an alleged witch over near Iserlohn about nine years ago, but it was a whole mob, not one man.'

'He probably isn't homicidal all the time then, or there'd be other cases on record,' said the inspector hopefully. 'It's usually some specific thing sets them off – a full moon or something.'

'It's the full moon tonight,' said the sergeant gloomily.

He did not know whether it was the full moon or not,

but he was unhappy and he felt that the inspector should be too.

The inspector was less unhappy than apprehensive, but at four o'clock that afternoon, while he was taking another nap in the detention cells, the case abruptly ended as Frank Hedemeier walked into the charge room at police headquarters and inquired when and where Rudolf Frentrup's funeral was going to take place.

Sent for observation to the psychiatric clinic in Eickelborn, Hedemeier devoted himself to further studies in the occult. He attempted to sell his soul to the devil by writing three wishes on bits of paper in his own blood and hiding them where they were ultimately found by the nurses.

There was a certain inconsistency in this, as he had sought to exorcise the devil from his friend by driving a stake through his heart.

Consistency was not, however, one of Frank Hedemeier's more prominent characteristics, and the psychiatrists came to the conclusion that neither was sanity. On 20 February 1988 he was ordered confined in an institution for the criminally insane until relieved of his mental problems.

It is thought that this may take some time, possibly longer than Frank Hedemeier can be expected to live.

2

THE MUMMY AND THE
VANISHING BATHROOM

It was past ten o'clock in the morning on that chilly Monday of 8 December 1986 when Olivier Belmont, student at the Sorbonne, descended from his attic room.

He was planning, with scant enthusiasm, to go for a walk along the Seine. There were over four hours to kill before his first lecture at two-thirty and he could not afford to sit in cafés.

Outside, it was snowing, and the high humidity of the Paris basin cut sharper than the barely freezing temperature, but the lack of heating, which eliminated the expense of a refrigerator in winter, made occupancy of his room untenable.

It was, of course, an old building. Ménilmontant is in the twentieth arrondissement, on the eastern edge of Paris, and the rue des Pyrénées, traversing it from northwest to southeast, has many decrepit rented properties.

It was an indication of the difficulty of finding any kind of housing in Paris that Olivier was usually delighted with his grubby little studio on the fifth floor of number 94, which, had it not been on the wrong side of the building and had there been any windows, would have enjoyed a view of the famous Père Lachaise cemetery.

His delight was, however, more intense in summer than in winter and it was in a decidedly grumpy humour that he felt his way down the dark, steep stairs.

He was bundled in nearly everything he owned – long underwear, woollen shirt, woollen trousers, thick sweater, boots, duffelcoat, scarf, ski-cap – all the result of hard bargaining at the Flea Market.

He did not yet know that he would be spending much of his day in the heated twentieth arrondissement police station. His first step in that direction occurred only when he arrived at the fourth-floor landing and found himself confronted with an alarming sight.

The door to one of the four flats was standing half open!

There are places in the world where an open flat door is not remarkable, but the twentieth arrondissement of Paris is not one of them. Even with the door locked, people sometimes return from an hour's shopping to find their flat bare as the interior of a blown egg.

Belmont did not know any of the tenants of the fourth or any other floor and, as a prudent big-city dweller, should have reacted to such an ominous scene by averting his gaze and hurrying on by, but Olivier Belmont came from the small southern town of Avignon and he had a dangerously well developed sense of civic responsibility.

He therefore went up to the door, knocked on it and called out, 'Hello there inside! Anybody home?'

There was no reply, but the knocking caused the door to swing wider open and he could see into the bedroom at the end of the short entrance hall.

A woman was lying half across the bed on her back, her nightgown up above her waist and her legs and arms sprawled. She did not look as if she were sleeping.

'Madame!' cried Belmont more loudly than he had intended, startled by the open door, the lack of movement and the immodest posture.

The sound of his voice was swallowed up by the unnatural stillness of the flat and an eerie sensation of strangeness swept over him. It was as if something was waiting silently there in those chilly, dark rooms and there was an odour which he could not identify, but which made his gorge rise.

Although neither big nor athletic, Belmont was courageous. Pushing the door completely open, he entered the bedroom and bent over to press his ear against the woman's chest.

There was no sound or movement and the flesh was icy cold. The woman was unquestionably dead and, although he could see no sign of injuries, her face was contorted in what looked like a grimace of pain. Taking into consideration the open door and the position of the body, it seemed probable that she had been raped and murdered.

The conclusion was oddly reassuring. Rape and murder were commonplace in Paris. There had been upward of thirty such cases reported in the newspapers within the past year and a half. Closing the door behind him, he went downstairs to the nearest café and telephoned the police.

To the surprise of the officer receiving the call, he identified himself and said he would wait outside the flat for the police to arrive.

This they did very quickly but, initially, only in the form of a patrol car, as it had first to be determined that there really was a dead woman at number 94 rue des Pyrénées and that the call was not the work of a practical joker, a cop-hating young revolutionary or someone under the influence of narcotics.

Once the accuracy of the report had been confirmed, the patrolman took Belmont into custody and radioed the station that they were at the scene of a murder.

In fact, they were not. An Inspector Jerome Saumier, a Sergeant Alain Rochereau and a Dr Yves Paulin soon arrived at the scene, but undertook no investigation as the doctor's examination of the corpse indicated that Mrs Colette Beulet had died of a heart attack.

'She probably felt it coming on and went to the door to seek help,' he said. 'Nobody heard her, and she staggered back to the bed.'

'No possibility of an induced heart attack?' said the inspector. 'I don't like that open door.'

'None that I can see,' said the doctor. 'There's not a

mark on the body. We'll have to see what the autopsy turns up.'

'Nothing seems to have been disturbed,' said Sergeant Rochereau, who had just finished going through the other rooms of the flat. 'Small amounts of money and some valuables lying about.'

'All right. Natural causes then,' said the inspector. 'What's that you have there, Alain?'

'Seems to be a diary for nineteen eighty-six,' said the sergeant. 'Probably nothing in it, but I thought I'd better check it out.'

There was little that the sergeant did not check out. A small, lean man with reddish-blond hair and sharp, foxy features, he suffered from an excess of energy which kept him coursing constantly about like a dog hunting rabbits.

Operations at the scene were concluded and the body transferred to the morgue, but Olivier Belmont was still going to miss his two-thirty lecture.

Even though the death was due to natural causes and there would be neither investigation nor suspects, Belmont was taken to the station and questioned at length.

The inspector, a tall man, raw-boned and bronzed as if he spent a great deal of time outdoors, although he was rarely able to leave the office, was Paris born and bred and he found it difficult to believe that any sane person would involve himself in the death of a stranger.

Mrs Beulet was fifty-nine and had some money. Belmont was twenty and had none. They lived in the same building. Under such circumstances arrangements sometimes arose, and Mrs Beulet's death might not be due to natural causes after all.

Belmont, who was conservatively minded, was mildly shocked by the inspector's insinuations, but grateful for the heated office and the free coffee and cigarettes he received while being questioned.

He therefore accepted his release almost reluctantly when Dr Paulin came over from the morgue to report that the essential part of the autopsy was completed and that the cause of death was definitely cardiac arrest. The time, he estimated, had been approximately three in the morning of that same day.

'Her head was as weak as her heart,' observed the sergeant rather callously, laying Mrs Beulet's diary on the inspector's desk. 'Read that when you get the time. The lady thought she was being molested by a mummy.'

'A mummy was it?' said the inspector. 'I'll take a look at it tonight.'

He was not surprised. A criminal investigations officer in Paris ran into things to make a mummy seem positively banal.

He was only marginally more impressed after having gone through the diary.

'She certainly had a macabre imagination,' he commented. 'A mummy trying to have sex with her while she was sleeping? No wonder she had a heart attack.'

'We could maybe sell it to television,' said the sergeant. 'I suppose I'd better turn it over to the heirs, though.'

The heirs were a fourth cousin named Paul Cartier and his wife, Mathilde. Neither had ever met Mrs Beulet, but they were her only living relatives and they were legally responsible for her burial expenses.

Consequently, they descended upon the flat in the rue des Pyrénées with the intention of plundering it of anything saleable and were pleased to find that Mrs Beulet's possessions would more than pay for her funeral.

'And,' said Mathilde, 'we should be able to get a good price for the lease. It's not a bad flat.'

Actually, it was a very bad flat – dark, gloomy, cramped and none too clean – but, in Paris, there were people who would kill to get it.

'Then somebody is going to have to stay here until we find a buyer,' said Paul. 'If the owner learns that she's dead, he'll grab it himself.'

The owner most assuredly would. He had probably

been trying to get the tenants out for years. It was the only way that he could hope to increase the rent.

'I'll send Gerda over,' said Mathilde. 'It won't hurt her to spend a few nights here.'

Gerda was the Cartiers' German au pair, a large girl with handsome features, a great deal of blonde hair, a startling figure and an apparently insatiable appetite for anything French.

Mathilde was glad of any excuse to get her out of the house. Paul was French.

He was less enthusiastic about the arrangement, but there was no alternative so Gerda packed an overnight bag and, on December eleventh, moved to 94 rue des Pyrénées.

She was back before dawn of the following day at the Cartiers' block of flats. She was let in by the concierge, who spent an agreeable two hours comforting her until the Cartiers got up.

She was in sore need of comfort. Never, she said, had she spent such a night. Every time she fell asleep, something tried to get into bed with her, and this had an effect on her bladder so that she continually had to get up and go all the way out to the bathroom in the hall and it was cold and she was afraid of being mugged and there was no toilet paper, etc., etc.

'Why didn't you use the toilet in the flat, noddle?' said Mathilde, who was fond of Gerda despite her appreciation of things French.

'There isn't any,' said Gerda.

The Cartiers thought it over and neither could remember any bathroom in the flat. Such a lack would, of course, severly depress the sale price, and they hurried to investigate.

Gerda was right. There was no bathroom, no toilet, no basin, no bath tub.

Astonished and mystified, the Cartiers went to the tenants of the other three flats on the floor to ask if they had bathrooms.

All did. Only the Beulet flat had none.

'She must have never had a bath in her life,' said Mathilde, who was out of sorts.

'She undoubtedly washed more than any of your relatives,' replied her husband, incensed by the attack on the personal hygiene of his cousin.

'It doesn't smell like it,' sniffed Mathilde. 'The place is absolutely foul.'

It was the same odour that had turned the stomach of Olivier Belmont and had also been remarked on by the patrol car officers, but, curiously, not by the homicide squad, the only ones who might have known what it was.

'It doesn't matter,' said Robert. 'We'll get nothing for the place without a bathroom.'

'There must have been a bathroom here when she rented it,' said Mathilde. Let's see if we can find her copy of the lease.'

The copy of the lease was with Colette's other papers, but, to the consternation of the heirs, it was in the name of a Mr Primo Dolfi, who had signed it on 1 January 1955.

'It wasn't even her flat!' exclaimed Mathilde. 'Who is this Primo Dolfi, anyway?'

It was the sort of question calculated to infuriate a harassed spouse, but Paul ignored it.

'Nineteen fifty-five,' he mused. 'This Dolfi could be a very old man. I wouldn't be surprised if he'd died. She was probably renting a room from him and she simply took over the whole flat without changing the lease.'

'No doubt,' said Mathilde, 'but we can't sell Dolfi's lease. I think all we can do is notify the owner and let him hunt for Dolfi.'

Paul was in agreement, but the owner of the flat – a property company and not an individual – was not. The manager came to inspect the premises, noted at once that the bathroom was missing and demanded that the Cartiers replace it.

'The flat was rented with a bathroom,' he said. 'See? It's listed right here in the lease. If it's not there, it's because your relative has done something with it and, as she is dead, you are responsible.'

The outraged Cartiers retorted that the lease had not been signed by their relative and that they had no responsibility for whatever Primo Dolfi might have done with his bathroom.

The manager did not hear with that ear, as the French put it, and relations rapidly deteriorated to the point where formal charges of theft of a bathroom were filed against the Cartiers.

This was not a terribly unusual charge. Amateur plumbers and professional thieves not infrequently made off with someone's bathroom.

Such operations normally concerned only the fixtures, however. The theft of the entire room was unprecedented.

The case, having aroused some hilarity within the twentieth arrondissement station, eventually came to the notice of Sergeant Rochereau, who remarked that the address was identical to that of the recently deceased Colette Beulet, and reported it to the inspector.

'A stolen bathroom?' said the inspector, wrinkling his brows so that he looked like a troubled basset. 'Bizarre. Do you remember if there was a bathroom in the flat?'

The sergeant did not.

'I'll run over and check,' he said, and he did – but he too was unable to locate the vanished bathroom.

'It seems now that the dead woman wasn't the tenant,' he reported. 'It was a man named Primo Dolfi.'

'Where is he?' asked the inspector.

'Nobody knows,' said the sergeant.

'Find out,' said the inspector.

The sergeant, who liked nothing better than nosing about in such mysteries, applied himself and soon produced a reasonably complete background report on Primo Dolfi.

He was a seventy-four-year-old Italian stonemason, who had emigrated to France in 1954 and acquired French citizenship five years later. He had retired on his social security pension in 1978. According to the records, he had never been married and there was no explanation of what Colette Beulet had been doing in his flat.

'Probably his mistress,' speculated the sergeant, 'if he was up to it.'

'I am less interested in his virility than his whereabouts,' said the inspector.

'He's missing,' said the sergeant. 'Nobody in the neighbourhood has seen him since March of this year.'

'Dolfi is missing and his bathroom is missing,' mused the inspector. 'This is either the greatest coincidence in the history of the French police, or they're missing together.'

'I haven't been able to find Dolfi,' said the sergeant.

'Then find the bathroom,' said the inspector.

Actually, it was not so very difficult. As in most such buildings, the floor plan of the flats on each floor was identical, and it was only necessary to determine the location of the bathroom in the flat on the floor below to find the one above.

The police then moved a wardrobe, pulled away the wallpaper and the sheet of plasterboard concealing the door, and the missing bathroom was found.

So too was Primo Dolfi.

He was lying in the bathtub, carefully wound with several hundred yards of narrow cotton bands torn from old sheets. The bands, and to an extent Dolfi, had been soaked in oil, turpentine and other substances.

He was in fact, a mummy.

But not a very good one. The stench when the bathroom door was opened was strong enough to fell an ox. It was, however, not the normal odour of putrefaction.

Dr Paulin performed a hurried autopsy and reported that Dolfi had died as the result of a fractured skull and internal injuries consistent with being kicked in the chest and stomach. The time of death was sometime in March, which coincided with the last reported sightings of the victim.

In the meantime, a positive identification of the body

had been made through fingerprints, the mummyfying process having preserved the fingerprints, and an active search for suspects in the murder of Primo Dolfi was under way.

The logical first suspect should have been Colette Beulet, but Dr Paulin, who had examined her body, was quite certain that she would not have been physically capable of inflicting the injuries which had led to Dolfi's death.

'A man or a very strong woman,' he said, 'and Mrs Beulet was not a strong woman.'

'She must have been an accomplice, though,' said the inspector. 'She could hardly have failed to notice the disappearance of another person living in the same flat, to say nothing of the bathroom, and it took some time to make a mummy out of Dolfi.'

'She told the people in the neighbourhood he'd gone back to Italy,' said the sergeant. 'No wonder she had dreams about a mummy trying to make love to her. She was a simple woman and she had a bad conscience.'

What little there was to know had by now been learned about Collette. Born in the village of Saint-Nicolas-de-Bourgeuil, she had come up to Paris at the age of eighteen. She had worked in Paris as a domestic servant and, at the age of nineteen, had married a man named Louis Judin. They had divorced six years later.

Mr Judin became an object of minor interest to the police until it was determined that he had died four years earlier.

'So,' said the inspector, 'despite the unusual aspects of the case, what we are confronted with here is a banal love-triangle homicide.

'Mrs Beulet was Mr Dolfi's mistress. She became involved with someone else who, with her knowledge and perhaps assistance, eliminated the obstruction to their love.'

'He could have waited a year or so and Dolfi would have died of old age,' said the sergeant.

'Love is impetuous,' said the inspector. 'Love cannot wait. If it could, our workload would be cut in half.'

'Not a very faithful lover,' remarked the sergeant. 'He turns Dolfi into a mummy, walls him up in the bathroom and leaves Mrs Beulet alone with him in the flat.'

'You've found no one who moved into the flat after Dolfi's murder?' said the inspector.

'No one,' said the sergeant. 'She was living there alone. The only person who came to the flat was a fellow named Joel Bastien, but he's close to twenty years younger than she was. He has a disability pension and runs errands for the old people in the neighbourhood to supplement his living.'

'An unlikely love triangle,' agreed the inspector, 'but check on him anyway.'

'I already have,' said the sergeant. 'The report's in the file.'

Forty-year-old Joel Bastien was no more exceptional than Primo Dolfi or Collette Beulet. Born in the rue des Pyrénées, he began his professional career as a baker's apprentice but, finding the profession not to his liking, joined the fire department. Married in 1966, he was divorced in 1978. In 1980, having changed jobs to become a welder in the Citroën car factory, he burned his eyes seriously and was granted a disability pension. As it was not enough to live on, he ran errands and did shopping for the old people in the rue des Pyrénées.

'Conspicuous appearance,' wrote the sergeant. 'Always wears white shirt, dark glasses, three wrist-watches on the same arm and carries a briefcase. Regarded by most as an obliging eccentric. No record of violence. He can hardly see his hand in front of his face.'

There was another report in the file over which the inspector lingered longer.

The sergeant was a thorough investigator and, having learned that Gerda, the Cartiers' au pair, had spent a night in the flat, he had taken a statement from her.

Gerda's experience bore an alarming resemblance to

those described in Collette Beulet's diary. Every time she fell asleep, she was awakened by something heavy lying on her and trying to force her legs apart. The first time, she had thought it a man wearing tights, but, when she had turned on the light, there had been no one there. It was a tribute to the stamina of her nervous system that it was only after the third such overture she had got up, dressed and gone back to the Cartiers'.

The girl did not know at the time that there was a mummy walled up in the bathroom [wrote the sergeant], nor did she know it at the time of the interview. Her stated movements for the night and following morning are corroborated by the concierge in the Cartier building and the Cartiers. No explanation suggested.

The inspector could think of none either, but he did think that Joel Bastien was a better potential suspect than the sergeant credited.

'If you're sure he was the only one calling at the flat, it has to be him,' he told the sergeant. 'Bring him in and we'll see what we can do with interrogation.'

Joel Bastien was brought to the inspector's office, but very little interrogation was necessary. Rendered so nervous by being taken into custody that he could scarcely speak intelligibly, Bastien soon confessed to the killing, although he denied vigorously that it had been murder.

'I never meant to kill him,' he said. 'We were all good friends and he couldn't do anything with Collette, anyway. He was too old. We'd all been living together for over two years. There was no need for him to go and get jealous.'

Rather incredibly, Joel Bastien had managed to live together with Primo Dolfi and Collette Beulet in the flat from February of 1984 without anyone suspecting it.

'It would have been bad for all our reputations,' he said earnestly. 'What would people have said?'

At the time he moved in, the relationship had been merely friendship between three somewhat lonely people, but before long he and Collette became lovers.

Dolfi had known of this and had, at first, raised no objections. He was, he had admitted frankly, no longer interested in sex, but if the others were, he would not stand in their way.

With the passing of time, however, he had become increasingly jealous and there had been frequent quarrels, terminating in the one on March the eleventh when it had come to a physical scuffle and Dolfi had been killed.

Not knowing what to do with the body, he and Collette had hit upon the original idea of turning Dolfi into a mummy and making the bathroom his tomb.

'We weren't able to make love after that though,' said Joel sadly. 'It was like he was there with us.'

The cause of Primo Dolfi's death was consistent with injuries received during the course of a scuffle and there was no evidence of premeditation. Joel Bastien's plea of unintentional homicide was accepted by the court and, on 8 May 1987 he was sentenced to ten years' imprisonment.

'Makes you wonder a little,' observed the sergeant. 'Was Collette Beulet's death really natural? The old boy may have been feeling a little vindictive, and a bad scare . . .'

'You can't get an indictment against a mummy,' said the inspector.

DANCE WITH THE DEVIL

For people with child-like faith in the advertising litera-
ture of travel agencies, the world is a single gigantic
resort, easily reached by air or bus and filled with quaint
native inhabitants who, despite minor differences in
speech and dress, are just like the folks back home.

Fortunately, this is not entirely true. Even within
the modern homogenized countries of Western Europe,
there are communities tucked away in forests and moun-
tains to which the tourist bus never comes. More sinister
than picturesque to the alien eye, they are the home of
people who may own cars and television sets, but whose
manner of thinking is very different indeed.

In the nineteen seventies, such a community was Retz,
a large village or small town with a population of under
four thousand near the Austrian border with Czechoslovakia, some forty miles north and slightly to the west of
Vienna.

Retz is the largest community in the area and serves
as a shopping centre for the even smaller villages around
it. Located in a shallow depression, it is surrounded by
dense pine forests and served by secondary state roads 35
and 215. No road crosses the border into Czechoslovakia.

Pine forests have many virtues. They grow rapidly;
they are easily cut; they look well on postcards and they
shelter various wild things.

A large pine forest can, however, give the impression
that it shelters altogether too many things. The foliage
of the older trees is so dark a green as to appear almost
black. The dense mass of the boughs tends to shut

the sunlight. The brown, springy carpet of dead needles seems to smother sound so that it is too quiet, and the endless rows of identical brown trunks can produce optical illusions of movement where there should be none.

Of course, it could always be a deer or a wild pig . . .

But on two legs and six feet tall?

In any case, many of the inhabitants of Retz do not like to go into the forest after dark and some do not like to go into it at all.

This is odd, for most of the families in Retz have lived there for centuries.

Or, perhaps, it is precisely because they have been there for centuries. With time comes caution.

And, with time, come also all the good things of civilization: telephones, jeans, trainers, electric toothbrushes, discotheques, tinned kumquats, television, marijuana, oral contraceptives and, above all, cars.

Cars require garages, and Retz has several – but only one in which the devil was employed as a mechanic.

This garage was owned by an Anton Schelzer and he found it perfectly normal to have the devil on his payroll. Teufel, the German word for devil, is not a terribly common surname, but it is not terribly unusual either.

This particular Teufel's first name was Karl and he was a good mechanic. He had arrived in Retz on or about 1 January 1971 and had immediately found employment with the garage. He did not say where he had come from, but his accent was not local. This was only to be expected, as there were few other garages in the region where he could have learned his profession.

What had moved him to settle down in Retz was not known, but he apparently intended to stay and, when not repairing Volkswagens, devoted himself to courting a Miss Gertrude Felsenbock, at the time of his arrival in Retz aged thirty-two and unmarried.

This was not Gertrude's fault. She was pretty. She had a fine figure. She had a pleasant personality. And she even had a small inheritance.

What was wrong was not Gertrude, but Retz. There being little employment and less excitement in such small, isolated places, the young males tended to drift off to the big cities. In Retz, women outnumbered men roughly three to two.

Karl Teufel was, therefore, welcomed with delight, particularly by Gertrude, for whom he was a near ideal match.

He was the right age – thirty-four – had a good job, was tall and well-built, drank little and was even handsome as the, uh, well – devil. Gertrude could hardly have done better by mail order.

Even so, the marriage only took place after nearly two years. The people of Retz are not given to rushing headlong into things and nobody knew anything much about this Teufel who had so suddenly shown up from nowhere.

Two years allayed any doubts there might have been. There was nothing wrong with Karl Teufel other than a rather harmless idiosyncrasy.

He took his own name too seriously.

This had become apparent at the beginning of the first carnival season.

Retz is, of course, solidly Catholic, and the carnival season before Lent is celebrated with fervour. There are fancy dress balls nearly every night, inhibitions are cast to the winds, drunkenness is a normal state and, nine months later, a graph of the birth statistics shows an abrupt and wholly explicable peak.

Karl Teufel attended the fancy dress balls disguised as the devil. He had brought with him from wherever he came a fine scarlet woollen devil's suit complete with impressive tail, boots designed to look like hooves, gloves with fearful claws, a horned devil's mask and a three-tined pitchfork. Thus accounted, he sent delicious tremors of terror coursing down the charming spines of the joyously squealing local maidens.

They were, however, the only sensations which they would experience at Karl Teufel's satanic hands.

Although he sometimes danced with others, he remained unswervingly faithful to his Gertrude.

A man capable of resisting the opportunities of carnival had to be sincerely in love and, on 26 December 1972, Karl and Gertrude were wed.

The couple immediately moved into a cottage which Gertrude had bought with her inheritance money. It was new, modern and on the outskirts of the village. Fifty feet from the back door, the forest began.

Karl and Gertrude proclaimed their happiness to anyone who would listen and, in the case of Gertrude, this was often her sister Eusebia, who was five years older and had more or less given up on the subject of marriage.

Nevertheless, she took a vicarious pleasure in hearing about her sister's, particularly the more intimate details. Gertrude was a healthy farm girl and her appetites were robust. So too, it seemed, were Karl's. According to what she told Eusebia, there was very little television-watching in the Teufel home. Every evening, it was a nourishing supper and straight off to bed.

This happy state continued for exactly eighteen days, and then the first ball of the carnival season took place.

It was on a Saturday night, 13 January 1973, and the Teufels attended, Karl dressed as usual, in his devil's costume.

Married devils are, however, less frightening than single ones. There were no delighted squeals of terror and some of the younger maidens were downright impertinent. One even ventured to pull the devil's tail.

'Nobody's afraid of you, you old fake!' she taunted. 'Your tail's limp!'

The word tail in German has a double meaning. In addition to designating the tail of an animal, it is the vulgar term for the human male sex organ.

The young lady was, therefore, making a mildly ribald pun.

All the other maidens in earshot laughed, and Gertrude laughed with them.

Karl did not laugh and he did not dance any more that evening.

On Monday morning, Karl, for the first time since his arrival in Retz, did not show up for work.

Anton Schelzer was unperturbed. Allowances had to be made for carnival. Half Retz was lying in bed with massive hangovers, and some were not even lying in their own beds. When Karl had recovered his wits he would return.

He did not return on Tuesday either.

Anton found this serious. There had been no balls on Sunday or Monday. Two days was too long for curing even the worst hangover.

As the Teufel's had not yet succeeded in getting a telephone installed, the only means of contacting them was to go there, and Anton got into his car.

Arriving at the cottage, which was the type known as Contemporary German Shoebox, he was relieved to see Teufel's car parked in front of it. It had occurred to him that no one in Retz knew very much about the man and that it was possible that he had cleared off altogether.

His relief quickly evaporated, however, for no one answered the doorbell, although he could hear it ringing inside the house.

Standing with his thumb on the doorbell, Schelzer could feel himself becoming frightened. It was a bitterly cold day and a winter fog lay over the village. Thick strands of it were drifting between the trunks of the trees, ghostly white against the dark shadows cast by the pines. It was still early and a faintly glowing disc low in the sky indicated the location of the invisible sun.

It was quiet – much *too* quiet. Like many old European towns, the original Retz lay huddled together for the protection needed in the Middle Ages. Only a few newer houses lay scattered beyond its sheltering walls.

What the devil could have happened to the Teufels? Could they both be sick? Food poisoning, perhaps?

Automatically, without expecting to find it unlocked, he tried the door handle.

31

The door swung open, and this alarmed him more than anything else might have done. There was little crime in Retz, but people did keep their doors locked, particularly out here where the forest was so near.

'Karl?' called Schelzer tentatively, leaning awkwardly so that his head and shoulders were through the open door, but his feet were still firmly planted outside.

The house was silent as a tomb, which was precisely the simile which sprang unbidden to his mind.

He did not call again, but straightened up and stood irresolutely, hesitating for several minutes while he tried to decide what to do.

Obviously, he realized, something was very wrong. Karl's car was there, so they had not gone away, but the door was unlocked and no one had responded to the doorbell or to his call. Perhaps the best thing would be to summon the police.

Retz has a police force – a rather large one, actually, as the little communities around it have none and depend upon the larger town for such services.

It was not so large, however, that Schelzer did not know every member of it, and he was not anxious to appear a fool. It was probable that the Teufels' absence had a perfectly innocent explanation and, if he ran off to the police simply because they were not at home, he would make a laughing stock of himself.

There was nothing for it but to enter the house and investigate, but, before he did so, he went back to his car and got the twelve-gauge shotgun which he used for hunting and which he carried in the car boot.

He had never been in the house and did not know the layout, but once he was in the entrance hall, it became obvious. The doors to the living room and kitchen were open and he could see that there was no one in either room. The door to the bathroom was also ajar and only the two doors to the right of the hall were closed.

He assumed that these were the bedrooms, and he knocked and then cautiously opened the first.

The room was empty and the bed was neatly made.

In the second, he could see nothing for the shutters were down and the room was in total darkness.

Leaning the shotgun against the wall of the hall, he reached inside to feel for the light switch.

The white light from the ceiling fixture made him blink and, as his eyes adjusted, he found himself confronted by Gertrude Teufel's naked posterior.

At least, he supposed that it was Gertrude's. It was the body of a young woman, half-lying, half-kneeling on the floor beside the bed, her arms stretched out above her head and the very short, very flimsy nightgown that she was wearing bunched up around her neck.

Schelzer took a step backwards. The room was overheated and it smelled of humans and of sex. Nothing in it was particularly disarranged. The covers of the bed were thrown back. That was all.

That and the woman on the floor. What was wrong with her? Was she drunk? Or was she sick and Karl had gone to get the doctor?

Schelzer suddenly felt extremely uneasy. Supposing Karl came back now and found him in the bedroom regarding his wife's naked bottom? How could he possibly explain?

But while a part of his mind was thinking these things, another part was noting that the woman lay unnaturally still and that it was an improbable posture for her husband to leave her in while he ran for help.

The woman's head was turned to one side and, with the stiff-legged reluctance of a dog being taken to the vet, he entered the room and got down on all fours to look into her face.

An instant later, he gave vent to an appalled yell, jumped to his feet and ran out of the bedroom, out of the house and down the road in the direction of the village, forgetting even his own car.

The face he had seen was like something out of a horror movie, black as coal, with red bloodshot eyes starting from their sockets and a swollen purple tongue protruding further from an open mouth than any tongue should ever protrude.

The police station was located on the square in the centre of town and, by the time he had reached it, he was so out of breath that he could only gasp, 'Dead! Gertrude dead!' at the startled desk sergeant.

There followed a short period of confusion. Schelzer had not said which Gertrude and, the desk sergeant having an aunt of that name, he assumed that Schelzer was bringing him news of her death.

In the end, however, it became clear that it was something quite different and that Schelzer was trying to report a murder.

Consequently, he was ushered to the office of the head of the Retz Department of Criminal Investigations, Inspector Josef Eichendorf.

Schelzer had by now recovered his breath and some of his composure and he described briefly the circumstances of his visit to the Teufel home and what he had found there.

The inspector, a large, dignified man with thick grey sideburns descending in a graceful arc to join a sweeping grey moustache, listened in grave silence and, when Schelzer had finished, asked a single question.

'Where is Karl?'

Schelzer started as if he had been jabbed with a pin. In his excitement, he had completely forgotten about the dead woman's husband.

'He wasn't there,' he said slowly. 'You don't think . . . They've only been married a couple of weeks!'

The inspector did not reply to his question, but got to his feet, summoned his assistant, Sergeant of Detectives Franz Waldmeier, and left the office without another word.

Schelzer, at something of a loss, followed them, but he did not go back to the Teufel's house. Instead, he went to the nearest tavern, where he drank three double brandies, one after the other.

Then he began to talk.

34

Less than forty minutes later, every soul in Retz knew that Gertrude Teufel had been murdered by the devil.

In the meantime, Inspector Eichendorf and Sergeant Waldmeier arrived at the house and found that Schelzer's report was essentially correct. The sergeant was sent to fetch Dr Peter Graff, who served as coroner and police medical officer as he was the only doctor in Retz.

A clean-shaven, professional-looking man who wore gold-rimmed glasses and parted his medium-blond hair in the middle, the doctor had performed his official functions for nearly twenty years, but had never before been called upon to examine a murder victim. Retz was not a community where many murders took place.

He was, therefore, a little uncertain as to how to proceed, but, with the assistance of the inspector and the sergeant, he got the corpse turned over on its back. Then the cause of death immediately became apparent.

Blood-red against the white skin of the woman's throat were the marks of two human hands, the outlines of the fingers as clear as on a blueprint.

'Red hands?' said Sergeant Waldmeier, nervously moving his long, lanky limbs and screwing up the leathery skin of his face in a curious expression which combined disbelief, shock and, possibly, even fear. 'He said he was the devil . . .'

'Nonsense, Franz,' said the doctor. 'We don't know that Karl is responsible for this and, anyway, the colour is simply the result of sustained pressure on the skin. Something like a blood blister, only bigger.'

'Can you tell anything else?' said the inspector. 'Franz, you go through the house and see if there's any indication of where Karl may have gone.'

'Well, it looks as if she was engaged in sex,' said the doctor. 'The pubic hair is matted and stiff. I think we should take her over to the morgue before we try to determine anything else.'

'Then it was either with Karl or she was raped,' said the inspector. 'I know Gertrude. She wouldn't have gone with another man, even if it is carnival.'

35

The doctor nodded in agreement. Like everyone else in Retz, Gertrude had been his patient.

'We'll have to keep this quiet,' he said. 'The man's a stranger and the name . . . We don't want a panic in the village.'

There was already panic in the village. As the inspector returned to his office to summon the ambulance and the two technicians who formed the staff of the small police laboratory, he encountered groups of men carrying shotguns, pitchforks and axes. Mothers were herding their children home from school although it was the middle of the morning, and some shopkeepers were putting up their shutters.

'Damn!' muttered the inspector. 'Schelzer.'

He regretted now that he had not thrown the garage owner into the detention cells before going to investigate the report, but it was obviously too late now. The devil was loose in the village and in a very literal sense.

Nearly everyone in Retz went to church. Nearly everyone believed in the existence of the devil. Surrounded by the dark, brooding forest and lost amidst the mists of gloom of winter, his appearance in their village did not seem illogical.

No one stopped to question why the devil should have especially chosen Retz when there were so many more suitable places or why he should have seen fit to murder the innocent Gertrude, whose soul was undoubtedly destined for heaven.

However, as the village settled into what amounted to a state of siege, the investigations at the scene of the murder were progressing.

The body had been transferred to the morgue, where Dr Graff was attempting a rather hesitant autopsy on it.

The Felsenbocks had been notified of Gertrude's death and were waiting outside the morgue, hugging each other and weeping bitterly. They had, of course, known Karl Teufel better than anyone else in the village and they did not believe that he had murdered his wife.

'They were crazy about each other,' said Eusebia. 'He's chasing the murderer, or he's been murdered too.'

It was a possibility that the inspector was prepared to admit. But if Karl Teufel was dead or chasing his wife's murderer, it was in a strange costume.

Examination of the house by the sergeant and the technicians determined that the only clothing missing was Karl's devil suit.

Missing too were his mask, his hoofed boots, his clawed gloves and his pitchfork.

'He must be insane!' exclaimed the inspector. 'You don't strangle your wife and then go running off across the countryside in a bright red devil's suit!'

'You wouldn't and I wouldn't,' said the sergeant darkly, 'but is this human being like you and me?'

'Try not to be stupid, Franz,' said the inspector sharply. 'Karl Teufel isn't the devil. That's just his name.'

'Then why did he go around dressed like one?' said the sergeant defiantly. 'And why did he leave his car and his personal identification papers behind if he's just a murderer on the run? He didn't even take any money. We found his wallet in the drawer of the night table.'

The inspector sighed. The identification papers were puzzling. Not only would it be nearly impossible for Teufel to go anywhere without them, but the ones he had left behind had no entry under place of birth – an unheard of omission in regimented Austria.

'I don't know,' he said. 'Something happened in that house on Sunday morning. According to Peter, she was killed at around one o'clock.'

'Close to two hours after they left the ball,' said the sergeant. 'Some of the people say he was out of sorts, but they aren't sure because he had his mask on. Gertrude was in fine form.'

'Two hours,' said the inspector, 'and Peter says they must have been – ah – making love the entire time. He says she was . . . well, you know . . .'

'Drenched,' said the sergeant. 'There's not the slightest indication that anybody else was in the house. Whatever he is, I say Teufel did it.'

'He's a man,' said the inspector, 'but, if he is guilty, he's dangerously insane and we have to find him before he kills someone else. His actions aren't rational. He must have been naked when he and Gertrude were making love, and that means he put on his devil suit after he killed her.'

'Why in God's name would he do that?' demanded the sergeant.

'You're invoking the wrong party for the question,' said the inspector.

He was prepared to invoke any party that could help remove this threat to public safety and, as locating Teufel was obviously paramount, he was anxious to get search parties out in the forest.

The number of police officers and off-duty firemen was, however, limited and there was a distressing paucity of volunteers from the public, such men as were willing to go being forcibly dissuaded by their wives.

'They think the devil is going to jump out and kill them,' said the inspector disdainfully.

'He killed Gertrude,' said the sergeant, 'and, even if he isn't the devil, he's a big, powerful maniac armed with a pitchfork.'

'True,' said the inspector. 'Only too true. How many volunteers do we have?'

'Six,' said the sergeant, 'and the minute they see something, they'll run like rabbits.'

'But you and I won't, will we, Franz?' said the inspector. 'Better check your service pistol.'

The sergeant had long since done so, and the mixed volunteer and police parties set off into the forest at a little after ten in the morning.

The sergeant had been quite right and, when one of the parties sighted something red moving in the fog between the tree trunks, two of the volunteers broke and ran for home.

The inspector and the sergeant were summoned and

the party advanced cautiously until a figure in a red suit could be seen skipping and capering about among the trees. It was wearing the devil mask and carrying the pitchfork.

Another of the volunteers left hurriedly.

No one blamed him. The red figure with the hideous grinning mask leaping erratically about in the fog-shrouded forest was an eerie sight.

'Hah!' cried Teufel, catching sight of the searchers. 'Beware! I am the devil! Kneel down! Show respect!'

'Put down the pitchfork, Karl,' called the inspector, walking down toward the man and holding out his hands to show that they were empty. 'It's time you came home now.'

'My home is hell. My home is hell. My home is hell,' crooned Teufel in a clear, high baritone, but he stuck his pitchfork into the ground and walked forward to meet the inspector.

Relieved of his mask and clawed gloves, he peacefully accompanied the search party back to Retz, where he proved to have a ravenous appetite.

His stomach full, he answered questions frankly. Yes, he had strangled Gertrude. Why? One should not laugh at the devil. Had she laughed at him? Yes, when the girl at the ball pulled his tail. He had shown her that the tail was not as limp as she thought. Then he had punished her. It was the devil's way.

Karl Teufel spent some very considerable time under observation at the psychiatric clinic for criminal medicine in Vienna and, although he failed to convince the psychiatrists that he was the devil, he did convince them that he thought he was.

Consequently, he was not tried, but committed to an institution for the criminally insane, where he is to remain until cleared of his dangerous delusions. It is expected that this will take some time.

There was one minor point which was never clarified and which troubles some of the people of Retz.

No one ever knew where Karl Teufel came from.

4

ONE ENCHANTED MORNING

Shortly before ten o'clock in the evening of 1 August 1982, forty-year-old Henri Kasprzak went up to his third floor flat in the Residence d'Evry and was pounced upon by an attractive coffee-coloured young man who tried to strangle him.

Kasprzak, astounded as there had been no one in the locked flat when he left it fifteen minutes earlier, fought like a tiger.

The young man responded by trying to hit him over the head with an empty wine bottle.

Kasprzak warded off the blows and knocked the bottle out of his hand.

Whereupon the young man pulled out a hypodermic syringe, which he tried to jab into Kasprzak's arm.

Having failed to do this, he left hurriedly through the front door.

The greatly wondering Kasprzak bolted the door, had a very large brandy to soothe his nerves and called the police.

He was still a little breathless when the patrol car arrived, the response speedy as Evry-Corbeil-Essonnes lies less than twenty miles to the southeast of Paris and the crime rate is relatively high, although the total population is under sixty thousand.

'Never saw him before in my life,' said Kasprzak. 'Can't imagine how he got in. I wasn't gone fifteen minutes.'

'What did he look like?' asked the senior of the two patrolmen, poising his pencil over his notebook.

'Black,' said Kasprzak. 'African of some kind, but light-skinned. Young, about twenty perhaps. He was well-dressed.'

'Did he get anything?' asked the second patrolman.

'Nothing, as far as I can see,' said Kasprzak. 'Probably didn't have enough time.'

'Who besides you has a key?' asked the first patrolman.

'Nobody,' said Kasprzak. 'Absolutely nobody.'

'Breaking and entering, assault with a deadly weapon and attempted murder,' muttered the patrolman, writing busily. 'Somebody from the department of criminal investigations will be coming to take your statement. In the meantime, we'll put out a pick-up order on him. Can you think of anything to add to the description?'

Henri Kasprzak pondered the question.

'Well,' he said. 'He moved as if he was stiff or there was something wrong with his coordination, and his eyes were sort of glazed. You know what he looked like? One of those zombies you see on television!'

'Thank you very much, Mr Kasprzak,' said the patrolman, closing his notebook with a snap. 'The criminal investigations department will be in touch.'

'A zombie?' said the junior patrolman as they were going down in the lift.

'Drug addict, more likely,' said his partner. 'We don't get a lot of zombies around here.'

Sergeant of Detectives Jean Lessieux was also inclined to suspect that the man had been a drug addict.

He had found the first information report form in his in-tray when he came to work on Monday morning and had immediately telephoned Kasprzak's flat.

The telephone was answered by a housekeeper, who said that Mr Kasprzak was at work in Compiègne, which was about as far to the north of Paris as Evry-Corbeil-Essonnes was to the south. He was employed in the engineering department of SNECMA, the Société National d'Etude et de Construction de Moteurs d'Avion.

41

It sounded as if it might be a sensitive sort of job, and it was. The switchboard operator at SNECMA would only grudgingly admit that the organization existed. She would not say if there was an engineering department of if Henri Kasprzak was employed by the company or not.

She would, however, take a message and, after a few minutes, Kasprzak called back to say that he would be at home and prepared to make his statement any time after six in the evening.

The sergeant, a stocky little man with a round, rather boyish face and a haircut which looked as if it had been given him by his wife, made an appointment for seven o'clock and spent the rest of the day on other matters. The Kasprzak case was not terribly important, but the building at 27 rue Claude Debussy was one of the most expensive in town and, in France, as perhaps in some other places, the reactions of the public services tend to correspond to the tax bracket of the citizen.

The interview with Henri Kasprzak produced nothing of significance. The man did have a sensitive job which required a high security clearance, but there was no reason to suspect that the attack had been connected with his work.

'How did he speak?' queried the sergeant.

'He didn't,' said Kasprzak. 'Never said a word. Too busy trying to murder me, I imagine.'

'He doesn't seem to have done a very good job of it,' said the sergeant. 'Are you trained in close combat? Judo? Karate?'

'I don't even play golf,' said Kasprzak. 'If I could get the best of him, he must be in terrible shape.'

'Do you have enemies?' said the sergeant. 'Are you married?'

'I am separated from my wife,' said Kasprzak, apparently taking the questions as connected, 'but we're not enemies. She lives with a friend in the next block. As a matter of fact, she was here on Sunday evening. That was why I left the flat. She lost her ring in front of the building and I went down to help her look for it.'

'You found it?' asked the sergeant.

'No,' said Kasprzak.

The sergeant concluded the interview, having learned nothing that he did not already know, and the following morning made a brief report on the case to his superior, Inspector Yves Poulain.

'It was probably an addict who saw Kasprzak leave the flat and thought he'd see what he could pick up,' he said. 'Kasprzak came back sooner than he expected and he panicked. The thing was too amateurish to be a deliberate murder attempt.'

'Kasprzak must have left the door open,' said the inspector, shifting his substantial bulk in the chair and passing a hand over the top of his head as if in search of long-departed hair.

'That's the mystery,' said the sergeant. 'It's a spring lock and the door shuts automatically. If you want it to stay open, you have to block it. Kasprzak swears that he's the only one with a key. Even the housekeeper doesn't have one. She comes before he goes to work and leaves after he gets back. The children are only seven and eight. They don't have keys. Very sophisticated lock. It would take a specialist with tools to open it.'

'Windows, balconies?' asked the inspector.

'Out of the question,' said the sergeant. 'I checked everything.'

'Then Kasprzak is wrong,' said the inspector. 'Somebody does have a key, and that rules out an amateur burglary by an addict.'

'The fellow tried to stab him with a hypodermic,' said the sergeant.

'If he was an addict, he'd have stuck it in himself, not Mr Kasprzak,' said the inspector. 'Keep an eye on this. We haven't heard the last of it yet.'

The sergeant assigned a junior detective to run up background reports on Henri Kasprzak and his estranged wife, in case the separation was not as amicable as Kasprzak had described it.

The detective, anxious to avoid being assigned something worse, did a thorough job and turned in exhaustive reports on both the Kasprzaks.

Kasprzak had been born of Polish immigrant parents in Fontenay-le-Fleury, a village to the west of Paris, five miles from Versailles. His father had earned his living as a gardener and the family had made great sacrifices to put Henri through university.

It had been worth it. Henri had been a brilliant student and he had a highly successful career.

He was a good son and had not forgotten his parents. Although they still lived in Fontenay-le-Fleury, it was in far better circumstances than when they were educating Henri.

On 1 November 1968, he had married Nadia Brznoz four years younger than himself, who came from the same village and whom he had known all his life.

The couple had moved to Saint-Étienne, where Henri was employed in a machine tool manufacturing company.

He had been so successful in this first job that he was soon offered a better one in Creusot, where he remained for several years, returning to the Paris region in 1980.

On 15 June 1982, Nadia had moved in with a thirty-four-year-old woman friend named Solange Mordenski, who had a flat a block from the Residence d'Evry, and had filed for divorce on grounds of incompatibility. The children had remained with Henri.

Despite his professional success and the accompanying affluence, Kasprzak did not appear to have enjoyed himself very much. He did not drink and, although he could easily have afforded it, he had never even acquired the customary French status symbol of a mistress. He had no close friends, no enemies at all, and it was hard to imagine why anyone would want to kill him.

As the wife of such a husband, Nadia's life had not been particularly exciting either, which was perhaps the real reason for the divorce action.

A pretty woman with curly blonde hair and striking emerald-green eyes, she had, it seemed, been a rather indifferent wife and mother who preferred sitting in cafés to housework and movies to child raising.

Her ancestry was less clear than Henri's. Her parents were dead and she had been raised by a great-aunt who had since died. It was thought that the family came from somewhere in the Balkans, but precisely where was not known.

She was regarded by her fellow villagers in Fontenay-le-Fleury as rather strange and a little disquieting.

From as far back as anyone could remember, she had been involved in the occult and was in some demand by people wishing to know what the future held for them. She told fortunes with cards, with tea leaves and with a crystal ball, but also practised the more sinister form of divination of gazing into a bowl of ink. Some said that she could not only tell the future, but influence it.

Otherwise, the only thing remarkable about Nadia Kasprzak was that she was undeviatingly faithful to her husband.

The detective had gone to some pains to determine this. When married people are the subject of assassination attempts, it is not infrequently the spouse who is responsible, and the fact that the Kasprzaks were separated only increased the probability.

However, Nadia Kasprzak had no lover and, as far as the detective had been able to determine, had never had one. She was not flirtatious and, aside from her occult activities, was generally regarded as good-natured, fond of good times and company, but slightly feather-headed.

Having learned nothing which might explain the attack on Henri Kasprzak, the detective was taken off the case and assigned to something less pleasant and more urgent.

The summer passed without further incident. The weather was excellent. In July, Nadia went to Saint Raphael on the Riviera for a week's holiday. She shared a flat there with a Miss Agnes Bouvier and Miss Bouvier's current lover. Miss Bouvier came from Fontenay-le Fleury and she and Nadia had been at school together.

Henri did not take a holiday. The children went to a summer camp.

Early autumn in the Paris basin was magnificent, as it so often is, but by the middle of November the skies had become overcast and there was a good deal of cold rain and some high winds.

It was on such a morning, with the wind whining about the cornices of the Residence d'Evry and the rain rattling against the windowpanes, that forty-year-old Jerome d'Estrel descended to the garage in the basement with the reluctant intention of going to work. It was shortly before eight o'clock of Tuesday, 23 November 1982, and it was completely dark outside.

It was not very light inside the garage either, as there were young people living in the building with their parents and they tended to vandalize the light fixtures, but he immediately noticed that the large, expensive Renault parked next to his own car had apparently attracted the attention of the young vandals as well.

The safety glass of the windscreen and the window on the driver's side had cracked into a thousand pieces and, although still in place, was ready to collapse at the touch of a finger.

There is something nearly irresistible about objects suspended in a state of delicate balance. A house of cards, a row of dominoes – few can resist the temptation to set in motion the mechanism of destruction.

Jerome d'Estrel was not one of the few. Stretching out his hand, he rested his forefinger on the crazed glass of the window.

It promptly collapsed in a clattering shower of fragments, and d'Estrel saw with consternation that someone was sitting in the driver's seat.

He realized, of course, who it was, for he had recognized the car even before the removal of the glass had permitted a view of the interior.

It was Henri Kasprzak, the engineer who lived on the third floor, and he had apparently been involved in an accident, for he sat with his head lolling forward on his chest and there was blood running down the side of his face.

D'Estrel instinctively stretched out his hand to open the door and try to help, but immediately withdrew it. Kasprzak was unconscious and obviously badly injured. D'Estrel knew nothing of first aid and decided he could do more harm than good.

Hurrying to the lift, he went up to his flat and telephoned the emergency ambulance.

The ambulance arrived even more quickly than the patrol car had in August, but the paramedic heading the crew did not open the door either. Reaching through the empty window, he felt for a pulse in the throat, lifted the head gently to examine the injuries and then stepped back away from the car.

D'Estrel, hovering anxiously in the background, inquired as to whether Kasprzak was all right.

'He's dead,' said the paramedic shortly. 'It looks to me as if he's been shot. Have you called the police?'

'No,' said D'Estrel.

'We will then,' said the paramedic. 'I advise you to remain here until they come.'

As there had been a previous case involving Henri Kasprzak, the name was tagged and the report from the ambulance crew was immediately routed to Inspector Poulain, who did not even stop long enough to say, 'I told you so', but departed immediately for the scene. The sergeant was to follow with the investigation detachment.

The inspector took with him only Dr Maurice Cremona, a thin, sallow, hollow-cheeked expert in forensic medicine, who began by attempting to determine the cause of death.

'Gunshot wounds all right,' he said, stepping back from the car. 'More than one in the head. Small calibre, apparently. It's homicide.'

This being established, there was nothing more that could be done until the arrival of the technicians who would photograph corpse and scene and secure any potential clues before moving the body.

While he was waiting, the inspector sent the ambulance back to its base and took a statement from Jerome d'Estrel, who then left for work.

A short time later, the homicide detail arrived, and for the next hour there was intense activity in the garage.

It was directed by Sergeant Lessieux, the inspector having gone up to Henri Kasprzak's flat with two detectives to see if they could find anything bearing on the murder there.

They found nothing and were presently joined by the sergeant, who reported that the investigations at the scene were completed, the body had been transferred to the morgue and the car was being towed to the police garage.

'Cremona's starting the autopsy immediately,' he said, 'but he doesn't expect to find much other than the bullets. He was shot three times in the head, once through the window and twice though the windscreen. Any one of the three would have been fatal.'

'There won't be anything in the car then,' said the inspector. 'The murderer never went near it. He was just waiting in the garage for Kasprzak to come down to go to work and he shot him as soon as he got into the car.'

'That's the conclusion the lab people came to,' the sergeant agreed, 'but the question is: How did he get into the garage? The door can only be opened by using a key in the command posts inside and outside.'

'He must have had a key,' said the inspector. 'It's the same thing as when Kasprzak was attacked in his flat.'

'The African?' said the sergeant.

'It would be a remarkable coincidence if it wasn't,' said the inspector. 'I didn't think that was an amateur burglary by an addict. The fellow was out to kill Kasprzak, and this time he's done it.'

'Anything about Africans here in the flat?' asked the sergeant.

'Nothing,' said the inspector. 'He read engineering manuals for entertainment.'

'But what about his kids?' said the sergeant. 'And the housekeeper? There was a housekeeper who came before he went to work.'

'Hmmm,' said the inspector. 'We'll have to find out about those things. They could be significant.'

It did not take long to find out and the things were not significant. The Kasprzak children had been enrolled in a boarding school at the beginning of September and, as they were no longer at home, the housekeeper came only twice a week, on Wednesdays and Saturdays.

She was interviewed, but was unable to shed any light on the murder. Mr Kasprzak, she said, was a quiet man who did little other than work. He often cooked his own supper and was a good cook. She did not believe that he had known any Africans.

Nadia Kasprzak had also been questioned, but had merely echoed what everyone else had said. No one she knew had any reason to murder Henri.

'She doesn't seem particularly grief-stricken,' observed the sergeant. 'She could have done it herself. Any woman can handle a twenty-two.'

The autopsy had shown that the bullets which had killed Henri Kasprzak were twenty-two calibre long rifle. The ballistics department reported no record of the gun but said that a mark had been cut into the tip of the bullets with a knife. They thought it looked like the number seven.

'Three bullets, three sevens,' mused the inspector. 'Doesn't that have some kind of an occult meaning, the triple seven?'

It did, and the trail led back again to Nadia Kasprzak, whose interest in the occult had been documented at the time of the first investigation.

'Logically, it has to be her,' said the inspector. 'If anyone had a motive, it was her. If anyone had the opportunity to obtain copies of Kasprzak's keys, it was her.'

'It certainly wasn't her who made the first attempt,' said the sergeant. 'That was a black.'

'Then Mrs Kasprzak must know a black very well,' said the inspector. 'We already know that she did not have the money to hire one.'

Kasprzak had been insured and he had had savings, but everything was tied up in a trust fund for the children. Mrs Kasprzak was not even the administrator of the trust.

'She's blonde . . . pretty . . .' observed the sergeant.

'Well, maybe,' said the inspector doubtfully, 'but if she was so strait-laced that she never had an affair, would she prostitute herself to get her husband murdered?'

'Have to, if she wanted it badly enough,' said the sergeant.

'I can't see Kasprzak as a man to inspire such intense hatred,' said the inspector. 'Their relations weren't that bad. I suspect the only reason she wanted to divorce him was because he was boring. You don't murder people because they bore you.'

'Millicent Perdonnet,' said the sergeant.

'Ah yes, Millicent,' said the inspector. 'Well, you may be right.'

Millicent Perdonnet had murdered her husband of twenty-four years in 1980 because he insisted on reading aloud the political speeches printed in the newspapers. She had been given a suspended sentence.

'If we could show that she had contact with an African during the past year?' suggested the sergeant.

'If *you* could show that,' corrected the inspector. 'Let me know when you do.'

The sergeant took this as an assignment and, although he did not work as hard as the junior detective originally checking the backgrounds of the Kasprzaks had, he was more experienced and soon produced an interesting item of information.

'Mrs Kasprzak was in Saint Raphael in July,' he reported. 'She stayed with a Miss Agnes Bouvier and her lover. The lover is black.'

'Ah?' said the inspector. 'And he is . . . ?'

'Serge Pognon, aged twenty-two,' said the sergeant. 'Only his mother is black. She comes from Dahomey. The father is French and Serge was born in Longjumeau. No criminal record, but he deserted from the army while doing his military service in August of nineteen eighty-one. He'd just met Miss Bouvier then. As he only had a week to do before his service was up anyway, they sent him to have his head examined. Verdict was that he was sane, but not too bright and easily influenced.'

'So he and Mrs Kasprzak . . . ?' said the inspector.

'Apparently not,' said the sergeant. 'She didn't like him and always referred to him as Agnes' nigger.

'He was scared to death of her and called her the White Witch. Told people she was putting spells on him.'

'Weird,' commented the inspector. 'Why do these things happen in our district? You weren't able to dig up any material evidence?'

The sergeant shook his head.

'We've already questioned everybody in the building about seeing a young black there that evening,' he said.

'It's pretty obvious now what happened in August,' said the inspector. 'Mrs Kasprzak was more bored with her husband than we thought and she persuaded Pognon in some way to kill him. She gave him the key to the flat and got Kasprzak to help look for her ring while Pognon let himself in. When he bungled it, she waited until November and then either had Pognon do it or did it herself. The question is: What do we do?'

'Well, if Pognon is as easily influenced as the army psychologists said he was, we could probably interrogate a confession out of him,' suggested the sergeant.

'Try it,' said the inspector. 'I don't see any other way we could hope to solve the case.'

Serge Pognon was, if anything, even more easily influenced than the psychologists had thought. Less that fifteen minutes of questioning produced the first admission.

It was quickly followed by others and, by the time that the sergeant had returned from picking up Nadia Kasprzak, the inspector had a detailed confession on tape.

Nadia, said Pognon, was a great sorceress who could turn people's bones into red-hot iron. She had told him that he was to frighten her husband so that he would give her a divorce and some money. Nothing had been said about killing.

In August he had gone to the flat and let himself in with a key that Nadia had given him. He was supposed to strangle Kasprzak a little, hit him on the head with a bottle and stick a syringe into his arm. That would frighten him.

Kasprzak had not cooperated and Nadia had been angry. She had made his bones get very hot and he had not been able to make love to Agnes.

'But to Mrs Kasprzak,' suggested the inspector.

Pognon looked at him with an expression of horror.

'No! No!' he exclaimed. 'Not with her.'

He was very convincing.

'Proceed,' said the inspector.

The first attempt having failed to frighten Kasprzak, Nadia had decided on stronger measures and had given Pognon a twenty-two calibre rifle. She had suggested that he could more easily conceal it on his person if he sawed off the stock and barrel, and he had done so.

His orders had been to hide in the garage and, when Kasprzak got in the car, to frighten him by firing exactly three bullets through the windows or the windscreen. Nadia had given him the bullets. Something had been cut into the nose of each one, but he had been afraid to look at them.

'It did not occur to you that firing a rifle through the windscreen of Mr Kasprzak's car might injure him?' asked the inspector.

'No, no, it was only to frighten him,' said Pognon. 'Nadia said so,'

Nadia Kasprzak confirmed this. She had only told

Pognon to frighten her husband. She had never told him to kill him, nor had she wanted him dead.

Pognon said this was true. Nadia had never told him to kill her husband.

'Then why did you?' said the inspector.

'I didn't,' said Pognon. 'It was the bullets. She did something to the bullets.'

'One of the most unusual defence arguments I have ever heard,' remarked the inspector.

The court thought so too, but Nadia's assertion that she had not wanted to kill Henri but merely frighten him into a little more rapid action about the divorce was also credible, particularly as she could show that she had known prior to the murder that she would not benefit financially from it.

One thing, however, was certain, and that was her power over the unfortunate Pognon, who cringed like a whipped cur whenever she passed near him in the court room.

Perhaps rather unfairly, he was sentenced to fifteen years' imprisonment on 10 February 1984, while Nadia got off with only twelve.

Seemingly unconcerned throughout the trial, Nadia became suddenly still and serious and she gazed fixedly at the judge as he pronounced the sentences.

A little less than five months later, the judge, who had no history of heart trouble, died suddenly of a heart attack.

The date was the seventh July, which is the seventh month of the year, and the time was seven o'clock in the evening.

5

EXORCISM MADE EASY

As a professional forester, Walter Egger really had no
business in the forest outside Singen on a Saturday.

Saturday 12 July 1986 was, however, a fine day along
the border between West Germany and Switzerland and,
anyway, Egger liked being in the forest.

He therefore set off at a little after nine o'clock in the
morning, dressed, as are all good Germans when they
go into the forest, in green loden knee breeches, braces,
stout boots and a green felt hat with a feather in it. He
was carrying a heavy walking stick and a light lunch,
prepared with his own hands as he was, although in his
mid-thirties, still unmarried.

He had intended to walk as far as the shore of Lake
Constance, a dozen miles to the east, but he had barely
got outside town when the walk ended.

Parked beside the logging trail leading into the forest
was a grey Volkswagen Rabbit with a long blue plastic
tube attached to the exhaust pipe. The other end of the
tube passed through the slightly rolled-down window on
the driver's side and the opening around it was stuffed
with rags.

'*Gott im Himmel!*,' cried Egger, running forward to
jerk open the door.

A stench of stale air hit him in the face. Carbon mon-
oxide does not smell, but the two men sitting in the
front seat had been in the confined space of the car for
some time.

They were obviously dead. The bodies were cold and
he could find no trace of respiration or heart beat. As

the men were dressed in black and wore large wooden crosses around their necks, Egger took them for two priests who had committed suicide together.

On the other hand, they seemed remarkably young to be priests, not much more than boys, he thought.

Whatever they were, this was a terrible tragedy and the obvious thing to do was summon the police.

Singen has as large a police force as might be expected in a town of fifty thousand, and the homicide squad came out immediately. Even if murderer and victim were identical, it was still legally homicide.

The victims were quickly identified from the personal identification cards in their wallets and neither was a priest. They were José Ferrero and Patrick Heilmann, aged respectively twenty-one and seventeen. Both were listed as resident at 23 Erzberg Strasse in Singen. The car, which had run completely out of petrol, was owned by Ferrero.

Even before identification, Inspector Max Lubbers had not taken the victims for priests. He had thought that they were homosexuals. Such people sometimes had emotional problems which made them prone to suicide pacts.

'Religious homosexuals?' said his assistant, Detective Sergeant Franz Brinkmann. 'What about the clothes and the wooden crosses and the ones painted on the car?'

There were two large white crosses daubed onto the door panels of the Volkswagen on either side.

'Homosexuals can be as religious as anybody else,' said the inspector, absently brushing back the tips of his drooping black moustache, which tended to get into the corners of his mouth. 'Rather more than most, I should think. Do you want to examine them here, Karl?'

Dr Karl-Heinz Paechter, the department's medical expert, said that he did not. This was not a crime where clues might be lost if the bodies were moved, and he could carry out the examinations more conveniently at the morgue. There would have to be a postmortem in any case.

55

'All right,' said the inspector. 'Let's get the photographs of the scene and take them in. We'll move the driver to the back seat so you can drive the car, Franz.'

The sergeant looked unhappy, but said nothing. He was a tall, skinny man with a long, thin nose which turned slightly down at the end and pale grey eyes set too closely on either side of it.

The inspector was, by contrast, remarkably handsome. His features were chiselled. His jaw was firm. His brow was lofty and he had a fine, clear complexion.

Dr Paechter was blond, overweight and wore glasses with such thick lenses that he resembled a frog peering through the bottom of a water tumbler.

He was, however, a highly competent medical officer and, three-quarters of an hour after the party's arrival back in Singen, he was able to make a report.

'Asphyxiation by the exhaust gases,' he said, resting a fleshy buttock on a corner of the inspector's desk. 'Death took place in both cases at around ten in the evening of Thursday. No signs of violence. Incidentally, no signs of homosexuality either.'

'Perhaps it was platonic,' said the inspector. 'All right, Franz. Nip on over to 23 Erzberg Strasse and notify the next of kin. They'll have to make arrangements with a funeral parlour for the burials.'

Erzberg Strasse is a long street beginning near the railway station and running generally north to the edge of the city. Many of the houses on it are villas, and number twenty-three is a particularly large one.

A sign over the front door proclaimed that this was the seat of The International Association for the Preservation of World Peace.

Reflecting that this seemed an imposing goal for an organization based in Singen, the sergeant rang the bell and, after a short wait, was startled when the door was opened by a young man wearing precisely the same black clothing and wooden pectoral cross as the suicides in the Volkswagen.

Informed of his mission, the young man took him

56

directly and without comment to a large, comfortably decorated room on the second floor where two old women, dressed in clothing similar to nuns' habits, were seated at a table eating sausages and drinking beer.

'This police officer says that José and Patrick have ascended to paradise, Holy Mother,' said the young man, inclining his head in a reverential bow.

'I am happy for them,' said the older of the two women, speaking as if the sergeant were not present, 'but why does he come to us?'

'We have no information as to their current whereabouts,' said the sergeant dryly. 'They committed suicide and someone has to bury them.'

'We can accept no financial responsibility,' said the Holy Mother quickly. 'We are a non-profit-making religious organization. Also, they were no longer members. They left us last week. I can give you the addresses of their families, and they will no doubt take care of funeral expenses.'

The somewhat bemused sergeant returned to police headquarters with the addresses of the next of kin, who, it seemed, lived in Munich.

'Some kind of a sect,' he said. 'The Holy Mother is a cool head. She caught on to the idea of the funeral expenses like a shot.'

'Have to have a cool head in that business,' observed the inspector. 'The competition is fierce. You didn't gain the impression that there was anything funny going on?'

'What could there be?' said the sergeant. 'The women must be in their seventies.'

The relatives of the dead boys were contacted. The bodies were sent to Munich for burial. The case was closed.

'I wonder what the motive was,' said the sergeant. 'They definitely weren't homosexuals.'

'Maybe they committed suicide because they weren't,' said the inspector. 'It's become so popular nowadays.'

The sergeant did not find this amusing. He had had a vaguely disturbing experience when he had gone to

The International Association for the Preservation of World Peace to pick up the dead boys' personal possessions which they had, oddly, left there.

He had heard a faint voice calling, "Help! Help!" and, when he had drawn this to the attention of the Holy Mother, she had said that it was her parrot, Hansi.

Perhaps finding the sergeant's expression sceptical, she had had the parrot brought in.

It was a red and green parrot whose wings had been clipped and it scrabbled about on the floor, crying out, 'Help! Help!'

'He is twenty years old,' said the Holy Mother, 'and he has never learned to say anything else.'

She was looking at the bird pensively and the sergeant had the strange impression that she was wondering what roast parrot might taste like.

'No wonder he keeps yelling "Help! Help!",' he muttered, seating himself at his desk in the inspector's office. 'Strange thing to teach a parrot to say.'

It would be a long time before the suppressed thought that had been troubling him rose to the surface of his mind.

The faint voice calling, "Help! Help!" had not sounded entirely like a parrot.

The sergeant was, by this time, working on another case, the disappearance and suspected murder of Mrs Anna Wermuthshaeuser, a wealthy sixty-six-year-old widow, who had neither friends nor close relatives, but who did have heirs who were very curious as to whether she was alive or dead.

They had not reported her disappearance very promptly, however, for when the sergeant began investigating, he was unable to find anyone who had seen Mrs Wermuthshaeuser since the beginning of 1983.

As it was now August of 1987, this meant that the woman had been missing for over four years without anyone reporting it.

'She was apparently a very retiring person who had trouble making contact with other people,' said the sergeant, reporting his findings to the inspector.'Once her husband was dead, she scarcely set foot out of the house.'

'What did you find in the house?' said the inspector.

The sergeant had supervised a detail which had carried out a search of Mrs Wermuthshaeuser's expensive villa.

. 'Nothing,' said the sergeant. 'There's no way of knowing what clothing may be missing, but her personal toilet articles are and the place was closed down as if she was going on a trip. The water, gas and electricity were ordered turned off as of 1 September 1982.'

'And she's not been seen since that date?' said the inspector.

'Several times in September, October and December, but nowhere near her home,' said the sergeant. 'Most of the sightings were in the Erzberg Strasse.'

'Strange, very, very strange,' mused the inspector. 'So she didn't go on a trip outside the city. She must have moved in with someone else, but why doesn't she or why don't they contact us? We've had appeals in all the newspapers and on the radio.'

'If she's dead, the only people who stand to benefit are the heirs,' said the sergeant.

'All right, check them then,' said the inspector, 'but if she hasn't been seen since the beginning of nineteen eighty-three, I doubt that we'll be able to determine much.'

He was right. The sergeant was not able to determine anything at all.

'What about the witnesses who saw her in late eighty-two?' said the inspector. 'Maybe they noticed something about her . . . ?'

'I'll ask them to come in and you can talk to them,' said the sergeant.

It was the second of four witnesses who made the puzzling remark.

'She looked as if she'd gone back into mourning,' she said. 'Everything black.'

'Dressed all in black?' murmured the inspector.

'Where have I heard that before. Didn't you say something about somebody dressed all in black, Franz?'

The sergeant could not remember. He too had the impression that there had been talk of somebody dressed in black, but he could not think who or when it had been.

The inspector had the witnesses brought to the station for new statements and it turned out that they had all seen Mrs Wermuthshaeuser wearing black.

The statements became something little short of an interrogation. The inspector's instincts were telling him that here was something of importance, if only he could put his finger on it.

'Maybe she'd been to church,' said one of the witness. 'She was wearing a cross. . . .'

'Cross!' shouted the inspector, nearly frightening the witness out of her wits. 'Black clothing! Erzberg Strasse! That's it!'

What "it" might be was less clear. Obviously, the connection that the inspector had been seeking was to José Ferrero and Patrick Heilmann, who had committed suicide while dressed in black and wearing wooden crosses around their necks and who had been members of The International Association for the Preservation of World Peace in Erzberg Strasse, but what had that to do with a sixty-six-year-old widow?

'The Holy Mother is older than that,' said the sergeant, 'but all of the other people I saw up there were young, under forty at any rate.'

'You never know about these religious sects,' muttered the inspector. 'Take as many men as you need and get me a complete rundown on everybody in that place. I think we may be on to something.'

They were, and the sergeant did not need many men to find it out. In order to be exempt from taxes, The International Association for the Preservation of World Peace had to be registered as a non-profit-making religious organization, and for such purposes the name of Holy Mother would not do. Consequently, seventy-year-old Maria Magdalena Kohler had had to make the registration under her own name.

The other old woman had also signed. Her name was Hilde Roeller and she was sixty-eight years old.

Neither name meant anything to the sergeant, but the inspector thought that he had heard the name of Maria Magdalena Kohler before.

'It was a long, long time ago,' he said. 'You would still have been in school. I'd just started in criminal investigations. Something in Switzerland. . . .'

'They're both German citizens,' said the sergeant.

'Run the names through the central registry file,' said the inspector. 'There should be something on them.'

There was a great deal. Twenty years earlier in Ringwil, Switzerland, Maria Magdalena Kohler and a man named Josef Stocker had been the joint heads of a religious sect specializing in, among other things, exorcism and the driving out of evil spirits.

Among their disciples was a family named Hasler, and the oldest daughter, Bernadette, was very pretty.

Although it was never proven, there were allegations to the effect that Bernadette had been diagnosed as possessed of the devil because she did not submit to Stocker's sexual demands.

In any case, the young student was turned over to the sect by her family in March of 1966 to be exorcised of her evil spirits.

Stocker and Kohler proposed to accomplish this by mortification of the flesh. Bernadette was stripped naked, bound to an altar and beaten for hours on end by the entire group of some twelve or fourteen people. She was deprived of food and water, left naked in unheated rooms and forced to humiliating confessions of lewd thoughts and actions.

Surprisingly, the treatmant failed to dislodge the evil spirits, whose presence could be detected only by Stocker and Kohler, and it was therefore continued and intensified until 14 May 1966, when Bernadette died.

Her parents, finally coming to their senses, called the

police, and Stocker, Kohler and a number of the other sect members including Hilde Roeller, who was Maria Magdalena's half-sister, were arrested and charged with murder.

The sect members all disclaimed responsibility on the grounds that they had only been following the orders of their spiritual leaders, whom they were sworn to obey.

Kohler and Stocker disclaimed responsibility on the grounds that they were only the instruments of God. The court had no jurisdiction over them. If it wanted to try someone, it should try God.

This defence was not entirely successful and both defendants were sentenced to ten years' imprisonment. The sect members were got off by the psychologists, who testified that when they had beaten Bernadette, they had sincerely believed that they were beating out the devil and that it was for her own good.

Ten years was not oversevere for slowly torturing a girl to death over a period of more than two months, but the murderers had not even had to serve that.

Both were deported to Germany, where Stocker assumed the title of the Holy Preacher and amassed a sufficient number of converts to die a wealthy man in 1980.

Maria Magdalena also founded a new sect and, after moving around Germany for several years, settled in Singen. She was able to buy the villa, which she christened "Noah's Ark", for cash. She was still accompanied by her sister.

As Germany is a country in which everything is neatly registered and recorded by competent civil servants, once the sergeant knew the Holy Mother's real name, he had no difficulty in tracing her movements and activities following her expulsion from Switzerland. As for the events in Switzerland, these were recorded in the Swiss court and police records. Copies had been sent to the West German central crime registry.

'Good God!' exclaimed the inspector. 'We should have checked that woman's identity long ago. This puts the

suicides of those two boys and Wermuthshaeuser's disappearance in a totally different light. We have to assume
now that the woman is dead.'

The sergeant did not reply. He was reading a report
written at the time of the investigation by one of the
Ringwil detectives and it was causing such queer
emotions that he was incapable of speech.

'Maria Magdalena Kohler [the investigating officer had written]
is the owner of a young green and red parrot which was present
at the time that Miss Hasler was being tortured. Her cries so
impressed it that its vocabulary became fixed on the words,
"Help! Help!" and it appears unable to say anything else. It
has been turned over to the Ringwil Society for the Protection
of Animals, where it will be kept until it can be restored to its
owner.'

'Hansi!' whispered the awed sergeant. 'My God! He's
still alive!'

Which was undoubtedly more than could be said for
Anna Wermuthshaeuser.

'It wasn't our fault,' said the inspector. 'She wasn't
even reported missing until this year, and she would
have been long dead by then.'

'Tortured to death,' said the sergeant. 'Is there anything we can do to keep this from happening again?'

'I don't know, Franz,' said the inspector. 'I don't
know.'

The problem was, of course, that a great deal of time
had passed since the presumed murder of Anna
Wermuthshaeuser and whatever traces there might have
been would long since have been effaced.

'The body could be anywhere in the country,' said the
inspector. 'By next month, she'll have had five years to
get rid of it.'

Next month was January of 1988. As might be
expected, it was cold, bitterly cold, and the slate-grey
bellies of the snow clouds hung low over the little town.
At night, the savage wind blowing down from the frozen
peaks of the alps, within sight to the south, whined and

snarled about the villa at 23 Erzberg Strasse. Sometimes, when its voice died, a faint voice could be heard calling, "Help! Help!"

Was it Hansi, desperate to recover the lost ecstasy of flight, flinging himself from his perch to scrabble, earthbound and despairing, on the cold floor?

But then, why did the voice sometimes cry, "Help me!"?

"Me" is a hard word for a parrot to pronounce.

The seventh of February 1988 was a Sunday, and neither the inspector nor the sergeant was at work. It was one of the advantages of the homicide squad. You worked around the clock when you were on a case, but when you were not, you had the weekends free.

Not this one, however. At a quarter to seven in the morning, the inspector's telephone rang.

The inspector, who was not yet out of bed, pulled the instrument out of its cradle and groaned, 'Lubbers' into the mouthpiece.

The duty sergeant at headquarters sounded apologetic.

'We've a report of an apparent homicide at 23 Erzberg Strasse,' he said. 'A woman named Wermuthshaeuser. I have a patrol car at the scene and—'

'What?' screamed the inspector, instantly wide awake. 'Oh my God! Why didn't we do something sooner?'

It took him less than fifteen minutes to arrive at 23 Erzberg Strasse, but Sergeant Brinkmann and Dr Paechter were there before him.

The sergeant had been the first to be called and he had literally dragged the doctor away from his breakfast table.

The two junior detectives on duty in the department of criminal investigations that Sunday morning were also at the scene, and so were the officers from two patrol cars. At headquarters, the dispatcher was calling in the specialists and technicians from the various departments that would be involved.

Maria Magdalena Kohler and Hilde Roeller were sitting in the living room where the sergeant had first seen them, looking calm but mildly offended. On the long table where they had eaten their sausages and drunk their beer, Hansi was staggering drunkenly up and down crying, 'Help! Help!'

Four of the disciples were on their knees in the room next door, engaged in prayer. The others had fled.

It was one of those remaining who had called the police, and he led the inpector down to the chapel in the basement where the body of Anna Wermuthshaeuser lay, still bound to the altar.

It was a bare and cheerless chapel with no ornamentation and no source of heat. The temperature was below freezing.

Anna Wermuthshaeuser had been left there naked, her flesh bruised and torn from an incredible five and a half years of beatings. A large, solidly built woman, she was unrecognizable and weighed less than seventy pounds.

'The evil spirit was very strong in her,' said the disciple. 'We were never able to get it out.'

'It's out now,' said the inspector.

Dr Paechter carried out a brief examination of the corpse and reported that Anna Wermuthshaeuser had died at around midnight on Saturday as the result of malnutrition and exposure. There was scarcely a square inch of her flesh which did not show the results of countless beatings.

The technicians poured into the house and began photographing the corpse, locating the rods with which the woman had been beaten and inventorying the over half a million dollars' worth of paintings, carpets and art objects with which the villa was furnished. Meanwhile Maria Magdalena Kohler, Hilde Roeller and the remaining disciples were taken to police headquarters for charging and questioning.

All proved to be cooperative and answered the inspector's questions readily.

Anna Wermuthshaeuser had come to Noah's Ark in

the late summer of 1982 seeking spiritual comfort. She was, she had said, lonely.

The Holy Mother had replied, 'You are not lonely. You are possessed.'

Anna had agreed to be exorcised of her evil spirits, but they had proved stubborn, and by the beginning of 1983 her physical condition had deteriorated to the point that she could not go out without people asking if she needed help.

She had from that time remained permanently in Noah's Ark, undergoing the mortification of the flesh deemed necessary to her redemption.

This had included spending nights naked on a balcony in the middle of winter, an extremely restricted diet and the ritual beatings administered by members of the sect – above all by the Holy Mother, who, despite her age, was possessed of a strong right arm.

José Ferrero and Patrick Heilmann had not been enthusiastic about the beatings and had either been forced out of the sect or had departed voluntarily. The circumstances were never entirely clear. The police theory was that the suicides were due to the conflict resulting from their unwillingness to denounce the sect and guilt over abandoning Anna Wermuthshaeuser to her fate.

The disciples were now also filled with guilt and repentance, but not Maria Magdalena Kohler.

'I am the instrument of God,' she said calmly. 'You have no right to interfere in God's work. I shall smite the demon wherever he is found.'

Neither Maria Magdalena Kohler, her sister Hilde Roeller nor any of the disciples ever came to trial. The Holy Mother was committed to an institution for the criminally insane, where she will remain for the rest of her life, and her sister and the disciples were found to be so completely under her influence that they could not be held legally responsible for their acts.

Hansi has been found a new home and is busy regrowing his wing feathers. His new owner has not been told his history or why he can say only, "Help! Help!"

She thinks it cute, but she might not be able to bear to hear him if she knew the circumstances under which he learned the words.

6

MENTALLY DISADVANTAGED VAMPIRE

Far down in the southwest corner of France, where the rock fingers of the Pyrénées dip their ribbed nails into the Mediterranean, a string of villages dots the coastal highway running from Argelès-sur-Mer to the Spanish border.

Collioure, Port Vendres, Banyuls-sur-Mer, Cerbère . . . charming little fishing ports where olives and grapes grow on slopes overlooking tiny sheltered harbours.

The people of the villages are not rich. Few are in the southwest of France, but there are compensations. The cost of living is relatively low and the climate is dry and warm.

Delightful as they are, the villages to the south of Perpignan do not attract large numbers of tourists. The hotels to house them and the restaurants to feed them are lacking, and no hotels and restaurants are built because there are not enough tourists to fill them.

However, few as they are, tourists, hotels and restaurants transform the summer atmosphere so that, as in all resorts, the off season is a little melancholy.

And the saddest place of all in the off season is a year-around amusement park.

Wednesday 14 December 1977 was off season, and the shabby little amusement park on the outskirts of Port Vendres was about as gay as the funeral of an impecunious aunt. Although there was no lack of visitors, most of them were children or adolescents with very little money to spend.

There was practically no other entertainment in Port Vendres, which has a permanent population of barely five thousand.

Winter comes late to the south of France. The afternoon was warm and, with the fall of darkness, the atmosphere became more cheerful. Neon lights flashed on, the music of the rides rose louder and wilder, and the roars of the monster hanging menacingly over the entrance to the fun palace took on a terror unsustainable in daylight.

He was a fine monster, a vampire, of course, but one with lovely long white blood-stained fangs, sunken dark eyes, lank stringy hair and a nose like a hook. His fingers were two feet long and each ended in a terrifying curved claw. For a creature constructed largely of polystyrene, he was formidable.

Even so, his roars did not attract many. There were few left in Port Vendres who had not ridden many times the battered little cars through the dark tunnels that were not really tunnels at all, with the imitation spiders' webs, the shrieking skulls suddenly popping up and the recorded bursts of mad laughter.

The funhouse monster was not, however, the only vampire at the amusement park. There was another, and he was neither wired fast to a booth nor made of polystyrene. With eldritch screeches, he pursued the ecstatically squealing adolescent girls through the dimly lit passages behind the attractions.

Only adolescent girls knew that there was a real vampire at the amusement park. It was not the sort of thing that a girl confided to her mother.

Alas! Even the most carefree merry-making has an end. Electricity costs money, and the amusement park consumed a great deal of it. By ten o'clock, there was scarcely a light to be seen and not a single customer.

The funhouse vampire roared no more. The real vampire had, presumably, gone home to bed, and so had the adolescent girls who squealed so delightfully.

All except one.

'I shall skin the hussy!' said Benito Tonetto. 'I shall

remove the skin from her posterior with my belt! I shall. . . .'

'Sylvie is only a child, Benito,' said his wife. 'She is not doing what you think. I am afraid.'

'She is twelve,' said Benito darkly. 'Very well. You are afraid. I shall go and bring her home, but woe unto her, if. . . .'

In fact, the stocky little olive-skinned stonemason was more than a little concerned. Girls in the south of France mature early, but Sylvie was an exception. She not only still looked like a child; she acted like one.

A delicately pretty little girl, with long straight black hair and huge dark eyes, Sylvie had two great passions in her life. The first was her dolls. The second was exploding balloons with darts.

This latter activity could be pursued at the amusement park and, whenever Sylvie had any money, she went there to throw darts at balloons. Having had a great deal of practice, she was very good at this and invariably won prizes, which she traded for more darts.

It might be thought that the owner of the concession would be unhappy over this, but he was, in fact, delighted. Other people seeing a rather small twelve-year-old girl winning prizes with ease were tempted to try their own luck, and few were as skilful as Sylvie Tonetto.

Benito was fully aware af all this and he suspected that if Sylvie had not come home by ten, as she was supposed to, it was because park she was throwing darts at balloons. The insinuations of less innocent activities were for his wife's benefit.

He was, therefore, startled and frightened when he arrived at the amusement and found it dark and deserted.

Sylvie was obviously not there, so where was she? Could he have been right about what she was doing without believing it himself?

But in his heart he knew that he had not been right.

Sylvie was not interested in sex. Wherever she was, it was not in bed with one of the local swains.

So where in the name of God was she? A car accident was improbable. At this time of year there was scarcely any traffic in the village.

A girl friend?

Abruptly, he felt much better. Of course. Sylvie was spending the night with a girl friend. All he had to do was go home and point this out to Daniele. She would know who Sylvie's girlfriends were. She would telephone and confirm. Everything would be all right.

But he returned home at a dead run and his heart was beating much harder than it should have been for such a short sprint by a healthy thirty-six-year-old man.

Unacknowledged but present in the back of his mind was the thought, why hadn't Sylvie come home first to say where she was going? And why hadn't the family with whom she was staying telephoned to make sure it was all right?

Daniele was also relieved by his solution of the mystery, but her relief soon turned to terror as she telephoned, one after another, every girl Sylvie knew, only to learn that none could say where she was.

At eleven o'clock, Benito telephoned the Port Vendres police department and reported his daughter missing. Daniele was, by this time, nearly hysterical.

The report was taken very seriously. Port Vendres does not have a large police department, but the officers know practically every soul in town and many of them knew Benito Tonetto.

Although it was now completely dark, a search was immediately organized and, at midnight, the police in Perpignan, a town of over a hundred and twenty thousand residents, were called in.

A party of off-duty firemen and police from the uniform branch arrived in less than an hour and joined what was now nearly the entire population of Port Vendres in the search for the missing girl.

It was already certain that something serious had taken

place. Sylvie was not with any of her girl friends and all the village's teenage boys were accounted for. Either there had been an accident or a crime had taken place.

If there had been a traffic accident, it had not been reported. Port Vendres had only a modest clinic, and no little girls had been admitted there that evening.

Otherwise, there was only the sea.

In some places to the south of town, a path runs along the top of the cliffs overlooking the Mediterranean. It is not dangerous and Sylvie would, like all of the local children, have known it well.

Still, in the darkness it was possible to stumble over the edge, which in places meant a sheer forty-foot drop to broken rock or surf below.

Although there was no reason for Sylvie to have been on the path at night, the villagers searched the cliffs for nearly a mile, shining flashlights down from the top while boats nosed among the rocks at the foot.

At two in the morning, Inspector Pierre Despres, the short, balding, cigar-smoking chief of the Perpignan homicide squad, was roused out of bed and informed that a presumed homicide or possibly kidnapping of a minor had taken place in Port Vendres.

The kidnapping theory represented unwarranted optimism. The Tonettos were not in a position to pay even the most modest ransom.

The inspector immediately drove to Port Vendres, where he found his second-in-command, Detective Sergeant Gerard Saverne, already present and engaged in questioning Sylvie's girl friends.

An attractive young man with an open, good-natured face and curly brown hair extending down below the level of his collar, he had determined that Sylvie had last been seen at the amusement park that afternoon.

'She apparently liked throwing darts at balloons,' he said, 'and I've been trying to locate the fellow who operates the concession, but he must be out with one of the search parties. Eighteen-year-old kid named Charles Moinceaux.'

72

'Local?' asked the inspector. 'The people who work the fairs and amusement parks. . . .'

'No, not local,' said the sergeant. 'He doesn't own the concession. Hippie down for the winter, from the description. Hasn't been here long.'

'We want to talk to him,' said the inspector. 'What about the girl? Precocious? Promiscuous?'

'By all accounts, neither,' said the sergeant. 'There'd be more reason for optimism if she was.'

'All right. Stay with it,' said the inspector, 'I'll see what I can do about getting some dogs down here, but with all these people running about, it's doubtful that they'll be able to pick up a scent. Who's that clown jumping around over there?'

The man to whom he was referring looked like anything but a clown. He was tall and painfully thin, but with huge hands and feet, and his face was as grotesque as that of the vampire over the entrance to the funhouse. It was a long, large face, but all the features in it were too small – the eyes tiny, shiny-black and darting, the nose a mere stub and the mouth pursed, thick-lipped and too red. Although the top of his head was completely bald, a fringe of straight black greasy hair hung down to his shoulders on both sides and at the back. He was dressed entirely in black, except for a red scarf, and the colours did not suit him.

'Robert Nivelles,' said the sergeant. 'He owns the local newsstand and sweetshop.'

'Apparently takes the loss of a customer seriously,' muttered the inspector.

Nivelles was in a state of almost frenzied excitement, waving his long arms and running from one group of searchers to the next. He appeared to regard it as a personal affront that there was no report of the missing child.

'Another one we'd better have a long talk with,' observed the sergeant.

At the break of dawn, a handler with two tracking dogs was flown in by police helicopter. The dogs were given articles of Sylvie's clothing to smell and led to the amusement park, the last place she was reported to have been seen.

The dogs were able to pick up the trail at the balloon and dart concession, but, as the inspector had feared, lost it again almost immediately. The entire population of Port Vendres plus a large police contingent from Perpignan had been milling around the area all night long and the spoor was too confused for even the most sensitive nose to detect.

The search had been suspended long enough for the searchers to get a little rest and some breakfast. Many had been searching without respite straight through the night.

At the amusement park, the purveyors of hot dogs, hamburgers and coffee had opened their stands and were doing a roaring business, with the inspector and Sergeant Saverne among the customers.

The officers were by now convinced that Sylvie had been taken out of the area altogether. Although it was possible that she was being held in someone's house, this was not thought likely considering the size of the community.

At a little before ten o'clock, just as the inspector had taken a very large bite of a hot dog and was wiping away the mustard running down his chin, there was a piercing yell and the gawky figure of Robert Nivelles appeared, galloping across the meadow adjacent to the amusement park.

He appeared to be more than half mad with excitement and, as he arrived at where the police officers were standing, he began to croak out, 'Sylvie! Sylvie!' Too out of breath to express himself coherently, he seized the inspector's arm in a surprisingly powerful grip and tried to drag him toward the meadow.

The inspector was rather too heavy for convenient dragging, but he immediately grasped that the missing girl had been found and, accompanied by everyone present, he followed Nivelles across the meadow and down a faint path to the bank of a small brook.

Sylvie was lying on the grass fifteen feet from the brook and, at the sight of the child, any hope still nurtured by the searchers died.

The little girl lay on her back, her arms and legs twisted under her and her green tights knotted tightly over her mouth. From the waist down, she was naked, and the black smears of dried blood on her thin, childs thighs and hairless genitals showed only too plainly what had been done to her.

Most horrible of all, however, were the bite marks, clear imprints of human teeth cutting deep into the flesh of the legs, the belly and the throat of the dead girl!

Some one whispered, 'Vampire!' and the word was taken up, passed through the crowd, passed through the amusement park, passed through the village. Within minutes, there was no one in Port Vendres who did not know that Sylvie Tonetto had been raped and killed by a vampire.

Everyone except Inspector Despres, who did not believe in vampires. His first reaction to the discovery was to order the area cleared and cordoned off. This done, he sent the sergeant to summon Dr Hercule Poincelles, the department's expert in forensic medicine, and the technical investigative specialists from the police laboratory.

Simultaneously, he took into custody Robert Nivelles and issued an order for the arrest of Charles Moinceaux, whom the sergeant had so far been unable to locate.

Dr Poincelles did not believe in vampires either, but he thought that the murderer probably did.

'The primary motive was sexual,' he said. 'She was raped, and very roughly too. The child was, of course, a virgin. There is extensive damage to the walls of the vagina in addition to the ruptured hymen. The bites are not typical of a sadist. The man was probably interested in vampirism and tried to act like a vampire. Very painful, but not dangerous.'

75

'But inflicted after death, surely?' said the inspector.

'I'm afraid not,' said the doctor. 'She was apparently alive for some considerable time after the attack. The actual cause of death seems to have been shock, exposure and the tights. He used them as a gag and they were pulled so tightly into her mouth that she eventually strangled on them.'

The sergeant said something savage in a low voice and even the inspector turned slightly pale and looked away.

The doctor was more than a little shaken himself. A clean-cut, carefully groomed man in his mid-forties whose dark, slightly wavy hair was beginning to turn grey at the temples, he had had wide experience in his field, but the brutal rape and slow murder of a little girl was something that no one became hardened to.

His examination of the corpse completed, he withdrew to where the inspector and sergeant were waiting, while the photographer made a pictorial record of the scene and the clue-detection specialists began going over the ground.

When they had finished working around the body, it was carefully lifted onto a stretcher, wrapped in plastic and taken to the waiting ambulance.

Lifting the body revealed that the child's hands and feet had been bound together behind her back with rusty wire. Trussed and gagged, Sylvie had been helplessly at the mercy of the vampire.

Which was what he was being called, even by the police, despite the inspector's objections.

'Maybe he isn't a supernatural vampire like Dracula,' said the sergeant, 'but, by God, he's vampire enough for Port Vendres.'

The residents of Port Vendres thought so too, and they were displaying a startling knowledge of the time-honoured methods for dealing with vampires.

Passing through the village on the way to his car, the inspector encountered men carrying pitchforks, sharp stakes, ropes, axes and shotguns.

'Silver bullets?' asked the inspector sarcastically.

'Salt,' said the sergeant. 'People who can't afford silver load shotgun shells with rock salt. Supposed to be nearly as effective.'

The inspector turned to look thoughtfully at his assistant. It appeared that the sergeant was better informed on the subject of vampires than he would have thought.

'Good thing we sent Nivelles to Perpignan,' said the sergeant. 'He looks altogether too much like a vampire to be safe here.'

'Nobody's safe here until this thing is solved,' said the inspector, 'and that means we'd better locate Moinceaux in a hurry. We're not the only ones who know that she was last seen at his stand and that she was killed almost within sight of the amusement park.'

'I still can't understand why she wasn't found before,' said the sergeant. 'As far as I'm concerned, that's the most tragic thing of all. If we'd found her last night, she might still have been alive.'

'Probably too careful reasoning,' said the inspector. 'They didn't believe anything could happen that close to all the people at the amusement park, so they checked the cliffs and the roads and didn't think to go over the open fields.'

'But Nivelles did,' said the sergeant. 'Strange no one else thought of it.'

'That's why he's in custody,' said the inspector, 'and he'll remain there until Poincelles determines the time she was raped.'

The time was of vital importance to Nivelles' standing as a suspect. If it was before five o'clock, he was in the clear, for witnesses had testified that he was in his shop up until that time.

However, even such evidence of his innocence would not be enough to permit his immediate return to Port Vendres. Nivelles was well known for his attachment to children and his shop had been a sort of social centre for them. Although he carried the usual newspapers, magazines and stationery supplies, he also stocked a large selection of toys, comics, sweets and ice cream.

Sylvie Tonetto had been a customer, and some of the girls said that she had been Nivelles' favourite.

The shopkeeper did not deny it. He had, he said, loved Sylvie as much as if she were his own child.

'I have no children of my own and I never will have,' he told the inspector sadly. 'Who would marry a man who looks like me? I love little girls. I could never harm one.'

The inspector was inclined to believe him, but there were stories in the village that Nivelles had sometimes exchanged sweets and ice cream for rather too intimate caresses, and there had been a formal charge of child molestation two years earlier. It had been dropped when the thirteen-year-old girl in question refused to make a statement.

Nivelles therefore remained a suspect, pending the findings of the autopsy, but the inpector was really much more interested in Charles Moinceaux, the operator of the balloon and dart stand.

It had been assumed that Moinceaux was out with one of the search parties. Now that the body had been found, the search parties returned to Port Vendres and broke up.

Moinceaux remained missing and, following interrogation of the searchers, it developed that he had not been with any of the groups.

This unexplained absence immediately elevated Moinceaux to the top of the suspect list and, twenty-four hours later, he became the only suspect when the autopsy report fixed the time of the rape as four in the afternoon, plus or minus fifteen minutes.

The cause of death was, as suspected, the gag – and Sylvie had taken a heartbreaking six hours to die.

Nivelles was released and the name of Charles Moinceaux was sent to the national crime registry, which replied with a terse "no record".

This surprised the inspector. Sex murderers, whether of children or adults, nearly always have a record of previous sex offences.

After mulling over the matter for a time, he sent a team of fingerprint experts to the balloon and darts stand, which was now closed for lack of someone to operate it.

Moinceaux had, of course, handled many things there and the experts were able to recover a nearly full set of his fingerprints.

Sent to the central registry, these produced a different response.

Charles Moinceaux was really Thierry Badru, a nineteen-year-old sex psychopath who had been released from detention on a rehabilitation programme and had immediately disappeared. The Paris police were still looking for him.

'Could be our man,' said the inspector. 'He's never raped a girl as young as Sylvie before, but he's not particular. They say he'll attack anything female.'

'But wouldn't he clear out anyway, with a record like that?' asked the sergeant. 'He was on the run and using a false identity. Then a girl that was coming to his stand all the time disappears and the police are called in to hunt for her. He'd be afraid of being exposed, whether he was guilty or not.'

'True,' said the inspector, 'but we still have to find him. In the meantime, you can continue with the investigation in Port Vendres. See what you can do with the teenagers.'

The sergeant could do a lot with teenagers and for the first time it was learned that there had been more than one vampire at the amusement park.

'Young girls' secret,' said the sergeant, reporting to the inspector. 'He's a good-looking dog and they got a lot of fun out of being chased by him.'

'And he never caught them?' asked the inspector. 'What is French youth coming to?'

'Apparently not,' said the sergeant. 'He may not have known what to do with them, if he had. The boy's twenty-two years old, but he's mentally subnormal. Illiterate, a drifter. He works the scooters at the amusement park.'

'You clearly don't regard him as much of a suspect,' observed the inspector. 'What's his name?'

'Patrick Crolbois,' said the sergeant. 'I don't see how he could have done it. He went to work on the scooters at two in the afternoon and he was still there when the park closed down at ten.'

'No, I suppose not,' said the inspector, frowning. 'Still, the rape took place less than five hundred yards from the amusement park. . . . Better go a little further into his background. He doesn't have a police record, does he?'

'Not if his name's really Crolbois,' said the sergeant, thinking of the missing Thierry Badru, otherwise known as Charles Moinceaux.

The name really was Crolbois and there was nothing of significance in his background. One of nine children, he was believed to have suffered brain damage as a child as a result of his father's habit of beating him over the head with a poker. He had never been arrested or charged with anything.

His impersonation of a vampire had apparently been nothing more than a rather childish game from which the girls had perhaps expected more than he had.

The inspector had, in any case, lost interest in Crolbois, for the fugitive Thierry Badru had been arrested in Marseille and was now on his way back to Perpignan.

Whether for once innocent or whether the thought patterns of sex criminals and detective sergeants resemble each other, Badru offered precisely the explanation of his disappearance that Sergeant Saverne had theorized.

'I already had a record,' he said, 'and they were looking for me in Paris. Then this kid disappears, and it's the very one who was blasting the balloons every afternoon. Of course I cut and run. Wouldn't you?'

The inspector was forced to admit that, under similar circumstances, he might have.

He did not agree, however, that Badru's job at the balloon stand was an alibi. He had since learned that the operators of the attractions at the amusement park often got one of their fellows to relieve them while they went to the toilet, had a beer, ate something, took a nap or went on one of the other rides. It was not unknown for an amorous adventure to take place in one of the caravans parked behind the stands while the concession operator was theoretically on duty.

Although none of them was local, most of the amusement park employees were young and what is called in France "marginals". Perhaps for this reason, they displayed considerable solidarity and none admitted noticing any absences at around four o'clock.

'Which means that we have no hope of an indictment,' said the inspector. 'It was probably Badru, considering his record, but it could have been Crolbois or even somebody we don't suspect at all. The worst part is that if he gets away with this, he'll try it again.'

'If he'd only stabbed her or hit her with a piece of pipe or anything that we could have got a fingerprint from . . .' said the sergeant. 'But he didn't leave a print anywhere at the scene.'

'Not a fingerprint,' agreed the inspector absently. 'He left enough prints of his teeth on the body.'

For a moment, there was total silence in the office, and then the inspector slowly turned his head to stare at his assistant.

Sergeant Saverne stared back.

'We could still get casts,' he said. 'Even if we have to exhume the body.'

'Exactly,' said the inspector. 'Even if both of them have perfect sets of teeth, they still won't have the same size jaws.'

Exhumation of the body of Sylvie Tonetto was not necessary. Dr Poincelles had thought of identification by the bite marks, even if the inspector and the sergeant had not, and he had conscientiously made precise casts of them.

Compared with sample bite marks by Patrick Crolbois and Thierry Badru, they fixed the identity of the murderer as clearly as would have fingerprints.

In one respect, Patrick Crolbois was an authentic vampire. His incisor teeth were exceptionally long and they had punched deep into the tender flesh of Sylvie Tonetto.

Crolbois, who up until this time had been clever enough to deny the murder, suddenly became much more mentally handicapped, and his court-appointed attorney claimed that the blows over the head by his father's poker had so addled his brains that he was not responsible for his acts.

A jury accepted this argument only to a limited degree, and on 17 March 1978 found Crolbois guilty of rape and murder and sentenced him to twenty years' imprisonment.

There was heavy security at the trial as the police did not want the residents of Port Vendres to shoot the accused full of salt or try to drive a stake through his heart, but there were no incidents.

It was accepted that Patrick Crolbois was a murderer, a rapist and a monster, but no one believed him to be a vampire.

After all, he did not look like one.

7

LUST BEYOND THE GRAVE

Sometime during the late summer of 1983, the terror
began.

It attracted little general interest. Vienna is a capital
city of over two million, and terror is commonplace.

Anyway, the victims of the terror were all old ladies
no longer capable of contributing anything to society. In
progressive, evolved countries, such people are ex-
pendable.

Young men, of course, are not. Even if they display
modest criminal tendencies at first, these can be ironed
out by the psychologists. A young criminal has the
potential to become a worker and a taxpayer. Old ladies
have no potential at all.

At the age of eighty-eight, Mrs Maria Diephold qualified as an old lady. Although she was not quite as alert
as she had once been, she was well aware of her slight
value to society and she was cautious. She did not have
much money, but what she had, she carried with her in
her handbag.

This was a mistake.

The young man who stepped out of the alley seized
the handbag and tried to tear it out of her hand.

Mrs Diephold resisted.

The man hit her twice very hard in the face.

Mrs Diephold's glasses were broken and so was her
nose. Even her dental plate was cracked.

Blinded and bleeding, she let go of the bag.

The young man left and a short time later a woman
came by and found Mrs Diephold leaning against the

wall. Her nose had stopped bleeding, but she could not see well enough without her glasses to make her way home.

The woman took her to the sixteenth precinct police station, where an ambulance was summoned to take her to hospital. Her injuries were not serious, but, considering her age, it was thought best that she have medical attention.

Mrs Diephold made a statement to the police in which she said that her assailant was young, under twenty perhaps, stocky, and stylishly dressed in a jeans suit and trainers. His hair was blond, straight and medium long. He was not bad-looking, but he had a rather dull-witted expression.

This was a remarkably detailed description for a woman of eighty-eight who had seen the mugger for only an instant, but, there being several hundred thousand people in Vienna of similar appearance, the police were not optimistic about finding him.

In fact, they did not try – nor was there any practical way that they could. Like any big, modern city, Vienna is full of idle young people who are neither qualified for work nor seeking any. Some are on drugs and all need money. Every few days or so, it occurs to one of them that old ladies are an excellent source of it.

Generally speaking, all the police could do was wait. If the mugger was greedy or had an expensive habit, he would strike repeatedly and frequently and thus increase the chances of his being taken in the act.

Not, of course, that this would help matters much either. Liberal-minded judges tend to look upon beating up and robbing old ladies as a sort of boyish prank, an indication of high spirits, of commendable initiative, even. The mugger would get a lecture, a suspended sentence, possibly a few weeks in detention. The victim would not even get her money back.

None the less, Mrs Diephold's mugging had been officially reported and it formed the subject of a police file. The file was dated July the twenty-eighth, and for nearly two months nothing was added to it.

Had the police been asked why, they would undoubtedly have replied that ninety per cent of such cases went unreported.

The old ladies knew how little good such a report would do them and saved themselves the trip to the police station.

They did, however, talk and, although it would be saying too much to suggest an old ladies' grapevine, the news of a mugging did get around in the neighbourhood where it took place.

As a result, the old ladies tended to be a little more cautious during that summer of 1983, but it did not help them.

At least, it did not help Louise Grundbauer, who was eighty-four years old and walked with a cane.

On the afternoon of September the twenty-first, the mugger took away her cane and hit her over the head with it. He then left with her handbag.

Mrs Grundbauer was knocked unconscious and ended up in the emergency section of the sixteenth precinct hospital. Her statement was added to the Diephold police file because the attack had taken place in the same area and the description of the mugger was roughly the same – blonde, stocky, stupid-looking.

Neither Mrs Diephold nor Mrs Grundbauer would have reported the muggings to the police had it not been for the medical treatment, which made a statement unavoidable – and it could be assumed that there had been a good many more such muggings by the same individual which had gone unreported.

Unreported to the police, that is. There were enough reports among the old ladies themselves so that by autumn they had become as rare on the streets of the sixteenth precinct as politicians interested in their plight.

One did venture out on October the seventh, and was promptly mugged. Her lack of caution was, however, excusable. Marthe Binz was eighty-nine years old and not in complete possession of all her faculties. Besides, her friends and relatives were all long since dead and she did not care very much what happened to her.

As she did not offer any resistance, she was not injured and the mugger got away with a handbag containing a great many rather strange items, but no money.

The pickings were getting thin in the sixteenth precinct. The old ladies were scarcely sticking their noses out of their houses and mugging anyone else could be dangerous. Muggers are not noted for their courage.

Something had to be done and, on the evening of December the thirtieth, the mugger did it.

Unlike Marthe Binz, Mrs Johanna Strobl still had a friend of her own generation, although she tended to look upon her as a little immature as she was ninety-two and Anna Huber was only ninety.

As a result of this age difference, it was usually Mrs Huber who came to visit Mrs Strobl and not vice versa.

At approximately ten-thirty in the morning of December the thirty-first, Mrs Huber came to visit Johanna Strobl in her ground floor flat at 13 Pallfy Gasse.

Mrs Strobl did not answer the doorbell, but the door was open, so Mrs Huber went in.

As she had expected from the moment she realized that the door was not locked, her friend was dead.

Mrs Strobl was lying just inside the door to the living room, her white hair stiff and dark with dried blood, her clothing pulled up to expose her body and her face coal black. There were a great many puncture wounds, particularly in the belly and thighs, from which blood had run and dried.

Mrs Huber was sad. She had known Mrs Strobl for a very long time. She was not frightened or shocked. Nothing can shock or frighten a ninety-year-old woman.

She therefore stepped over her friend's legs, made use of her telephone and called the police.

The homicide squad responded promptly, sending a sergeant of detectives named Franz Graumann to the address.

Mrs Huber had not seen fit to describe the body over the telephone and there had been a question as to whether this might not be one of the domestic accidents which terminate the lives of so many old people.

However, the sergeant had only to put his head round the door to determine that this was indeed homicide. Mrs Strobl was not only dead, but the entire flat had been turned upside down.

'Typical robbery-murder of an elderly woman,' said the sergeant, reporting to his chief at headquarters over the telephone. 'We'll need the full squad.'

He was very matter-of-fact about it. A stocky, neatly dressed man with the face of a medium-level civil servant, he had investigated more murders of old woman than any other kind. Even cab drivers and whores had a lower homicide rate.

Logically, Inspector Walter Brecht, the officer-in-charge of the homicide squad, should have been even more objective. He had been ten years longer in criminal investigations than the sergeant and, aside from some grey at the temples and a certain swelling of the waistline, looked very much like him.

But the Inspector was of a different nature and, although he could no long count the number of elderly murder victims he had seen, was invariably shocked and outraged.

'Something should be done!' he exclaimed. 'A ninety-two-year-old woman! There's no sense of decency today! These addicts prey on old women like wolves on rabbits.'

'You think it was an addict?' asked the sergeant. 'I see nothing to indicate that.'

'So much the worse if it wasn't,' said the inspector. 'What do you find, Julius?'

'Dead about thirteen or fourteen hours,' said Dr Julius Tetsch, a short tub of a man with a thick moustache who looked as if he smoked a pipe and, when he was not examining corpses, did. 'Say nine o'clock yesterday evening.'

'Strangulation, I suppose?' said the inspector. 'I've never seen one as black in the face as that.'

'Well, no,' answered the doctor. 'It's paint. Her face has been spray painted. The cause of death was either a fractured skull or internal bleeding from the stab wounds. I should be able to tell you which once I've completed the autopsy.'

'Spray painted?' said the sergeant. 'Why in heaven's name would he do that?'

'You'll have to ask him,' said the doctor. 'Graffiti artist maybe.'

'Madman!' muttered the inspector. 'I suppose she was raped too?'

'Doesn't seem to have been,' said the doctor. 'He may have pulled her clothes up to make it easier to stab her. He didn't use a knife. It was some kind of relatively dull tool.'

'A screwdriver,' said one of the technicians from the laboratory. 'He hit her over the head with a hammer and he stabbed her with a screwdriver. They're both here in the kitchen.'

'Hers?' said the inspector.

'Doubtful,' said the technician. 'They're both new. We also have one spray can of black enamel.'

'Weird!' said the inspector. 'Utterly, utterly weird.'

He returned to his office, leaving the sergeant and the technicians to complete the investigations at the scene. He did not expect them to find very much and in fact, they did not.

But they were able to arrive at a tentative reconstruction of the murder.

The killer had rung Mrs Strobl's doorbell and, when she opened the door a crack, had sprayed the black enamel into her face.

Blinded, she had staggered back towards the living room, possibly with the intention of calling the police, and he had come through the door to knock her unconscious with the hammer. He had then stabbed her to death, ransacked the flat and departed. It was not possible to say how much money he had got.

The results of the autopsy tended to confirm this theory of the murder. Either the hammer over the head or the screwdriver in the belly would have been fatal, which was not surprising considering the victim's age.

There were no clues which could be connected directly to the murder, but there was one interesting detail of information.

In her statement to the police, Anna Huber said that Mrs Strobl had told her only the preceding day that she had been followed in the street by a suspicious-looking young man.

He was stocky, she had said, with straight blond hair and a vacant sort of expression.

It did not occur to the sergeant that he himself had straight blond hair, was stocky and had, on the authority of his wife, a slightly blank expression. He ran the description through the central computer, which promptly produced the Diephold file.

'It's possible,' said the inspector. 'Normal progression really. They start with bag-snatching and move on to burglary, robbery and murder. Doesn't sound like an addict though. He's too fast on his feet.'

'Fast enough that he's not left a clue to his identity,' said the sergeant. 'What do you want to do?'

'What can we do?' said the inspector. 'I wouldn't want to arrest everybody in Vienna with that appearance.'

He had noticed the sergeant's resemblance to the description, even if the sergeant had not.

'Then wait for the next one,' said the sergeant stoically. 'It shouldn't be long.'

It was longer than he expected. Although there were a number of muggings in the sixteenth precinct, some reported and many more not, the next murder of an old woman did not take place until 18 April 1984.

The police, however, only learned of it at ten o'clock in the morning of the next day.

Fifty-eight-year-old Dieter Spengler had come to visit

his mother in her ground floor flat at 3 Detter Gasse in the sixteenth precinct.

Spengler visited his mother every day and, when he saw her on the afternoon of eighteenth, she had been in good health and spirits. Although she was eighty-six years old and lame so that she walked with a crutch, Franziska Spengler had not had so much as a cold in twenty years.

Her son was therefore alarmed when she did not answer the doorbell and even more so when he was unable to insert his key into the lock. It seemed that a key was sticking in the lock inside.

The problem with the key instantly brought to his mind an incident which had taken place a week earlier. His mother had forgotten her keys and left them sticking in the door outside. They had disappeared.

Dieter had insisted that she immediately have the lock changed, and she had said that she would, but perhaps she had not got around to it yet. As a matter of fact, it had also slipped his mind that the lock was to be changed.

In any case, the situation was alarming and, after hammering vainly on the door with his fist, he ran to the nearest public telephone booth and called the police.

Normally, an Austrian needing to get a door open would call the fire department, which handles such matters, but Spengler was badly frightened and he wanted someone in a hurry.

A patrol car is never far away in Vienna and within a matter of minutes one arrived in the Detter Gasse.

The officers were, however, no more able to get the door open than Dieter Spengler had been.

'We can break it down,' said the senior patrol officer, 'or we can try to get in through the windows. Which do you prefer?'

'Try the windows,' said Spengler. 'The door is very solid.'

The officers left the building and, followed by the

distraught Spengler, crossed the small front garden to the side overlooked by the windows of Franziska's flat.

Although the morning was decidedly chilly, one of them stood wide open, the white voile curtains lifting out in the breeze.

'Mother!' yelled Spengler, his voice breaking with terror.

Franziska Spengler was of the old school which believed that fresh air was bad for you. She tended to overheat her flat and she would never have left a window wide open on such a cool day.

He ran forward to try to clamber through the window, which was well over his head, but the officers pulled him back. They too now thought that something serious had taken place in Mrs Spengler's flat and that there might be fingerprints on the window where the intruder had entered.

It was necessary to gain entrance to the flat immediately. Mrs Spengler could be injured and prompt action might save her life.

The patrolmen therefore returned to the front door of the flat and, after an unsuccessful effort to break it down, shot out the lock.

While one patrolman remained outside with Dieter Spengler, the other entered the flat with his service pistol at the ready, calling out Mrs Spengler's name.

There was no response and, having gone through the living room and kitchen, he found her in the first bedroom he entered.

She was lying on her bed, wearing her nightdress – which was stained in several places with dark, dried blood. The handles of a pair of scissors stood stiffly up from her chest and her face was blue from the effects of strangulation.

The patrolman holstered his pistol, returned to the hall, told his partner not to let Spengler enter the flat and went to telephone the homicide report to headquarters.

Twenty minutes later, Inspector Brecht, Sergeant

Graumann and Dr Tetsch arrived, followed immediately by the twenty-two members of the full homicide squad.

The doctor's inspection was brief and unsurprising. Franziska Spengler, he said, had died at approximately ten o'clock the preceeding evening as the result of manual strangulation. She had been stabbed after death with the kitchen scissors and with two kitchen knives, one of which had broken off in the body. She had been in bed at the time.

The technicians' report was more startling.

'Somebody spent the night in bed next to the corpse,' said the chief specialist. 'He or she hasn't been gone an hour.'

'Are you certain?' asked the inspector. 'That could mean he was still in the flat when the patrolmen got here.'

'See for yourself,' said the technician.

He had turned down the covers next to the corpse to display a dent the size and shape of a human body in the mattress.

'Feel it,' he said. 'It's still warm.'

'The patrolmen trying to get in the door must have woken him up,' said the sergeant, 'and he went out of the window. We thought he came in there.'

'No,' said the technician. 'He came in the front door. There was a set of keys sticking in the lock on the inside before the patrolman shot it off, and Mrs Spengler's are still in her handbag.'

The circumstances surrounding the murder of Franziska Spengler were clear. She had gone to bed at her usual hour of around ten o'clock. The murderer, who had, perhaps, been waiting to see the lights go out, entered with the stolen keys and, apparently, immediately murdered the woman in her own bed, using the shears and knives from her own kitchen. He had then got into bed next to the corpse and had slept through the night. He had still been in bed when Dieter Spengler arrived and had been aroused by either his or the patrolmen's efforts to get the door open. Realizing that someone was trying to enter the flat, he had simply gone out through the window and fled.

The only thing that was not clear was why.

In so far as could be determined, nothing had been stolen from the flat, nor were there any indications of a search. Mrs Spengler had had a sum equal to several hundred pounds in her handbag and in the drawer of a chest. The money had not been touched.

'It was probably because he didn't know about the son coming to visit every day,' said the inspector. 'Many old people like that are completely alone. If someone comes to visit them once a month, it's a lot. He thought he could take all the time he wanted.'

'And he simply hadn't got around to searching the place,' said the sergeant. 'That makes sense, but couldn't he be a psychopath whose motive was the murder itself? I can't see any normal person murdering a woman and then spending the night in bed with the corpse.'

'The murder would have shown more signs of sadism in that case,' said the inspector. 'Julius says that there was no sadism in it. He just strangled her to death and the stabbing was to make certain she was dead. There's no indication that he took any pleasure in it.'

'In short, just an average twenty-year-old youth from the Juvenile Care Centre,' said the sergeant.

The police knew that the murderer was twenty years old and they even knew his name and a great deal more about him.

He had carelessly gone away leaving his wallet with his personal identity papers lying on the night table beside the bed in which he had spent the night with his victim's corpse.

According to the papers, his name was Oswald Sibrol and he had spent most of his life in homes for orphans and abandoned children.

His history was on record with the juvenile department of the social welfare office and it was not remarkable by modern standards.

Sibrol's parents had never bothered to marry,

although Rudolf Sibrol acknowledged paternity of the boy. As they had not been interested in founding a family, they had put him into a home at an early age. He had been taken out and cared for by his mother briefly when he was eleven, but she had died and he had been returned to the home.

He was not regarded by the staff of the centre as difficult or violent and he had been within a few weeks of completing an apprenticeship as a pipefitter when he had, on 11 July 1983, suddenly run away.

The centre had heard nothing of him since and had not reported him as a runaway to the police because he was already twenty and would have been free to go in a few months anyway.

There were recent pictures of Sibrol, and, it appeared that he was stocky, had straight blond hair and looked somewhat stupid.

'Diephold, Grundbauer, Binz, Strobl,' said the inspector, 'and undoubtedly a few dozen more. Well, I suppose it beats pipefitting.'

'You think he's an addict?' said the sergeant.

'I think he's just the latest youth to hit upon this easy way of making a living,' said the inspector with bitter irony.

With his identity known and every police officer in Vienna looking for him, Oswald Sibrol could not remain at liberty for very long. Arrested while trying to snatch a handbag on 15 May 1984, he proved no match for the police interrogators and quickly confessed to the murders of Johanna Strobl and Franziska Spengler, plus a few dozen muggings and thefts.

Examined by the state psychologists, he was declared sane and fit to stand trial, but remarkably stupid. He really had no idea, they said, why he had killed the women, but he knew very well that it was wrong. His reason for spending the night in bed with the corpse was stupefyingly logical. He had been tired.

It was over a year before Sibrol came to trial and he

had by then discovered an understandable excuse for his acts.

It was, he told the judge, the fault of his grandfather, Gottlieb Sibrol, who had died three years earlier at the age of eighty-four.

Grandfather Sibrol, it seemed, was a man with a strong sex drive and he had retained it to the last. Indeed, he had carried it with him into the hereafter.

Heaven, or wherever it was that Grandpa was, did not, however, have any suitable sex partners and he was becoming very hard up.

As a result, whenever his grandson was engaged in his chosen profession of robbing old ladies, he had whispered into his ear, "Kill her! Kill her! I can use her up here."

Oswald had resisted manfully most of the time, but Mrs Strobl and Mrs Spengler had appealed particularly to Grandpa, and what could an obedient grandson do?

The dazzled court did not know what an obedient grandson could do in such cases, but they knew what they could do. Although Sibrol had legally been a minor at the times of the murders, they tried him as a result and, on 14 June 1985, sentenced him to twenty years in prison, where it is reported he has resumed his studies in pipefitting.

He harbours no resentment against his grandfather for getting him into trouble and has been quoted as saying that he hopes he is having a good time with Mrs Strobl and Mrs Spengler.

8

BLACK MASS

Nine-year-old Christel Devilet was in heaven. The impatiently awaited summer holiday had finally arrived and the Devilets were off to the seaside.

She was not the only happy one. The Devilets were a young family and they enjoyed their holidays. Michel was thirty-six, his wife, Denise, thirty-one and the two boys, Frederic and Michael, were thirteen and seven.

On the morning of Friday 7 August 1987, they set gaily off from their home in Luettich – a small village with a large castle, in the east of Belgium – and, as Belgium is not a very large country, soon arrived at Coxyde, a seaside resort a mile and a half north of the French border.

Hotel accommodation for five people being expensive, the Devilets had, like many European families, rented a summer house for the last three weeks of August. After they had got themselves installed, they all went for an exploratory stroll down the esplanade.

On the land side, the esplanade was a solid row of hotels, restaurants, cafés, discotheques, fun houses, video arcades and similar forms of entertainments.

One of these was called Luna Park, and a concerted family effort was required to extract Christel from it. It was an arcade featuring mechanical games and rides and she had a weakness for such diversions.

Although the children were almost too excited to sleep, the trip had been a little tiring and they eventually drifted off into happy holiday dreams.

Even in August, the weather is not always good along

the Belgian coast, but this year it blazed with sunshine and there was just enough breeze to raise an interesting surf.

The following morning, immediately after breakfast, Christel went off alone. She was not a girl to tag after her brothers. As she was wearing her bathing suit, her mother assumed that she was going to the beach.

Christel did not return for lunch, but her mother was not alarmed. On the first day of the holiday it would have been surprising if any of the children had come back for lunch.

Christel did not return for dinner.

Denise was puzzled and concerned. Christel had had enough money to buy a hot dog for lunch, but she did not have enough to pay for dinner. In any case, why would she spend her pocket money when she could eat at home?

The boys had also missed lunch, but they had come back for dinner. Had they, Denise asked, any idea where their sister might be?

Frederic and Michael said the last time they had seen Christel was at around three o'clock. She had been standing in front of the Luna Park talking to a fat woman. The fat woman had given her a balloon.

'You're sure it was a woman?' said Denise. 'Did she go away with her?'

The boys were certain that it had been a woman. They had gone on down the esplanade so they did not know whether Christel had left with the fat woman or not.

At nine o'clock, Michel Devilet went to the police. There were still a great many people about and even some children, but he did not think that Christel would stay out so late without saying something to her mother. She was quite a serious, responsible little girl.

The Coxyde police were not unduly alarmed. The town was small, only a little over thirteen thousand permanent residents, and there was not much that could happen to a little girl. It was probable that, in the excitement of the first day of the holiday, she had not noticed how late it was.

However, Devilet was insistent, and the evening duty constables were alerted to keep an eye out for a pretty, dark-haired little girl with delicate, elfin features.

Some were sighted, but not the right one, and by eleven o'clock there were very few nine-year-old girls still running about.

The matter began to look more serious and a police car equipped with a loud speaker was sent to patrol the esplanade and the main streets of the town, blaring out Christel's name.

This produced no result either and, at midnight, Inspector Hans Louks, head of the small department of criminal investigations, was informed that a child was missing and that an accident or worse could not be ruled out.

The inspector came at once to the station, where he found his assistant, Detective Sergeant Piet Van Dam, who had been called in two hours earlier, directing the search operation.

Van Dam, a young, round-faced man with sun-streaked, blond hair and a heavy tan, reported that practically every place of interest to a child along the esplanade had been checked without result. He had obtained a recent photograph of the girl from her parents and copies of it were being made for the detectives to show to concession operators and employees.

'When and where was the last sighting?' asked the inspector.

He was a man in his late fifties, stocky, square-faced, impassive and slow of speech.

The sergeant reported the statements made by Christel's brothers.

'No known sighting since,' he said.

'A fat woman,' said the inspector pensively. 'That's not enough for an identification. See how many people you can find who were at the Luna Park this afternoon.

We need a better description. Coxyde is full of fat women.'

It was a slight exaggeration. Coxyde is in Flanders, and Flemish women are often solidly built, but fat ones are not all that common.

This one, it seemed, had not been fat enough to attract attention, for although the sergeant's men were able to find some teenagers who recalled seeing a stout woman in her middle or late thirties at the Luna Park, she had been more conspicuous by her age than her weight. Very few of the Luna Park's clients had yet seen their eighteenth birthday.

'We can't even be sure that it was the same fat woman,' said the sergeant. 'Apart from the brothers, we've found no one who saw her with the girl.'

'She gave her a balloon,' said the inspector. 'Check with the balloon sellers. See if one of them remembers selling a balloon to a fat woman accompanied by a little girl.'

It was Monday morning and the disappearance of Christel Devilet had now become an affair of major importance. Despite the efforts of the entire Coxyde police force, no trace of the child had been found.

Already, early that morning, the inspector had quietly sent out a circular to all police units along the French-Belgian border requesting reports on any bodies of female children found, and had queried Interpol, the European supranational police organization, concerning possible white slave activity in the area. Christel was pretty and exactly the right age for an African or Middle Eastern harem or brothel.

No bodies had been reported, but Interpol responded with the name of a man believed to be associated with a white slave ring. He was a twenty-eight-year-old Fleming named Albrecht Martens who had been convicted on charges of pandering and abduction for immoral purposes on four occasions in the past three years.

'Interpol only thinks he's in the area,' said the inspector. 'We'll have to determine if he is here. They're sending us the file with his mug shots.'

'If it was him, he wouldn't be in the area now,' said the sergeant. 'I think we'd do better to look for sex deviates with a record of offences against minor females.'

'I've already had records pull the files,' said the inspector. 'Locally, we've nine of them, but four are in jail or in the psychiatric clinic. He needn't be local, though. Even if he hasn't a car, the tram runs along the whole coast from Holland to France.'

It was not a great distance. From Knokke in the northeast to De Panne in the southwest is only thirty-five miles, although there are dozens of little communities along the way.

'He couldn't have carried her off on the tram,' objected the sergeant.

'He could have enticed her,' said the inspector. 'The white slave people are always handsome and smooth talkers. They don't force the girls. The girls think it's true love and go with them voluntarily.'

'Nine is a bit young for true love,' muttered the sergeant. 'Still, I suppose he would have other inducements to offer.'

He went off to look for balloon sellers and found one who had sold a balloon to a fat woman at around one-thirty in the afternoon of the day in question. He was unable to describe her other than to say that she was ordinary-looking and pretty fat.

Interrogation of personnel and passengers on the coastal tram produced several reports of fat women, but none of a little girl resembling Christel Devilet. By Monday evening, the investigation was at a virtual standstill.

It remained at a standstill until Saturday, when, at about four o'clock, Nicco Laplume, an unemployed lathe operator, came strolling rather morosely along the towpath of the Canal de Bourbourg at Dunkirk, five miles southwest of the Belgian border in France.

Although best known for the evacuation of the British Expeditionary Force during the Second World War,

Dunkirk is also a seaside resort and Laplume was on holiday.

It was not, however, a paid holiday and, the French economy not having recovered from its savaging by the socialists, he was much inclined to doubt that he would ever see a paid holiday again.

Indeed, industrial activity was so much reduced in this northwest corner of France that the water in the canal was only moderately polluted.

The body of the naked child just below the surface was therefore clearly visible and, as she was floating on her back, Laplume could see that she was a little girl, her long hair spread out in the water around her head like a dark halo.

Laplume swore savagely. He was not married and had no children of his own, but he was appalled by the sight of the body, which was covered with raw red wounds and purple bruises.

Even from the bank of the canal, it was obvious that Christel had died a violent death and, such things being common in civilized countries, he assumed that she had fallen into the hands of a psychopath.

His immediate concern was that the body not be lost altogether. At this point the sea was over a mile away, but although the current was not strong, the body was drifting steadily seawards.

He realized the water in the canal would be over his head, and he did not know how to swim. There were no boats or people in sight and he could see no pole or anything else with which he could hope to snag the body.

He followed helplessly the slowly drifting corpse, casting about for help and calling out from time to time.

He had covered close to a quarter of a mile along the towpath when, to his relief, a river police launch, returning from an inspection tour, hove into sight.

Minutes later, the little body of Christel Devilet lay on the towpath beside the canal, and a detachment from the Dunkirk department of criminal investigations was on the way to the scene.

Very shortly thereafter, Inspector Louks was notified that the corpse of a female child corresponding to the description of Christel Devilet had been recovered at Dunkirk.

The inspector and the sergeant left immediately, taking with them the Coxyde coroner, Dr Wilfried Poltens, and Michel Devilet.

The corpse was still lying on the towpath surrounded by screens and, while the sergeant waited in the car with Devilet, the doctor and the inspector covered all of it except the face with a sheet. The body was mutilated and the inspector did not want Devilet subjected to a sight that he would not be able to bear.

The sight was almost more than the doctor and the inspector could bear and, having cleaned the face and made it as presentable as possible, they summoned Devilet, who made a formal identification and then collapsed.

He was driven back to his family in tears by the sergeant.

Dr Poltens was not far from tears himself. An elderly, white-haired man with a thick white moustache and gold-rimmed spectacles, he had held the position of coroner for many years, mainly because no one else wanted it, and, violent crime in the little community being relatively rare, he was unaccustomed to such terrible sights.

'What is it?' asked the inspector uneasily. 'Did she get caught in the propeller of a barge?'

The doctor's voice was thick as if something was constricting his throat.

'The injuries are deliberate,' he said. 'The child has been ritually tortured and, I think, raped.'

'All right,' said the inspector, sounding less impassive than usual. 'No need for you to continue with the examination. We'll take her over to the morgue here in Dunkirk. They'll have people who are trained in this sort of thing. You have no objection to them performing the autopsy, I suppose?'

'They'll have to,' said the doctor. 'I'd resign before I'd do it.'

Dunkirk is a city of close to eighty thousand, and the police did have experts in forensic medicine capable of carrying out the autopsy of the body of Christel Devilet.

Even they, however, were appalled.

The child, [they wrote] has served as sacrificial victim and altar for what appears to have been a black mass. Symbols connected with devil worship were burned into her skin in several places (see diagram) and a fire was kindled on her abdomen, four inches above the navel.

The body is covered with cuts and bruises, many placed in a manner indicating occult significance, and there are traces of electric-shock torture on the genitals and elsewhere.

Index and middle fingers of the right hand and the ring finger of the left hand have been broken, probably deliberately.

There are cuts at the corners of the mouth caused by a gag, and marks on wrists and ankles indicating restraint by hard, smooth bonds, probably handcuffs.

The victim was an intact virgin and the fully consummated rape by an adult male ruptured the hymen and caused extensive damage to the walls and entrance of the vagina. Traces of not yet decomposed semen have been recovered, but in insufficient quantities to permit identification of the rapist's blood group.

No water was present in the lungs and the immediate cause of death was manual strangulation. Time is estimated at seven in the evening of 8 August 1987, plus or minus forty-five minutes. The victim had been dead for a minimum of one hour before she was placed in the water.

Christel Devilet's last holiday had soon been over, but it must have seemed unbearably long to her.

'This is not only the worst case I have ever handled; it is the worst case I have ever heard of,' said the inspector grimly. 'We're going to get them if it's the last thing I ever do.'

'Them?' said the sergeant unsteadily.

He had just finished reading the autopsy report and he was still cold with horror.

'I've never heard of anybody celebrating a black mass alone,' said the inspector. 'It's always a group.'

'I've never heard of anyone celebrating a black mass

around here at all,' said the sergeant. 'I thought that was something from the Middle Ages.'

'Devil worship has never really died out,' said the inspector. 'It just went underground, and now that the Church no longer has the power to do anything about it, it's coming out in the open. It's the modern trend to equate and tolerate all religions.'

'But, my God, not torturing and murdering little children!' said the sergeant.

'It's generally more harmless,' said the inspector. 'An excuse to run around bonfires at night and engage in group sex. But some people take it seriously, and that's the sort that murdered this little girl.'

'Do you think the fat woman is one of them?' asked the sergeant. 'It seems to me impossible that a woman would take part in something like that.'

'Ever heard of equality of the sexes?' demanded the inspector sarcastically. 'In our business, they really are equal. Yes, I think the fat woman was involved. She was the last person seen with the child and it was probably she who procured her for the black mass.'

'Right place and the right sex, I suppose,' said the sergeant. 'The Luna Park is a hangout for young kids, and the child wouldn't have been suspicious of a woman.'

He was pale under his tan and he was sweating, although it was not particularly warm in the office.

'What's to stop them from doing it again?'

'Nothing,' said the inspector. 'All we can hope is that they're local and not just passing through. If they are local, we may be able to identify them.'

'I don't see how,' said the sergeant.

'If there's a devil-worshipping group here in Coxyde, we can identify it,' said the inspector. 'You couldn't keep such a thing secret in a place of this size. There would be traces.'

'What kind of traces?' asked the sergeant. 'I don't follow you.'

'I'm not sure,' admitted the inspector, 'but it seems

to me that devil-worshippers would have some special needs in the way of clothing, implements, uncommon substances connected with their rituals that we could trace. I want you to go to Brussels and see if they have an expert on satanism at the university. You're to find out what we have to look for.'

It was under an hour's drive to Brussels, and the sergeant was back the same day. He did not, however, have a great deal to show for his trip.

Many modern devil-worshippers, it seemed, were neither orthodox nor traditional and might require almost anything or nothing. They were devil-worshippers for money, thrills or sex, and their rituals owed more to imagination than to knowledge of the subject.

If they were traditional and had any idea of what they were trying to do, they would be buyers of certain objects and substances, the nature of which the experts recommended should not be revealed by the police.

'Right,' said the inspector. 'Get everyone who can walk to ask questions. If stuff like that is being sold here, we'll find it out.'

"Everyone who can walk" meant the entire Coxyde police force, whether uniform or plainclothes. The inspector had been authorized by his superiors to spare no efforts. Such a tragic murder was disastrous for the tourist trade, and Coxyde lived from tourism.

The effort proved to be not enough. Most of the items were not even available in the area, and there had been no unusual trade in the ones that were. Either the devil-worshippers were unorthodox or they were merely in Coxyde on holiday and had brought their supplies with them.

Fortunately, the Dunkirk police were also working on the case.

Beginning with the assumption that the child's body had been brought to the canal after dark in a car, all accessible points were ascertained, in the hope of finding witnesses who had seen a vehicle on the night in question. The area along the canal was sparsely populated and even more sparsely trafficked, especially at night.

The entire canal did not have to be canvassed as it was possible to calculate minimum and maximum distances the body could have been carried by the current.

Based on an estimate of approximately sixteen hours in the water, Christel had been thrown into the canal at around midnight of Saturday.

This finding placed the point of entry somewhere within a half-mile section of the canal along which there were only four places accessible by car.

Three of these places had occupied buildings nearby, and from one there was a report.

A man taking his dog for a toilet stroll a few minutes before midnight on Saturday had seen a white Peugeot with a Belgian licence plate parked on the towpath at the edge of the canal. A man, standing looking down into the water, had got hurriedly into the car and driven away.

The dog had acted strangely, whining and whimpering as if it were afraid, and the man had felt oddly frightened himself. Although he had thought the matter suspicious, he had not noted the licence number of the car, nor had he had a very good look at the man's face despite bright street lighting along the canal.

'Well, it's something, at least,' observed the inspector, handing the report by the Dunkirk police to his assistant. 'Average height. Average weight. Dark hair. No beard or moustache. Has access to a white Peugeot with a Belgian licence plate. The first thing will be to identify the owners of white Peugeots in or near Coxyde.'

This was not as formidable a task as it sounded. Coxyde was small enough for the total number of car registrations to amount to only a little over four thousand.

Of this number, seven hundred and four were Peugeots, of which twenty-nine were white.

The owners were checked, and seventeen were immediately eliminated. Some had had their cars in a garage for repair. Some were women with no close male contacts. Nine had been driving their cars home from restaurants at around midnight. Many Belgians go out for dinner on Saturday night.

The remaining twelve were investigated individually, not so much for the whereabouts of the owners, which would be difficult to establish at that time of night, but for the whereabouts of the cars.

A further seven came off the list. Witnesses had been found who saw the car close to midnight somewhere that made the trip to the canal impossible.

However, of the five remaining, one was an outstanding suspect. A thirty-three-year-old bachelor named Didier Goossens, he had served seven years of a fifteen-year sentence for the violent rape of a twelve-year-old girl in 1978. He had been released on parole, following successful psychiatric treatment, at the beginning of 1987.

Goossens was arrested and brought to police headquarters, where he provided the inspector with an unpleasant shock.

Although of average height and weight, with black hair, he was bearded to the eyes – and the beard was much too long to have grown since the murder!

None the less, the dog-walker from Dunkirk was brought to Coxyde, where he emphatically confirmed that Goossens was not the man he had seen by the canal on the night of August the eighth.

Goossens was released with the apologies of the police, and the potential-suspect list was down to four.

'If we're on the right track at all, we must be getting close,' said the inspector. 'Let's just hope that the rest of them aren't bearded.'

There were no other beards, but one man did have a moustache too long to have been grown in the time elapsed. He was not arrested; nor were two of the others, for the fourth suspect turned out to have a qualification none of the others possessed.

A fat wife.

Thirty-five-year-old Claude Bouck was clean-shaven. He was of average height and weight. He owned a white Peugeot. And his wife Nicole, two years older than himself, was substantially overweight.

The couple was taken into custody and their house on the outskirts of the town was searched.

The detectives found an extensive library on black magic and the occult and, in the basement, a sort of torture chamber equipped with knives, pincers, branding irons and a device for administering electrical shocks.

Traces of human blood were recovered from the floor of the basement and from wooden planks laid across trestles to form a rough altar. The blood group corresponded to that of Christel Devilet.

The Boucks at first denied all knowledge of the crime, but gave up when Nicole was tentatively identified by Frederic and Michael as the fat woman they had seen talking to their sister on the day she disappeared.

Claude and Nicole did not appear to feel their crime was very serious. After all, they said, it was only a child, and human sacrifice was a part of their religion. It was clear, looking around the world, that the forces of evil were infinitely stronger than those for good and, unfortunately, cruelty was a part of what their master demanded of them. It had been a question of their immortal souls.

Apparently blessed with remarkably strong stomachs, after having tortured Christel to death, they had gone for a fine dinner in an expensive restaurant before returning to dispose of the body.

The only regret they expressed was that the body had not washed out to sea. They had believed the current in the canal to be stronger.

During their trial, which ended on 19 February 1988, they added their regrets that true freedom of worship did not exist in Belgium, but did not deny the crime and were sentenced by a horrified court to life imprisonment without possiblity of early release.

9

THE POWER OF THE PENDULUM

On Saturday 13 November 1982, Anne-Marie Fasolato did not turn up for lunch. This was surprising, but not alarming.

Anne-Marie, a pretty, blonde girl of twenty-six, had moved out of her parents' home in April of the preceding year, but only a few blocks away to the ground floor of a two-family house at 121 Grand Rue in the same village of Vernet, and she continued to take most of her meals at home.

Unless, of course, she had a luncheon date in Saint Leon, where she worked in a retirement home. This happened occasionally, and Jean and Marie Fasolato assumed that this was the explanation for her absence on Saturday.

Anne-Marie did not turn up on Sunday either.

Could she have found a boy friend? wondered her mother.

Anne-Marie was very pretty, but she was a little too serious for the boys even in this conservative southwest corner of France. She had had two unsatisfactory romances, one in 1978 and the other in 1980. Since then, she had been a little cautious with boys.

There was no point in calling the retirement home on Sunday, as this was Anne-Marie's day off, and she did not yet have a telephone in her flat. Public facilities were a little slow in the largely rural region to the south of Toulouse.

On Monday, Marie Fasolato called the retirement home in Saint Leon, less than five miles away, and was dismayed to learn that they too had seen nothing of Anne-Marie since Friday. The administrator had thought that she was sick and that she had not called in because she did not have a telephone.

Marie Fasolato found the explanation unsatisfactory. Vernet had a population of three hundred. It was impossible for Anne-Marie to be sick without the neighbours knowing, and any of them would have been glad to telephone her place of work and her parents.

Now thoroughly alarmed, Marie Fasolato walked quickly to her daughter's flat, returned even more quickly and telephoned her husband at work.

The door to the flat was locked, she said, a little breathlessly, and no one answered the doorbell. The upstairs neighbour was not at home and Anne-Marie's nearly new red Fiat was not parked anywhere near the building. She was frightened.

So was Jean Fasolato, but he did such a good job of calming his wife that he succeeded in allaying his own fears, to some extent. Anne-Marie was not a child and this was not Paris or Berlin. There would be some innocent explanation for her absence.

And, to his and his wife's initial relief, it appeared that there was.

He went to the flat after work to find that, although Anne-Marie did not answer the doorbell, the upstairs neighbour had returned.

Thirty-year-old Christian Impina told Fasolato that he had indeed seen Anne-Marie, on Saturday afternoon. She had told him she was going to Spain and had left with two strange men in a yellow Mercedes. He was annoyed because she normally baby-sat with his two-year-old son, Serge, at weekends and on some evenings.

Jean had known nothing of the baby-sitting, but he went home with the good news that Anne-Marie was all right. She had merely gone to Spain, which was, after all, less than a hundred miles away.

'Why?' demanded Marie. 'Why would she go to

Spain? She doesn't know anybody there. She's never been more than twenty miles from Vernet.'

'Two men took her away in a Mercedes,' said Jean. 'Friends, no doubt.'

'You call that good news?' said Marie.

Actually, Jean did not find the news all that reassuring either. The question of what Anne-Marie could be doing in Spain with two strange men had occurred to him too and, knowing his daughter, the obvious answer seemed to be excluded.

For a week, the Fasolatos tried everything they could think of to determine where Anne-Marie had gone and why. They called all her girl friends. They talked to her colleagues at the retirement home and they spoke again to Christian Impina.

Impina repeated what he had already told Jean and added that Anne-Marie had given him the keys to her Fiat, so that he could drive it while she was in Spain. It was not good for the car not to be driven at all. Impina knew about cars. He worked for a garage in Saint Leon.

Finally, on Monday, November the twenty-second the Fasolatos, worried to the point of madness, gave up. Jean went to the gendarmerie station in Muret, ten miles west of Vernet.

Anne-Marie, he said, had left with nearly two weeks' pay still due to her. She had not sent them so much as a postcard from Spain. In another week the rent would fall due on her flat and she had made no provision to pay it. He was very much afraid that something unfortunate had taken place.

Gendarmerie Captain Leon Bordreau, a rather dapper man with closely trimmed black hair and a small black moustache, listened silently to the story of Anne-Marie's sudden departure and then asked what Fasolato thought the gendarmerie should do about it. Anne-Marie was an adult. If she chose to go off to Spain, that was her business.

Yes, said Jean, but they had talked to absolutely everyone who knew her and she had not mentioned Spain to anyone. She was on very close terms with her parents and he could not believe that she would worry them by going away without saying anything.

The captain said that if the parents wanted to file a formal missing-person report, he would send someone to force an entrance to Anne-Marie's flat. Perhaps there would be some indication of her whereabouts inside. At worst, they could determine whether she had taken her clothes and toilet articles with her.

Jean promptly filed the report and the captain summoned his assistant, Sergeant Jerome Cressy, explained the situation and told him to go Vernet with Mr Fasolato and get into the flat by whatever means necessary.

The sergeant, a bulky young man with a drooping brown moustache and large hands which looked clumsier than they were, found the lock so simple that there was no need to break it and soon had the door open.

Everything inside was in perfect order. Anne-Marie's clothing was hanging in the wardrobe or lying in the chest of drawers. In her father's opinion, it was practically everything she owned.

Her only suitcase lay on top of the wardrobe and, in the bathroom, her toothbrush and other toilet articles were neatly laid out on the shelf over the basin.

The sergeant told Fasolato to go home, plastered a paper strip marked *Muret Gendarmerie. Do not enter* across the door and went back to Muret.

'The girl didn't leave voluntarily,' he reported. 'Could be kidnapping. Could be white slavers. The yellow Mercedes sounds like it.'

'In Vernet?' said the inspector. 'You aren't letting your imagination run away with you, are you, Jerome? Maybe you've been watching too many crime movies on television.'

'There's hardly anything else,' said the sergeant, 'but that's my report. When a serious, middle-class girl like this walks away without so much as a toothbrush and leaves part of her pay on the books, it's suspicious.'

'Yes, I suppose so,' said the captain. 'Well, if you

think something's wrong, set up a detail and see what you can find out.'

The sergeant set up a detail, but he was unable to find out anything more than the Fasolatos. This failure had a beneficial effect, however, for it convinced the captain of the seriousness of the case. By the end of the week, the detail had grown to over fifty men, the operation had expanded to cover an area fifteen miles in diameter and the search was tacitly for a body.

The captain was still optimistic, if it could be called that.

'She's probably been picked up by one of the gangs supplying the North African brothels,' he said. 'Impina says the men were dark and handsome.'

'She's too old,' said the sergeant. 'For the North Africans, anything over sixteen is a senior citizen.'

'Well, maybe Holland or Belgium then,' said the captain. 'We'll file with Interpol.'

Interpol is the supranational police organization which helps in cases extending over national boundaries. They are often called in on missing-person cases.

They are often successful, but not this time. Interpol could find no more trace of Anne-Marie than could the Muret Gendarmerie.

They had, by now, scoured the countryside with the assistance of great numbers of volunteers from all the little villages in the region. Community spirit is strong in the rural southwest, and a missing girl was a matter of concern to everyone.

Jean and Marie Fasolato had not given up hope completely, but both were physically ill from the strain of fear and uncertainty.

Jean had taken leave from his job to devote himself full time to the search for Anne-Marie, crisscrossing the countryside on a bicycle, which he found more practical than a car in getting down narrow paths and between fields. Like the gendarmes, he was looking for a body, but praying that he would not find it.

The gendarmerie was eventually forced to give up.

In so far as was possible, they had examined every hole, crevice, abandoned building and patch of brush in the entire area. No trace of Anne-Marie had been found. The conclusion was that she was not there.

Jean Fasolato did not give up. He was emotionally incapable of it. All through that winter of 1982 to 1983, he continued to peddle his bicycle through rain, sleet, freezing cold and, sometimes, snow in search of his daughter.

He did not find her and, by spring, he was reduced to grasping at straws. None of the ordinary methods had served to find Anne-Marie. He would try the supernatural.

This involved a trip too long for a bicycle. Paul Bady, the famous dowser and clairvoyant, lived in Aubiet, nearly forty miles west of Toulouse.

Bady, a retired farmer, was seventy years old, but physically robust and with the appearance of a man in his fifties. He had been practising his gift for nearly half a century, during which time his reputation had spread throughout the whole of the south of France.

Bady had begun as a young man with dowsing – locating underground streams of water with a forked willow or elm rod – and had been highly successful. Where Paul Bady said to dig, the well-digger could be assured of finding water.

It is not an unusual gift. Dowsers have been in demand for locating water everywhere in the world since time immemorial and, as successes greatly outnumber failures, they often command relatively high fees.

The procedure is simple. The dowser walks slowly over the area where water is being sought, holding his forked stick in both hands parallel to the ground. When he arrives at a place where there is water, the tip of the fork dips.

The dowser then makes several more passes across the site to confirm his findings before indicating the point at which the well is to be dug.

Usually, the dowser works on a pay-by-results basis. If there is no water, there is no charge.

There have been many explanations offered for this ability to locate water underground, some occult, some scientific. None is entirely satisfactory, but the system works and the well-diggers, being practical people, ask no more.

Some dowsers, however, go beyond dowsing for water and attempt to locate mineral deposits or lost articles. A few look for missing people – as a rule, dead ones.

It was due to his success in this field that Paul Bady had become famous. A specialist in drownings, he had successfully located the bodies of no less than four hundred victims since 1955.

His efforts were not commercially motivated. For locating a body or for healing by the laying on of hands, which he also practised, Bady never charged anything, and his fees for water divining or finding lost objects were based on what the client could afford.

All that he needed for his work was a photograph of the missing person and a scale map of the area in which he or she had last been seen, and that was what Jean Fasolato brought to him on 11 March 1983.

Bady did not ask him what he wanted. He already knew, but not through clairvoyance. The mysterious disappearance of Anne-Marie Fasolato had been on the front pages of every newspaper in the south of France.

A gentle, compassionate man, the old dowser added no more to the suspense, but immediately spread the map out on the rough kitchen table, propped Anne-Marie's photograph up against a water tumbler and got out his pendulum, a small metal weight like a plumb bob attached to the end of a short cord.

His eyes fixed on the photograph, he began to move the pendulum slowly over the map, the end of the cord grasped between his thumb and index finger.

Fasolato waited, unconsciously holding his breath.

Presently, the pendulum stopped following the direction taken by the dowser's hand and began to turn in a small, tight circle.

Fasolato let out his breath with a whoosh, but remained silent for fear of destroying the dowser's concentration.

Bady continued to run the pendulum back and forth over the map. Sometimes it oscillated from right to left; sometimes it swung in a wide circle; sometimes it remained motionless. Its movements seemed to have no correspondence with the movements of the hand.

Abruptly, Bady terminated the operation, rolled the string around the pendulum in a businesslike manner and put it away in the table drawer.

'I am sorry, Mr Fasolato,' he said gently. 'Your daughter is not in Spain. She is dead.'

'Where . . . ? How . . . ?' said Jean Fasolato in a strangled voice.

That he had long anticipated it did not make the news less hard to bear.

'I do not know how, Mr Fasolato,' said the dowser gravely. 'I only know where. Her body is not far from Vernet in a place called Naillou.'

He closed his eyes.

'I see a ravine,' he murmured. 'There are broken cement blocks, construction materials of all kinds, insulation. . . .'

'That's the building-material dump at Naillou,' said Fasolato. 'The gendarmerie has already searched it, and so have I. She is not there.'

'She is there,' said the old farmer. 'You did not find her, but she is there.'

Jean Fasolato went home to Vernet. It was too late to go to Naillou that day, but the following morning he set off immediately after breakfast for the dump.

It was a bad day for anything. The early spring weather was cold, wet and windy, the gusts so strong that they nearly knocked Fasolato off his bicycle. Overhead, the sky was a tortured mass of rolling, livid clouds fleeing wildly eastward from the storm-lashed Bay of Biscay. At eight in the morning, it was still dark.

Jean Fasolato had seen worse. It would take more than bad weather to deter him in his search for Anne-Marie, or whatever might remain of her. He did not expect to find her alive. Even before the visit to Paul Bady, he had abandoned hope of that. What he sought now was certainty. He had to know what had happened to Anne-Marie.

Despite Bady's reputation, he was dubious about finding her body in the construction materials dump. The gendarmerie had searched it, he knew, and so had he, but he had not been as thorough as he could have been and, perhaps, the gendarmes had not been either. In any case, he had no better place to look. He had already looked everywhere possible.

He went over the dump again, dragging aside cement blocks, sheets of corrugated plastic, giant cardboard cartons and enormous chunks of insulating material light as air. The rubbish, he realized was very deep – over ten feet in places. The dump had been in use for a long time and construction materials were bulky.

At eleven o'clock, it began to rain heavily. Fasolato, who had not brought his raincoat, sought shelter under a tree. He was cold, wet, disheartened and sick with grief, but he would not give up. If Anne-Marie was in the dump, he would find her, if he had to move every item in it.

After half an hour, the rain stopped, the clouds parted and the sun shone through. The temperature rose abruptly half a dozen degrees.

Fasolato left the dripping tree and began to pick his way wearily across the dump again.

A swarm of flies rose from around his feet and he waved his hands to drive them off.

Suddenly, he stopped dead in his tracks.

Flies? This was a building-materials dump. What were flies doing here? What did they find to eat?

His mind gagged away from the answer and he fell to

his knees, scrabbling with his hands at the broken concrete blocks where the flies were thickest.

Two feet down was a slab of cracked concrete. He heaved it up and away. Beneath it, long blonde hair lay spread over the rubble. The flies were very thick and there was a ghastly odour.

It is ten miles from Naillou to Muret, and the roads are not ideally suited for cycling. Jean Fasolato covered the distance in an impossibly short time. He did not need to. There are telephones in Naillou. But he was not thinking clearly. The culmination of his seven-month search had proved too dreadful for rational acceptance.

Captain Bordreau, Sergeant Cressy and most of the gendarmerie department of criminal investigations raced to the scene, where they carefully removed the concrete blocks and other rubble to find the leathery, dried-out, mummy-like remains of Anne-Marie Fasolato.

Her face was unrecognizable, but her parents were able to identify her because of three missing teeth, the result of a motorcycle accident ten years earlier.

The corpse was completely naked and the preliminary examination by Dr Fabien Paussac, the gendarmerie medical officer, revealed no obvious cause of death.

'She may even have been stabbed or shot,' said the doctor, a tall, sturdy man in his fifties who looked like an athlete, although he in fact detested sports. 'It's going to take more detailed examination at the morgue before I can say anything.'

The body was wrapped in plastic, placed in a metal coffin and taken away to the morgue, accompanied by the doctor. Nearly the entire personnel of the department of criminal investigations remained behind, sifting through the debris for possible clues.

The captain returned to Muret, leaving Sergeant Cressy in charge of the operation. He did not think, considering the length of time that had elapsed, anything significant would be found, and he was worried about the press reaction to the discovery.

Relieved as he was that the mystery of Anne-Marie's

disappearance had been at least partially solved, the fact that the body had been found by her own father with the help of a dowser and in a place previously searched by the gendarmerie was certain to provoke caustic comment in the newspapers, which were always delighted to depict the gendarmerie as idiots or worse.

There was no help for it, however, and the matter was made even worse when Dr Paussac was unable to establish the cause of death, or anything else, for that matter.

'Probably strangulation,' he said, 'but, after seven months. . . .'

He could not even say with certainty that Anne-Marie had been dead for seven months. The condition of the body made precision on anything impossible.

As the captain had expected, nothing was found at the dump either, although the sweating gendarmes moved every stick in it.

'She wasn't killed there,' said the captain. 'The body was just brought there and dumped.'

'By the men in the Mercedes?' said the sergeant.

'If they ever existed,' said the captain. 'I want you to take a good, hard look at Impina. He's the last person known to have seen her, and his statement about her going to Spain is beginning to sound like a fairy tale.'

The sergeant went with six investigators to Vernet, where he had little difficulty in finding out everything he wanted to know about Christian Impina. There were few secrets in a community of under three hundred people.

Impina had been born in Tunisia of Italian parents, but held French nationality and had lived most of his life in Marseille, where he had supported himself by various odd jobs.

He had come to Vernet in 1978 as a seasonal fruit-picker, had met a local girl named Martine and had married her. Their son, Serge, had been born in 1980.

There being little work in Vernet outside the fruit-picking season, Impina had been more or less permanently on unemployment compensation, which, in France, is not wildly generous.

The resulting financial stress had taken whatever magic there had been out of the marriage, and in April of 1982, Mrs Impina had departed, leaving Serge with Christian.

Too late, Christian had found work in a garage, and had depended on Anne-Marie for baby-sitting when she was not at work.

This had resulted in some gossip in the village. Before her departure, Martine and Anne-Marie, who were approximately the same age, had been close friends, and Anne-Marie had become very attached to Serge. Now, however, Martine was gone and Anne-Marie was still spending much time in Impina's flat.

Some of Anne-Marie's friends had heard the gossip and had come to her with it. She had assured them that there was nothing between her and Impina, but that she felt it her duty to look after the child.

'There's nothing against Impina,' said the sergeant. 'No police record and, if he's not very ambitious, neither are half the men of his age in France.'

'Have you checked with the people where he works?' asked the captain. 'You might pick up something there.'

The sergeant had not and, when he did, the result was an exceedingly bizarre tale.

Impina, it seemed, had blandly stolen a customer's white Renault R5 from the garage and sold it to Anne-Marie for the bargain price of three thousand francs.

Unfortunately, Anne-Marie had decided to trade it in for the red Fiat, and the garage had recognized their customer's property.

The garage had been taking the three thousand francs off Impina's salary at the rate of two hundred francs a month, and they had not fired him because he would then have been unable to pay them back. For the same reason, no report of the matter had been made to the gendarmerie.

'Very interesting,' said the captain. 'And now he's driving her red Fiat. See what else of hers he has.'

What else he had was Anne-Marie's cheque book. The girl had been frugal and she had had a substantial bank account. Impina had been cashing her cheques all over the region ever since her disappearance.

Impina was promptly taken into custody and charged with theft of the cheque book so that he could be held indefinitely while being interrogated on the subject of the murder.

He proved to be astounding consistent, clinging like iron to his account of Anne-Marie going off in a yellow Mercedes with two strange men.

He denied stealing the cheque book. Anne-Marie, he said, had left it with him for safekeeping and, when she had not returned after seven months, he had thought he might as well make use of it.

Unfortunately for this version of the events, the cheques were dated, and he had cashed the first one four days after Anne-Marie disappeared.

Impina explained this by charging that the captain himself had altered the dates of the cheques. He was, said Impina, desperate for a suspect and obviously had no qualms about railroading an innocent man.

In fact, the captain was desperate, not for a suspect – because he thought he had one – but for evidence that would lead to a certain conviction. Without a confession, the case against Impina was weak.

The confession was never forthcoming, nor was the evidence, but the prosecution presented the statements of every adult resident of Vernet to the effect that no yellow Mercedes had ever been seen in the village, and the jury found Impina guilty of murder.

He was sentenced to life imprisonment on 21 September 1984 and immediately appealed the verdict.

The appeals court was no more understanding and, on 10 January 1986, confirmed verdict and sentence.

While the appeal was being heard, it occurred to one of the newsmen that Paul Bady might be able to throw some light on the mystery of Anne-Marie's death, but it turned out that he had since died.

Captain Bordreau believes, however, that he knows the motive for the murder.

Christian Impina wanted to get rid of the monthly payments being taken off his salary.

10

LUCIFER'S OUTLAWS

The adventure began prosaically enough. In the living room of a modest flat in Northampton, the indifferently manicured thumb of a twenty-eight-year-old housewife and mother descended firmly on the transmit button of the citizens' band radio set.

'Joan of Arc calling,' she crooned into the microphone. 'Joan of Arc calling. Let's hear a male voice. Somebody sexy . . . horny . . . ready to go. . . .'

It was early evening of a grim January day and husband Ian had gone off to his job as a printer. The kids were in bed. Sue Turner was looking for action.

With Ian's approval. Although only four years older than his wife, he was no more capable of satisfying her raging appetite for sex than were the lovers she found so easily through the miracle of modern communications.

Miracle or no, the search had been never-ending. Not once had she ever found a male so virile, so skilful, so insatiable that the relationship could become anything more than passing. Once the wild, initial excitement of the new conquest was over, the plaintive, eager voice of Joan of Arc would again be heard, calling, calling, calling over the short waves for that ultimate, that unattainable, that all-encompassing orgasm that would finally still the fire of her loins.

Although she did not suspect it, tonight would mark the end of her quest. The purring growl that issued from the speaker was not the mewling of some half-female, decadent weakling, but the full-throated, seductive voice of a dominant male.

'Gnasher here,' it rasped. 'If you've got something to offer, I've got what it takes to shake the chill out of your knickers.'

Sue went into her sales pitch. She was not beautiful, she admitted, but she was built – big, firm breasts, generous hips, blonde hair down to her shoulders – and she knew what she was doing.

She went into detail about what she could and wanted to do, feeling the excitement mount in her as she sensed it mounting in her listener. The performance was intended to be stimulating. Sometimes, she and – she had no doubt – he literally achieved orgasm over the radio.

However, Gnasher was not interested in long-distance sex.

'I know what you need,' he interrupted. 'Hold on. I'm coming over to give it to you.'

He switched off and Sue, trembling with excitement, went to search her wardrobe for the sexiest clothes she owned, but she was in such a state of arousal that she was unable to decide and, when the doorbell rang, she opened the door half naked.

The man outside was big, thick-shouldered, slim-hipped and muscular. He had a short black beard and moustache and, when he removed his leather jacket, his forearms were covered with tattoos.

The strength of his personality struck her with almost physical force so that she staggered back a step.

'Not afraid, are you?' said the man. 'I'm Mick Bardell. Gnasher to my friends.'

He walked casually across to the bedroom, kicked off his boots, pulled off his jeans and lay down on the bed.

'Ready?' he asked, a cigarette dangling from the corner of his mouth.

She was ready.

The experience was a revelation. Never in her life had she encountered so skilled so inexhaustible a lover. For what seemed hours, he kept her teetering on the brink of her climax before bestowing such blessed relief that she lay limp, wet, drained and sated with pleasure.

When he stated upon leaving, 'Tomorrow night, you come to me,' there was no doubt she would come.

The address he gave her turned out to be a block of brick council flats. It was not a very desirable residential district and most of the other tenants seemed to be punks, rockers or immigrants.

Mick's flat was decorated in keeping with his personality and interests. A huge swastika covered the end of the entrance hall, and the walls of the living room were hung with Nazi emblems, portraits of Adolf Hitler and weapons.

One wall was covered with bookshelves containing, as she would later learn, an impressive collection of works on sorcery, black magic and necromancy.

Mick, dressed completely in black leather, led the way into the bedroom, where the walls were papered with thousands of obscene photographs and drawings cut from magazines and the ceiling was filled with a gigantic picture of a nude girl.

The ecstasy this time was even greater and, when she had slightly recovered her wits and was able to focus her eyes again, Sue saw that someone had entered the room and was standing watching them.

The voyeur was a handsome woman with brown permed hair. Sue, with the uncanny accuracy of the female in judging the age of a member of her sex, took her to be as old as Ian. She was obviously enjoying the spectacle, for her mouth hung wetly open and her eyes were bright with lust.

'Meet Babs, the missus,' rumbled Mick. 'She's going to make it with you. You'll see. It'll be nice.'

Babs was already pulling off her blouse and skirt, stripping down to her panties.

It was nice. Almost too nice. There was little that Sue did not know about sex with men, but this was her first experience with a woman.

'They're a smashing couple!' she told Ian. 'You've just

got to meet them. Babs is two-way. She makes it with men or women.'

On his next night off, Ian accompanied Sue to the Bardells' place. Mick and Babs were everything that Sue had promised and, before very long, they were all four locked in a sweating, panting, naked tangle on the bed.

Broad-minded Ian had been a little shocked when Sue and Babs began making love to each other, but 'Gets you up, don't it?' said Mick conspiratorially, and went to join in.

It did, and although Ian was no equal to the super performances of the others, he had a wonderful time and he became an unconditional admirer of thirty-four-year-old Mick Bardell.

After that, it was accepted as only natural that Sue should spend most of her nights in the Bardells' flat and bring with her the Turners' two sons.

The arrangement was especially convenient as the Bardells had five children, with whom the Turner boys could play before going to bed.

Mick was, in the meantime, still working the citizens' band radio and he presently made contact with a thirty-two-year-old unemployed sex fanatic named Steve Parkinson.

Like Mick, Steve was a motorbike enthusiast and, after a few group-sex sessions with the Bardells and the Turners, he brought along another couple of bikers.

Their names were David Cox and Debbie Fallon and they were considerably younger than the others. David was twenty-three and Debbie, a lovely, uninhibited brunette, was barely nineteen.

Both immediately succumbed to the charisma of the "guru", as they now began to call Mick, and the group-sex sessions began to take on the aspects of a Roman orgy.

Or the perverted dreams of the Marquis de Sade.

Mick Bardell was a man with a taste for violence. Graduate of a course in paramilitary training, he was a skilled marksman with rifle or pistol, a close-combat fighter and an acknowledged artist with the commando knife. Stimulated by the absolute, unquestioned power which he had come to exercise over the group, he began to introduce sadomasochistic practices into the sex games.

The group-sex sessions became increasingly interspersed with whippings, cuttings with a straight razor and burnings with a lighted cigarette, particularly on the more sensitive parts of the women's bodies.

The torture was undergone voluntarily. The weaker wills of the group's members were so overwhelmed by the powerful personality of their guru that they actually vied with one another in causing and enduring the greatest suffering.

Terrible rituals of black magic were performed and the slippery slope of sadism grew ever steeper. The group was rapidly approaching emotional free fall when events would no longer be under their control, but in the hands of . . . what?

'We're going to form a chapter of Hell's Angels in Northampton,' announced Mick. 'I've been in touch with the head office in London and we're authorized to call ourselves Lucifer's Outlaws.'

The group was delighted. It was a great thing to become members of such a famous and distinguished organization.

'There'll be tests. We'll have to prove ourselves,' warned Mick. 'We have to be ready for anything.'

Lucifer's Outlaws were. All swore undying loyalty to the Hell's Angels principles, whatever they were. Democratic elections were held and Mick was chosen Absolute Dictator. Steve was made Assistant to the Chief. Ian and David became Freedom Fighters.

They were, in fact, not very convincing fighters. David was frail, immature and had not yet succeeded in growing a moustache. Ian was skinny, sallow and nervous-looking. Only Steve, who was burly and had a moustache, looked the part.

In any case, there was nothing to fight, and they con-

tinued to divide their time between copulation and torture until, towards the beginning of March, Mick called
together Steve, Ian, Babs and Sue for a secret meeting.

The London administration of the Hell's Angels had
handed down a decree, he announced. To prove their
worth, they had to perform certain chastisements within
the group. Someone had been talking too much. They
were to be sacrificed.

As everyone was present except David and Debbie, it
was obvious who the victims were to be.

'But they're our chums!' protested Ian.

'A real Hell's Angel has to be ready to sacrifice his life
or anybody else's,' said Mick coldly. 'We've sworn the
Angel oath. You want us to break it?'

The question was put to the vote and it was decided
that Lucifer's Outlaws would keep the faith. Ian was
still doubtful, but he had no choice but to accept the
majority decision.

'Ten o'clock tonight,' said Mick, 'in the woods beside
the MI approach. Everybody in dress uniform.'

At the appointed hour, the full complement of Lucifer's Outlaws was assembled in a clearing in the stunted
forest which could be reached by a dirt track leading
down from the service area beside the motorway.

The motorcycles were drawn up in a circle, their head-
lights focused on the Leader, who was dressed from
head to foot in black leather and chains, with the great
commando knife swinging from his belt.

At a sign from him, Steve seized Debbie and chained
her to a tree. The girl did not struggle, assuming, no
doubt, that this was the beginning of another of the
perverse sex games. David, however, made a move as if
to come to her defence.

'Are you with us or against us?' roared the Leader
threateningly.

David bowed his head in silent surrender, but
remained near his companion.

Mick made another sign to Steve, who responded by
stripping away Debbie's clothing. Naked in the chilly

night air, she still offered no resistance and it was apparent that the situation was beginning to excite her.

Drawing the long, razor-sharp commando knife, Mick walked unhurriedly up to the unsuspecting David and, without warning, drove it to the hilt in his stomach.

Blood spurted over Mick's leather-gloved hand, and David gave a deep groan of pain. Chained to the tree a scant six feet away, Debbie began to scream.

Mick jerked the blade upwards, slicing into David's heart and lungs, and the dying body slid off the blade to lie jerking in death throes on the ground.

Without giving it a second glance, Mick turned to the chained girl, who was screaming and writhing against her bonds, her eyes starting from her head with fear and horror.

At another sign from Mick, Steve seized the girl's hair and pulled back her head. Dropping the knife, the Leader locked his huge hands around the girl's throat with such force that her neck was broken and her larynx crushed.

A stream of blood spurted from her mouth and ran down between her breasts and over her pale belly to form a dreadful red loincloth between her thighs.

The Leader seized the knife, turned to face his diciples and held it high.

'Look!' he commanded. 'My hand ain't even shaking!'

Babs smiled a silent, secret smile and Steve went off to get the Polaroid camera, with which he took a series of photographs of the bodies of David Cox lying on the ground and of Debbie Fallon, hanging in chains from the tree.

Sue, however, was close to fainting and Ian had turned and walked away in a paroxysm of horror and revulsion.

Mick eyed his retreating back.

'I had to do it,' he said to Sue. 'It was orders from the Hell's Angels. If I hadn't, they'd have killed all of us and the kids too.'

Sue was incapable of a response.

'That's not all either,' continued the guru. 'The

Angels want another sacrifice. It's going to have to be Ian. I've booby-trapped his car. When he gets in to go to work tomorrow, he'll be finished. Not a word, mind you. The lives of the kids depend on it.'

With his bloody, gloved hand, he took her by the throat and raised her lips to his.

Sue's knees gave way under her. Even the knowledge that Mick was planning to murder her husband was not enough to free her from his spell.

Mick, fortunately, was not as expert in explosives as in some other fields, and the car bomb failed to go off.

Having learned of this, he came to the Turners' flat and invited Ian to go for a walk with him.

'We have some unsettled business,' he told Sue.

They left, and for over two hours Sue was torn between loyalty to her guru and concern for her husband.

Then she could stand it no longer and went running wildly off across the dark fields in search of them.

She found Ian dragging himself across a piece of waste land, leaving a trail of blood behind him. He had been stabbed in the back, but he was not dead.

Sue got him to the hospital and, nearly hysterical with fear and grief, telephoned Mick.

'Leave my husband alone!' she screamed into the receiver. 'Leave him alone, or I'll tell everything to the police.'

Mick said that he would consult the Hell's Angels, and two days later he announced their verdict.

Ian was to be spared, but, as penance, he was no longer allowed to live in Northampton. He was to move to London and had permission to visit his wife and children only at weekends.

Incredibly, the Turners accepted this verdict. Although Ian knew that Mick had tried to kill him, he was not resentful, believing that the Leader had acted unwillingly on the orders of the London Hell's Angels.

Sue too, after that one explosion of revolt, had been forced to accept that she could not free herself of Mick

Bardell's influence. Her sexual dependence on him was so great that he could do with her what he liked.

However, on Easter Sunday of 1983, the bodies of David Cox and Debbie Fallon were found by two men going for a walk, and the investigation began.

It promptly established that, on one count at least, Mick had been right. The young victims had talked about Lucifer's Outlaws and about the group sex sessions.

As a result, it did not take long to identify the other members of the group and the Bardells, the Turners and Steve Parkinson were taken into custody.

All denied any connection to the murders, but a search of the Bardells' flat produced the pictures that Steve Parkinson had taken of the bodies, plus a great many pornographic studies of Babs and Sue separately and together.

Babs was the first to break, admitting that she had been present at the murders, but defending her actions by saying that she had been afraid of her husband.

'If I hadn't gone along with him, he'd have killed all of us,' she said.

Her confession was followed by those of Mick Bardell and Steve Parkinson and, in the spring of 1984, they were brought to trial on charges of murder and aiding and abetting to murder respectively.

Mick Bardell's claims that he had been acting on the orders of the Hell's Angels brought a categoric denial by a spokesman for the group.

Bardell, he said, had been acting on his own initiative. The Hell's Angels had never heard of Lucifer's Outlaws until the story appeared in the newspapers, and Bardell had never contacted them.

Steve Parkinson said simply that he was the chief's assistant and he did whatever the chief said. He had sworn an oath to that effect and he intended to keep it.

The remainder of the testimony was more interesting. Babs Bardell began by telling the court that she was prepared to stand by her husband no matter what he had done.

'We have been together for over ten years,' she said, 'and we have five children. A more gentle or affectionate husband and father never lived.'

She then progressed to the subject of her bisexuality, going into such detail and making use of such graphic terms that a great many useful quotes had to be cut out of the newspaper reports.

Ian Turner, who had rejoined his family in Northampton, said only that he had been convinced that Mick Bardell was a great spiritual leader and that whatever he did was in the best interests of the group; but Sue was even more voluble than Babs.

Before a spellbound courtroom, she described at length her relationship with Mick Bardell, how he had turned her from a liberated woman into a sort of sex slave and the techniques by which he had accomplished this. Even after the attempted murder of Ian, she had not been able to free herself from his sexual spell, she said.

Throughout the trial, there had been frequent references to bewitching, enchantment and supernatural powers, but Sue went further. She described her former lover and master as, if not Satan himself, the devil's most faithful disciple.

Mick Bardell's parents testified for the defence, asserting that Mick was a good boy and kind to animals, but it did not help and, having been found guilty as charged, he was sentenced to life imprisonment on 6 March 1984, with the recommendation that he serve a minimum of twenty years.

Steve Parkinson, who had helped but had not actually killed anyone, was sentenced to life imprisonment, but without recommendation for a minimum time served.

11

INTERVIEW WITH A MURDER VICTIM

What was it about Galina Terhaerst that distinguished her from any other young West German girl?

It was not her appearance. She was very attractive, wholesome and cheerful-looking, but not really beautiful. Perhaps it was her plump-cheeked, frequently smiling face, which always seemed so filled with the joy of living.

And yet, Galina thought often of death.

Not death in general. Murder. Her own murder.

'Murder is predestined,' she told Herta Bollmann, her twenty-year-old friend, that Friday evening of 11 September, 1987. 'The paths of murderer and victim are fixed and, at the appointed time, they cross.'

'Don't be so morbid, Galina,' said Herta. 'You give me the cold shivers when you talk and look that way.'

It was almost exactly what Galina's mother, Nina Terhaerst, had said a few nights earlier.

Galina had taken on that strange look as if she were gazing into some other world altogether and she had said something stranger yet.

'A murder victim must be prepared to help her murderer, Mother.'

'You're always talking about death and murder, Galina,' Mrs Terhaerst had said nervously. 'Ever since you were a child. I do wish you'd stop it. You have no earthly reason to think that you are going to die young.'

No earthly reason? Perhaps not, but might there not be other reasons that had nothing to do with this earth?

September the eleventh was a beautiful late summer day. In the lovely lake country to the southwest of Munich, the flowers were still blooming. It was warm, but the year was advanced and by seven o'clock it would be dark.

On the field paths between the villages of Planegg, where Herta Bollmann lived with her family, and Gauting, where Galina lived with hers, there were no street lights.

Galina did not need any. She had ridden her bicycle from Planegg over Stockdorf to Gauting so many times that every bump in the path was registered on the map in her mind.

At fifteen minutes past eight, she mounted her bicycle, gave Herta, standing in front of the house, a cheery wave and disappeared into the darkness.

Herta watched her go with a greater feeling of uneasiness than she had ever experienced before. There was something about that September night. . . .

Someone else out there in the darkness, which the rising quarter-moon fought vainly to dispel, also had a feeling about the September night.

It was a hunting night, and he had not hunted for a long time. Was it for months or was it for years that he had been caged, watched, tested?

He had been clever. He had learned what they wanted and he had pretended to give it to them. It was only a matter of finding the right answers. They were so anxious to cure him, as they called it, that they had coached and hinted, helping him to get it right.

He had got it right, and on Monday they had let him go. He was all right now, they said. Ready to take his place as a useful member of society. They urged him to come and visit them. They liked to keep in touch with their cured psychopaths.

So now he was free, free to lope the dark fields, to crawl through bushes, to hide in ditches, to look for something . . . What was it he was looking for anyway?

Frank Hedemeier in court
(Amateur Exorcist)

Right: Joel Bastien *(The Mummy and the Vanishing Bathroom)*

Far right: Karl and Gertrude Teufel at their wedding *(Dance with the Devil)*

Below: Oswald Sibrol at his trial *(Lust beyond the Grave)*

Right: The canal in which the body of Christel Devilet was found *(Black Mass)*

Left: Claude Bouck *(Black Mass)*

Below: Nicole Bouck *(Black Mass)*

Below: Police recovering the body of Anne-Marie Fasolato *(The Power of the Pendulum)*

Left: Lina Boseggia *(Never Get Your Fortune Told)*

Below: Rolf Steckmann entering the courtroom *(Lucifer's Outlaws)*

Above: Georges
Sauveur *(Saviour)*

Right: Michael Labbé
(Dr Hyde, I Presume)

Above: Francine Sauveur *(Saviour)*

Right: Domingo Ponessa (Tailor to Tart)

Warm, wet, soft, frightened, he would know it when it came.

His path led west and north, Galina Terhaerst's south and east. Four hundred yards from the edge of Gauting, they intersected.

Herta Bollmann had not slept well. She had thought repeatedly of telephoning Galina's home to see if she had arrived safely, but she had not done it. There were no grounds for her feelings of disquiet and she did not know how to explain her call. After all, Galina had ridden her bicycle hundreds of times between Planegg and Gauting and nothing had ever happened, so why now?

Later, she would reproach herself that she had not telephoned, but there was no reason to. It would not have altered anything.

Perhaps Galina was right. Perhaps nothing could be altered. If murder there was to be, it was predetermined. Nothing could alter the paths of murderer and victim leading them inexorably to the fatal intersection.

September the twelfth being Saturday, there was no school for third-year high school pupils Willi Trichter, Karen Elsauer and Gottlob Schmidt, who were all eleven years old.

The weather was, if anything, even better than the day before, and the three inseparable companions set off early from Gauting for a day's wandering along the shores of Lake Starnberg. They were carrying a picnic lunch and they did not propose to return home until that evening.

In fact, they would be back within three-quarters of an hour and they would not see the shores of Lake Starnberg at all that day.

Four hundred yards from the edge of the village, they came upon a bicycle lying in the path. It was not damaged, but it was a woman's bicycle and Karen found this alarming.

'A woman wouldn't leave her bicycle lying out here,' she said. 'Something's happened.'

'Probably drunk and fell off it,' scoffed Willi.

'And she couldn't find it again in the dark so she had to walk home,' added Gottlob.

They were both big boys for their age and inclined to bravado, particularly in the presence of Karen, who was half their size but more than a match for either of them.

'We'll look,' she said firmly.

Neither Willi nor Gottlob had any objections and they began running about in the bushes beside the path, yelling and making a great deal of noise. Beyond the bushes was a sort of a briar patch, but with the wild blackberry vines so far apart that it was possible to walk between them.

Karen followed more slowly, her eyes on the ground. Suddenly, she stopped and called out, 'Look here!'

The boys came running.

Lying on the round near a bush was a large handbag.

Willi and Gottlob immediately became serious. The combination of the bicycle on the path and the handbag lying a dozen yards away was sinister. Something really had happened.

Silent and staying close together, the three children began to go over the area systematically and, after a few moments, came upon the body of a young girl.

She was lying near but not among the blackberry bushes, her pleated skirt ripped away, the crotch torn out of her underwear, her blouse pushed up above her breasts and her legs bent at the knees and sprawled wide apart. It was obvious even to eleven-year-olds that she had been raped.

It was equally obvious that she had been murdered. Her long brown hair, worn loose over her shoulders, was stiff and matted with dark, dried blood and there were smears of it on her face and forehead. Incongruously, her features were composed and her expression was almost happy.

Without hesitation, Karen stepped forward, knelt down and laid her ear against the girl's naked breast.

'She's dead,' she said, rising to her feet. 'I can't hear

her heart. Two of us will have to stay here while the other one goes for the police.'

'He could still be around here,' said Gottlob. 'You go for the police, Karen. You shouldn't stay here.'

Karen did not argue. She was a fast runner and she arrived at the Gauting police station in less than fifteen minutes. The time was exactly seven minutes past nine.

Gauting is a community of under fifteen thousand residents and the police force is not large. A team of constables armed with a walkie-talkie accompanied Karen to the scene, where they found the boys back to back with stones in their hands. In a modern society, boys often get raped too, and they knew it.

The constables took the names of all three and sent them about their business. The dead girl was no sight for children.

It was hardly a sight for constables, and their report over the walkie-talkie left no doubt at police head-quarters that a particularly savage crime had taken place outside Gauting.

The chief of the Gauting police reacted by immediately alerting the department of criminal investigations in Munich, a city of a million and a half, less than fifteen miles away.

As there were special homicide units for the rural areas around the city, the response was rapid, and by ten o'clock a complete homicide squad was at the scene.

The investigation began with the photographing of the corpse, the bicycle, the handbag and the general area surrounding the scene of the crime.

This completed, Dr Wilhelm Henkel, the squad's stout, blond and bespectacled medical expert, proceeded to examine the body. He had previously only approached it enough to make certain that the victim was definitely dead.

His first concern was confirmation of the apparent motive and, after having examined the dead girl's sex organs, he reported that there appeared to have been penetration, but that he could detect no traces of semen.

137

'Minor damage to the entrance and walls of the vagina,' he said, 'but he apparently failed to achieve orgasm. May have been incapable of it.'

Inspector Rudolf Berger nodded in understanding. The ability to rape, but not to climax would be an important factor in establishing a profile of the killer.

The doctor continued with the examination, carefully parting the dead girl's hair and probing with sensitive, rubber-gloved fingers.

'Multiple fractures of the skull,' he said. 'The immediate cause of death, in all probability. She put up a fight. There's bruising of the hands and forearms, and some of the fingernails are broken.'

'No bruising of the insides of the thighs, though,' remarked the inspector.

He was a tall man, heavily tanned, with a long, lined face which gave him the sorrowing look of a bloodhound.

'Possibly because she was dead or unconscious when he raped her,' said the doctor. 'I think that's about it until we get her over to the morgue. Time of death would be around nine o'clock last night, but that's only a guess until I've completed the autopsy.'

'Close enough,' said the inspector. 'Do we have an identification yet?'

'Yes,' said Detective Sergeant Klaus Friedel, handing over a standard identification card such as is carried by most Germans. 'It was in the handbag.'

The inspector opened the folded card, looked briefly at the smiling photograph of the dead girl and read aloud, 'Galina Terhaerst, age twenty, single, student nurse, resident at 38 Grofeld Strasse, Gauting.'

He closed the card and put it into his pocket.

'You keep an eye on things here,' he said. 'I'll notify the family.'

The sergeant's round, normally cheerful face clouded. A comparatively young, rather easy-going man with a snub nose and large brown eyes set wide apart, he disliked telling people that their son or daughter or husband or wife had been murdered.

138

As the inspector did not know the village, he took one of the local constables with him as a guide and drove to the Terhaersts' house in Grofeld Strasse.

As it was Saturday, both Thomas and Nina Terhaerst were at home, and their first reaction was simply disbelief. It was true, said Nina, that Galina was not home at the moment, but she had spent the night with her friend, Herta Bollmann, and, if she was not there now, it was because she had already gone off shopping or something like that.

'It must be a case of mistaken identity,' insisted Thomas Terhaerst.

The inspector silently held out their daughter's identity card.

The Terhaersts abruptly turned pale and Thomas put his arm around his wife's shoulders.

'Are you sure?' he said in a low, pleading voice.

'One of you will have to come to the morgue this afternoon for the formal identification,' said the inspector, not answering the question directly. 'No need for both.'

The Terhaersts both came and made the obligatory identification, Mrs Terhaerst rather woodenly as she was under the influence of a massive dose of tranquillizers administered by her family doctor. Neither had the slightest explanation for Galina's death.

'A madman,' said Thomas. 'Only a madman.'

'She saw it coming,' wept Nina. 'She always said she would be murdered.'

The inspector pricked up his ears. When people predicted they would be murdered, they usually had some grounds for the belief. Perhaps there had been previous contact between Galina and her murderer.

If so, it went a long way back. When questioned, the Terhaersts said that Galina had been predicting her own death by murder since she was a small child.

'Talk to her friend Herta Bollmann,' they said. 'Talk to Pastor Haberle. They know all about it.'

The inspector did talk to Herta Bollmann and to

139

Christof Haberle, pastor of St Benedikt parish church, and both confirmed what the Terhaersts had said. Galina had been talking about dying young and being murdered since she was in primary school.

'It's of no significance for the investigation,' said the inspector. 'It wasn't that she knew some specific person she thought might kill her.'

'But don't you find it strange?' asked the sergeant. 'She appears to have had an accurate premonition of the manner of her own death. There are a great many people who recall her mentioning it for at least the last ten years.'

'I find it exceedingly strange,' said the inspector, 'and I think that's one mystery we'll never solve. I expect the murder will be easier.'

It did not strike the sergeant as easy. Despite an extremely careful examination of the scene of the crime, no clues to the identity of the murderer had been found and none of Galina's circle of friends, relatives and acquaintances came in question as a potential suspect.

The murder had taken place near where the body was found and, judging from the marks on the ground, Galina had simply been pulled off her bicycle as she rode past the bushes.

She had fought with her attacker, but he had been much stronger and had struck her a total of thirteen violent blows over the head with a stone weighing close to two pounds which was found lying near the body. It had definitely been the murder weapon for it was covered with dried blood in which some of Galina's hair was still sticking.

It was thought that she had failed to mark her murderer, for although three of her fingernails were broken, there were no traces of skin or hair beneath them.

'A weapon of convenience, no previous contact between victim and murderer and no clues at the scene,' said the sergeant. 'I don't see how we can hope to solve this.'

'It's not that hopeless,' said the inspector. 'The man

is seriously deranged. This could not possibly be his first offence. The chances are that he has been in prison or in a psychiatric institution and, if so, there is a record on him.'

'Yes, but there are a great many such people,' said the sergeant. 'How are we to tell which one it is?'

'Well, we know some things about him and we can deduce others,' said the inspector. 'To begin with, he's strong. The girl was athletic and healthy and she was fighting for her life. She would have got the better of a weaker or less determined assailant.

'Secondly, he has a heterosexual sex drive because he wanted to rape her, but he's sexually abnormal because he couldn't achieve orgasm.

'Finally, he doesn't have any transport. The only way to reach the place where she was murdered is by foot or by bicycle, and there were no other recent bicycle tyre marks on the path.'

'Also, he must have just got out of wherever he was,' added the sergeant. 'A man that crazy wouldn't be able to wait very long before attacking some woman.'

'An intelligent observation, Klaus,' said the inspector. 'We'll start with that. Put half a dozen people on to checking recent releases from all the penal and mental institutions in the area, and have the files sent to this office. We'll establish profiles on each one and run them against our assumed profile of the murderer to see whether we get a match.'

Considering the urban population of Munich and its surrounding communities ran well over two million, this was a massive task and, without computers and computer files, one that would have taken years to complete.

As it was, it went slowly and the potential-suspect list was still two pages long when information from an unexpected source was received.

The source was none other than the victim herself, and she had been discussing her case with Elisabeth Kroll, a famous medium and the author of a book entitled *Contacts With the Hereafter*.

The medium, a young and remarkably attractive woman, reported that Galina had described her murder in detail.

'He wanted to rape me,' she had told the medium, 'but he was impotent. He's insane, a loner, I fought with him, but I didn't have the strength. After six minutes, my body was dead.

'I told him when he was attacking me, "Don't hurt me. I'll give you a hundred marks. I have a hundred-mark note in my bag."

'I knew that he would kill me. I've always known someone would. I realize now that I was a medium while I was still on earth.'

The inspector called on Miss Kroll. He was anxious to hear whether the victim had mentioned her murderer's name or could describe him. He did not particularly believe in spirits or life after death, but he was a thorough man and he was not going to neglect any possibility of solving the case. After all, the proven fact that Galina had predicted her own murder years in advance was evidence enough that some things not accepted by conventional wisdom were possible.

There was also something concrete. The police had found a single one-hundred-mark note (worth over thirty pounds) in Galina's handbag, but the press had been told that there was no money at all. It was a routine provision for information which, being known only to the police and the murderer, could be used to exclude false confessions or confirm a true one.

The inspector was, therefore, much impressed by the medium's mention of the hundred-mark note.

The interrogation of the victim ended in failure, however. Galina was cooperative, but said that she did not know the man's name. She did not think that she had ever encountered him before in her life and she could not describe him because it had been dark.

'It doesn't matter,' she said, speaking through Miss Kroll. 'Where I am now is a wonderful place and there is no hate here. I don't hate my murderer. I only regret that he can never be where I am now and I weep for him. Tell my parents and friends that they need have no fear. The soul lives on!'

The inspector took the failure philosophically.

'We'd never have got any of it admitted before a court, anyway,' he said.

'It wasn't all lost,' said the sergeant. 'I've added the fact that he wasn't interested in money to the profile and it's cut out three-quarters of the potential suspects. Apparently, a psychopath has to be completely off the deep end before he loses interest in money.'

The psychopath who killed Galina Terhaerst had been so little interested in money that he had not even opened her handbag, although, according to the dead girl, he had known that there was a hundred-mark note in it.

The inspector regretted this pecuniary disinterest. The surface of the handbag was smooth enough to retain fingerprints which might have rendered unnecessary much of the patient, boring sifting of information that had, finally, reduced the potential-suspect list to twenty-one men.

'None of whom will ever stand trial for anything,' he observed, 'because they are all officially certified mad.'

'Then they should be in madhouses,' said the sergeant.

'That is what I think,' said the inspector, 'and that is what you think, and that is what the public, the jury and even, sometimes, the judge thinks, but the psychologists think differently – and they are accountable to no one.'

'A curious system for protecting the public,' said the sergeant, who knew all about this state of affairs but thought that agreement with his chief could do no harm. 'Do you have any ideas on how we can cut the list down further?'

'Not really,' said the inspector. 'If you've eliminated as many as you can, take the rest of them into custody. Normally, they won't make any difficulty about confessing because they know they're safe. All that can be done to them is send them for some more psychiatric treatment.'

The inspector was speaking from experience, but he had overlooked one thing. Having eliminated another three, the sergeant arrested eighteen suspects – and fourteen of them confessed!

The sergeant was dismayed.

'We're back to where we started,' he said. 'I don't know which one of these confessions is true, or if any of them are.'

'I do,' said the inspector, who had just finished listening to the tape recordings of the confessions. 'It's Barsch.'

'Thomas Barsch?' said the sergeant. 'Why him? He's no crazier than the rest. It's true that he was let out of the psychiatric clinic at Haar four days before the murder and it's true that he's attacked other females at night, but the same applies to many of them. They've been let out recently from some institution not far from the scene and they have a record of violence against females.'

'But none of the others mentions a hundred-mark note,' said the inspector. 'They either say nothing about money or that she didn't have any. Listen.'

He changed cassettes and pressed the button of the tape recorder. The eerie, singsong voice of twenty-seven-year-old Thomas Barsch filled the office.

'I did it to her! I did it to her!' he chanted. 'Her hundred marks didn't help her. I did it to her! I did it to her! I–'

The inspector tapped the off button.

'You see?' he said.

'Well, there was a hundred-mark note in the handbag,' said the sergeant, 'but he could have got that detail from the newspapers.'

'No, he couldn't,' said the inspector, 'because we told the press that we found no money on her.'

'Of course,' said the sergeant. 'It slipped my mind.'

His face suddenly took on a startled look.

'Do you realize that this is confirmation of what the medium said?' he demanded. 'Only the police, the murderer and . . .'

'. . . the victim knew about the hundred-mark note,' finished the inspector. 'I'll leave you to work that out. In the meantime, have all of Barsch's clothing sent to the laboratory. They should be able to find traces of blood on it.'

The laboratory came up with the evidence and the inspector proceeded to a re-enactment of the crime, in which Thomas Barsch participated enthusiastically. In fact, he became so excited that it was necessary to place him under restraint. Although neither big nor burly, he was astonishingly strong.

Armed with the re-enactment, Barsch's confession – worthless because he was certified insane – the traces of blood on the clothing and the mention of the hundred-mark note, the inspector brought his prisoner before an alienation panel, which examined his record and sent him back to the psychiatric clinic at Haar with the recommendation that he be cured a little less swiftly this time.

12

EGG POWER

There are good streets in the sixth arrondissement of Lyon, but the rue Sainte-Génévieve is not one of them. Situated in an old part of the city of nearly half a million, many of its neglected buildings are occupied by North African immigrants, often clandestinely.

However, even a dingy street can look cheerful on a high summer morning, and this was 17 July 1986, three days after the Fête Nationale and a day away from the weekend.

Yves Courreau, municipal sanitation worker third class, was therefore whistling as he made his way along the rue Sainte-Génévieve, dragging the huge plastic dustbins to the kerb for emptying into the following dustcart.

The dustbin in front of number 117 was exceptionally heavy.

Courreau opened the lid and peered in.

Sixteen inches from the tip of his nose was a pair of naked female buttocks.

Courreau, a stocky man in his late thirties, let out a yell of alarm and dropped the lid. A French dustman is not easily startled, but there are limits.

The other members of the refuse collection crew came running, everyone had a look and, finally, someone called the police.

Five minutes later, the first patrol car arrived, and within half an hour the street was blocked off for a hundred yards on either side of the bin in which the body lay. By this time, the advance unit of the sixth

146

arrondissement homicide squad had already arrived at the scene.

Although there was no doubt the woman was dead, regulations required that Dr Charles Lenfant, the squad's medical expert, look for signs of life.

As he had anticipated, he found none and, rather than continue with the examination of the body at the scene, he recommended that it be brought in the dustbin to the police morgue where it would be easier to remove it and where any clues there might be would not risk being lost.

Inspector Jules Pichon, the sturdy, broad-faced and bushy-browed officer in charge of the squad, agreed. The sooner the area was cleared, the better.

'She's been dead some time, I assume?' he said. 'It's not something that just happened.'

'Five or six hours at least,' said the doctor, prodding the flesh of the buttocks with a long, elegant finger and gazing, with professional detachment, at the tuft of brown pubic hair protruding from between the close-pressed thighs.

He was a carefully groomed man with a stylish haircut, a neatly trimmed little moustache and gold-rimmed glasses which he frequently removed to wipe.

The inspector summoned two hefty detectives, who lifted the dustbin into a police van and drove it off to the police morgue. The doctor went with it, looking slightly offended at having to ride in a common van.

Half an hour later, the street was cleared, statements had been taken from the dustmen, and the homicide squad had returned to headquarters.

There would, of course, be further investigations in the rue Sainte-Généviève, but they could not begin until the body was out of the dustbin and, if possible, identified.

Upon his return to headquarters, the inspector went straight to the morgue, where he found that Dr Lenfant had experienced no difficulty in extracting the body from the dustbin, but was finding examination of it more difficult. Rigor mortis had set in and it remained bent double, the face pressed against the legs, and the arms wrapped around them.

'Not much prospect of an identification, I'm afraid,' said the doctor. 'She's completely naked and there wasn't anything in the bin other than a little rubbish stuck at the bottom.'

The bin had already been taken away to the police laboratory, where it would be examined for fingerprints and other potential clues.

'Can you get her legs far enough apart for us to take a photograph of the face?' said the inspector. 'I want to start my people canvassing the street as soon as possible.'

'I doubt that she lived there,' said the doctor. 'This is a high-class, expensive woman. Look at the fingernails and toenails and the hair. Very good flesh tone. She's had expert care.'

He turned the corpse so that it was lying on its back, bent the arms slowly back and, with some difficulty, parted the legs.

The face that peered out between them was beautiful and it still bore skilful make-up. The expression, however, was one of horror.

'Strangled, I expect,' said the doctor, as the police photographer stepped forward and levelled his camera. 'No blood, in any case.'

'And the motive?' said the inspector. 'Was she sexually assaulted?'

'Tell you in a minute,' said the doctor, prying open the genitals and reaching for the speculum. 'Well! What's this?'

He bent forward, peering between the folds of stiff flesh, probed with his fingers and produced a small, dirty-white oval object, which he held up for the inspector's inspection.

'What in God's name is that?' said the inspector, staring at it in perplexity.

'An egg, I should say,' said the doctor, laying it in a glass dish and removing his glasses to polish the lenses with a small square of cloth intended for that purpose. 'A hard-boiled egg.'

'There's hair threaded through it,' said the inspector unbelievingly. 'What in the devil . . . ?'

'Ju-ju,' said the doctor calmly. 'African magic. Probably a love charm, considering where she had it.'

'You mean she wore this thing there because she thought it would make somebody love her?' said the inspector.

'That was the general idea, I expect,' said the doctor. 'It would, no doubt, have been removed before any demonstration of its efficiency. Only guessing, of course. I'm not a witch doctor. My degree is in forensic medicine. You can probably get a better opinion from one of the Africans in business here. There are a few thousand of them.'

The inspector was aware of this. He did not believe in witch doctors and magic charms himself, but he knew that such superstitions were widespread in France. The preceding year, an informal census of magicians, soothsayers, witch doctors, fortune-tellers, readers of cards and sellers of good-luck charms and amulets and other less conventional practitioners of the black art had produced a figure of over fifty thousand for the Paris region alone. Many were successful enough to afford full-page advertisements in magazines and newspapers.

'I hope this isn't going to be one of those crazy cases,' muttered the inspector. 'Get her prints, Maurice. The first step is still identification.'

Maurice, the technician from the fingerprints department, took the dead woman's fingerprints.

'Beautiful woman,' he said. 'How old do you think she was?'

'Around thirty,' said the doctor.

He too was led astray by the care that Marie-France Dunoyer had taken of her face and body. At the time of her death, she had already turned thirty-six.

'Husband is *the* Dunoyer, the one in the TV commercials,' said the inspector. 'Hard to imagine that a woman like that would be doing in the rue Sainte-Génévieve.'

'Probably brought there after death,' said Sergeant Lucien Davoine. 'We found no one in the street who admitted to ever having laid eyes on her. Of course, not many people in that street are prepared to admit to anything.'

The sergeant was the inspector's number two, a neat, compact, smiling, blond man who was as hard as nails, but regarded by his colleagues as too compassionate with the undeserving.

'Maybe the husband will be able to offer some explanation,' said the inspector. 'You can interview him. It'll give you an opportunity to mix with the rich and famous.'

It was Marie-France's husband, a wealthy and prominent businessman, who had been responsible for the identification. When he was unable to locate his wife on the afternoon of July the seventeenth, he had reported her missing to the police and provided a photograph. The inspector had recognized it immediately.

'Should I mention the egg?' asked the sergeant.

'By all means,' said the inspector. 'Ask him if he knew that his wife was running around with a boiled egg in her private parts, and if so, why. The fact is, it was probably intended for him. My sources on witch doctors say that it's a charm for regaining lost affection.'

'Then I might as well look into the identity of Dunoyer's mistress while I'm about it,' said the sergeant. 'You don't consider Dunoyer a suspect, do you?'

'The husband is always the top of the list,' said the inspector, 'but, somehow, I can't see a man in his position stuffing his wife into a dustbin. People with that kind of money don't need to do such things. He could afford a divorce, so why have her killed? He surely didn't do it himself. Besides, she was his third, and he didn't strangle the other two.'

Dr Lenfant had stated in the autopsy report that Marie-France Dunoyer had died as the result of manual

strangulation and that she had engaged in sexual intercourse with a man whose blood group was O not long
before her death.

There were no indications that she had tried to defend
herself, but certain traces, too small to be analyzed, in
the bloodstream were possible indications of drugs which
might have rendered her unconscious, or at least help-
less, at the time she was murdered.

This time was fixed at approximately one o'clock in
the morning of July the seventeenth.

The sergeant interrogated the bereaved husband and
looked discreetly into his private life.

Dunoyer had not one mistress but two, the second
only sixteen years old. They were the latest in a long
series and there was no reason to suspect that he had
taken them any more seriously than their predecessors.

Marie-France had apparently thought that he did,
however. She had been particularly jealous of the six-
teen-year-old and had alternately made scenes and tried
to seduce him.

'He says he didn't know anything about the egg,'
reported the sergeant, 'and that if she was that crazy,
she may have strangled herself.'

'It's not possible,' said the inspector morosely.
'Anyway, the egg was a ju-ju. The lab says the hairs
threaded through it are her own pubic hairs. It was a
love charm. She was trying to pry him off the sixteen-
year-old.'

'Him or someone else,' said the sergeant. 'She may
have had a lover.'

'I'm sure you'll find out if she did,' said the inspector.

The sergeant did find out. Marie-France had had no
lover. According to all accounts, she had been virtually
obsessed with her husband.

'Her one true love, it seems,' said the sergeant. 'It
wasn't the husband. It wasn't the lover. What does that
leave us?'

'One of the mistresses?' asked the inspector hopefully.

'They're small women,' said the sergeant. 'All his

mistresses are. He likes them smaller than his wives. Something psychological, no doubt. The two of them together couldn't have stuffed Mrs Dunoyer into that dustbin. Of course, they could have hired somebody, but strangulation isn't typical of a professional killer.'

The inspector sighed.

'No, it isn't,' he agreed. 'So, about all that's left is the witch doctor. I was afraid of that.'

'Looks like it,' said the sergeant. 'We've gone into her background enough now to know that there wasn't anyone with a motive for murdering her. Incidentally, Dunoyer's blood group is B.'

'Meaning that it wasn't he who had sex with her just before she was killed,' said the inspector, 'and you tell me she didn't have a lover so. . . .'

'Again, the witch doctor,' said the sergeant. 'Probably got carried away applying the ju-ju and slipped her something to keep her quiet while he took care of his own problem. Wasn't enough, so she realized what he was doing to her and, when she threatened to go to the police, he killed her.'

'Something like that,' the inspector concurred. 'Now, which witch doctor?'

'Well, not one that lives in the rue Sainte Génévieve,' said the sergeant. 'Even a witch doctor wouldn't be stupid enough to discard the body in his own bin.'

'And, presumably, he's an African,' said the inspector. 'The egg with the pubic hairs is typically African, so they tell me.'

'Which narrows it down to five or six thousand people.' The sergeant sighed.

The inspector looked at him thoughtfully.

'I wonder how she could have got in touch with him,' he said. 'They'd hardly have moved in the same circles.'

'Recommended by another woman?' suggested the sergeant.

The inspector thought it over.

'No,' he said finally. 'Another woman wouldn't want

to admit that she'd had to resort to a witch doctor to keep her husband.'

'Small ad then,' said the sergeant. 'The newspapers and magazines are full of them. The trouble is: How can we find out which one she answered?'

'We can't,' the inspector told him. 'Ads like that usually give nothing but a phone number. There's no address, so she couldn't have written to him – and that means no record.'

'I have the feeling that you expect me to check four or five thousand witch doctors,' said the sergeant.

'Only one at a time, Lucien,' said the inspector, retaining a perfectly expressionless face.

Checking four or five thousand witch doctors, half, at least, of whom were in the country illegally, was manifestly impossible, whether one at a time or simultaneously, but it was becoming obvious to the sergeant that there was going to be a great deal of legwork and unpaid overtime connected with the case, and this tended to sharpen his wits.

'Look,' he said three days later, 'I've been doing some research on the witch doctor business, and the love egg isn't all that common.'

'I was told it was very common,' said the inspector.

'The egg itself, yes,' said the sergeant, 'but where it was, no. The approved practice is to put it under the target person's mattress and, in theory, he goes mad with lust for the woman whose pubic hairs were used. With the egg where Mrs Dunoyer had it, there would have been an obstacle to consummation or, at least, an awkward retrieval problem.'

'You have a graphic turn of mind, Lucien,' remarked the inspector. 'Continue.'

'I think there may be only a relatively small number of witch doctors practising this unorthodox application of the magic egg,' said the sergeant. 'Small enough, perhaps, for us to investigate them individually and determine which one was treating Mrs Dunoyer.'

'Perhaps,' said the inspector, 'but how do you propose to separate the orthodox from the unorthodox?'

'Even the most talented witch doctor must have some failures,' the sergeant explained. 'The charm couldn't work every time, and these highly trained specialists charge the eyes out of your head. It's possible that there have been complaints by dissatisfied patients.'

'You mean, to the police?' said the inspector. 'Why haven't you checked that already?'

'I have,' said the sergeant. 'A Mrs Michele Vaux, aged forty-three, unhappily married, filed charges of swindle and assault on April the seventh against Mr Abdul Fahdi Raschid, aged twenty-four, an Algerian national and, according to the advertisements, the seventh son of a line of seven generations of sorcerers.'

'Assault?' the inspector queried.

'She charged he pulled out some of her pubic hair to put in an egg,' said the sergeant. 'Seems, in this case, he put the hairs in an empty eggshell. The charge sheet doesn't say what else he did to her.'

'And what was the disposition?' asked the inspector.

'It was investigated by Section Four,' said the sergeant. 'There was an indictment and the case is awaiting trial. Raschid denies receiving more than a nominal fee for marital advice and, as Mrs Vaux was unable to produce a receipt or the egg, he'll get off for lack of evidence.'

'Clandestine?' wondered the inspector. 'If so, he could be quietly eased out of the country and. . . .'

'His papers are in order,' said the sergeant. 'He has a residence permit and a work permit.'

'As a witch doctor?' said the inspector.

'As a street sweeper,' said the sergeant.

'Sounds promising, so far,' said the inspector, 'but was Mrs Dunoyer one of his patients?'

'I haven't been able to determine that as yet,' admitted the sergeant, 'but I'm seeing Mrs Vaux this afternoon, and it could be that she knows the identity of some of the doctor's other patients.'

Michele Vaux turned out to be an extremely valuable witness. She was now divorced and still furious with her incompetent witch doctor.

She denied, however, that he had done anything physical to her other than pull out seven of her pubic hairs.

'That's the extent of his occult powers,' she said bitterly. 'The advertisement said that he had never failed in regaining affection and there were dozens of testimonials, so I thought, "Well, maybe there really is something in it." Anyway, I was desperate. I knew Jerome was seeing another woman and I'd already tried everything else I could think of.'

'You had only the one – ah – treatment?' asked the sergeant.

'I was there four times,' said Mrs Vaux. 'Mumbo-Jumbo isn't the boy to let a paying customer get away with a single visit. It cost me a thousand francs each time, but I thought it was worth it if I could get Jerome back.'

The sergeant cleared his throat sympathetically.

'And he ah – pulled out . . . er, that is . . . he carried out the physical part of the treatment on each of these occasions?' he inquired delicately.

'Do I look like a bear?' snapped Mrs Vaux. 'I'm not covered with hair. I'd have ended up as bald as his stupid egg. It was only the last time.'

A somewhat irascible woman, she impressed the sergeant as having a not much higher opinion of police competence than she had of her former witch doctor.

She was, however, very anxious to injure Raschid in any way she could and she left no details out of her statement.

Raschid's advertisement, she said, had listed only a telephone number, and she had called for an appointment.

She had been given one for three days later and, upon arriving at the address – which turned out to be a slum building near the junction of the Saône and Rhone rivers in the old part of town – had been ushered into a room, the walls of which were covered with black cloth decorated with supposed magic symbols in silver paint.

Raschid was dressed in a long, flowing garment with more occult symbols painted on it and was wearing a sort of crown.

The only furniture in the room was a tripod supporting a copper bowl in which incense sticks were smouldering and a mattress lying in the exact centre of the floor.

Raschid had instructed her to sit down cross-legged on the mattress and, after walking around her seven times in an anticlockwise direction while muttering incantations, had announced that she was there because her husband loved another.

This was not a spectacularly brilliant revelation by the spirits as she had already explained her problem to the doctor over the telephone. Even so, Mrs Vaux was impressed.

So much so that she returned three more times, paying cash and asking for no receipt. Mr Vaux was a very wealthy man and Mrs Vaux was desperate.

Each visit had produced further startling revelations and promises of help, and although the sergeant, familiar with the tricks of fortune-tellers, was more impressed by Mrs Vaux's naivety than her doctor's somewhat primitive performance, she herself had become convinced that Raschid really did possess mysterious powers.

By the fourth visit, however, she was beginning to display a certain amount of impatience and Raschid, apparently judging that there was no more milk to be obtained from this particular cow, had said that it was time for the infallible charm.

Although somewhat doubtful, she had allowed the magician to pull out seven of her pubic hairs, which he placed in an empty eggshell and sealed with plastic tape. He had instructed her to place the charm under her husband's mattress and recommended that, if she made use of a contraceptive device, she should be wearing it as Mr Vaux would be in a hurry.

He had then pronounced her cured and said that no further treatment would be necessary.

Mr Vaux, who was in his late fifties and had a very young mistress, had fallen exhausted into bed and had been sound asleep within a matter of minutes.

The eggshell containing the pubic hairs had been destroyed the following day in the course of an unsuccessful attempt by Mrs Vaux to force it up her witch doctor's nostrils.

Although Mrs Vaux did not know the identity of any of Abdul Fahdi Raschid's other patients, the sergeant was able to locate several similar complaints concerning him and other prominent practitioners of alternative medicine, some involving eggs and pubic hair and some less savoury practices. He was not, however, able to establish any connection to Marie-France Dunoyer until a complaint was filed in May of 1987 by a Mrs Christine Ramourelle.

Mrs Ramourelle was thirty-nine years old and her husband, a wealthy businessman, was having an affair with a nineteen-year-old secretary in his firm. He had informed his wife that he had found true love at last and that he was filing for divorce.

The despairing Mrs Ramourelle had answered an advertisement by a Mr Kandioura Sylla which read, 'Love regained. Frigidity and impotence cured. Results guaranteed.'

Mr Sylla, who came from Senegal and had entered France illegally, claimed vast experience in the solution of problems such as Christine's, although he was only twenty-three years old. He explained, this, however, by saying that much of his experience had been gained in former lives, of which he had had a great many.

Sylla had given Mrs Ramourelle a green liquid to drink, which had made her feel very strange. He had pulled out some of her pubic hairs, threaded them through a hard-boiled egg and told her that he was going to put the egg into her vagina, where she was to keep it until shortly before going to bed with her husband. He had then charged her five hundred dollars.

Mrs Ramourelle had been half-unconscious, but she had a confused recollection of Sylla first putting something into her other than an egg. An examination following removal of the egg confirmed her suspicions, so she had gone to the police to charge her doctor with rape.

What made Mrs Ramourelle's case of exceptional interest to the police was that the egg had actually been placed in her vagina, which was, it seemed, not often the case.

Sylla was being held in the detention cells and the inspector ordered an immediate search of his practice, which was, contrary to expectation, in the rue Sainte Génévieve, although at number six, a considerable distance from where the body of Marie-France Dunoyer was found.

Sylla's appointment book was located, and in it, among nearly three hundred other names, all of women, was the entry, 'Mrs M. F. Dunoyer. 16 July 1986 10 p.m.'

The inspector had hoped that this material evidence would produce a confession, but it did not. Even under intense interrogation, Sylla denied all knowledge of the murder and of Marie-France Dunoyer. He was, he insisted, an honest sorcerer whom the police were persecuting because they were racist Christians and he was black.

M. F., he said, stood for Martine-Felice, and this was proof that he had not murdered Marie-France Dunoyer because he had had an appointment with Martine-Felice Dunoyer at that time. He did not, however, know where Martine-Felice lived or how to contact her.

Whether Kandioura Sylla was a good witch doctor or not, he was an excellent lawyer. Influenced by fear of the standard charges of racism when dealing with Africans, French judges tend to reverse discrimination, and the name M. F. Dunoyer in Sylla's appointment book was held to be insufficient evidence for handing down an indictment without an accompanying confession.

None was forthcoming and, on 6 July 1987, Kandioura Sylla was quietly deported to his own country on charges of entering France illegally, residing in France illegally and practising medicine without a licence.

The rape charge was dropped, as Sylla's claim that sexual intercourse was part of the treatment – and that Mrs Ramourelle had consented to it – could not be disproved.

13

PRACTICAL HYPNOSIS

At a little before seven-thirty in the early autumn evening of 12 March 1981, thirty-eight-year-old Harley Brown rose from the dinner table and headed for his chair, his newspaper and his pipe. A supervisor in a local textile mill, he had put in a hard Thursday.

In the dining room of the comfortable house at 144 Kirsten Avenue, Mathilda Brown, four years younger than her husband, busied herself with clearing away the dinner dishes.

Both the Browns were looking forward to a quiet evening, but Harley had barely seated himself when there came the sound of an anguished scream from outside.

Anguished screams are not common in Paarl, a modest community of under fifty thousand residents twenty-five miles to the northeast of Cape Town. A summer resort stretching along the Great Berg Road, Paarl produces wine, fruit and tobacco and manufactures flour, lumber and textiles. Many of its residents work in Cape Town, however.

This was the case with forty-four-year-old Alan Mitchell, an employee of the South African railway system, whose house was next door and from whose yard the scream had come.

Rushing out of their kitchen door, the Browns saw twenty-eight-year-old Penelope Mitchell standing in the path leading from the Mitchells' garage to the house. She had not screamed again and stood as if paralyzed, her eyes riveted to something on the ground.

As there was a hedge bordering both sides of the path, the Browns could not see what it was and thought that one of the Mitchell daughters, ten-year-old Natalie or her two-years-younger sister, Jane, might have hurt herself.

However, when Brown forced himself through the hedge, he saw that the body lying on the gravel of the path appeared to be that of Alan Mitchell. The man lay sprawled face down and his shirt, his head and a large area of the gravel around him was drenched with fresh blood.

Utterly dumfounded as he could not imagine what kind of an accident might have produced such fearful injuries, Brown ran forward, dropped to his knees and turned Mitchell's head to one side to get his nose and mouth out of the blood.

To his horror, he felt the bones of the skull part beneath his fingers and he shouted to his wife, 'Call the ambulance! Alan's hurt bad!'

Mathilda ran back into the house and Brown gently but quickly led Penelope in the direction of hers. It was obvious to him that he could do nothing for Alan. The man's injury was so severe that any attempt at first aid might kill him.

'My God, Penelope!' he exclaimed. 'What happened?'

'I don't know!' wailed Penelope. She was shaking violently and her knees were buckling under her. 'I heard his car stop in front of the garage like every night, but he didn't come in and there was a sort of thump. When I want to see what he was doing, there he was lying in the path all blood!'

She was obviously on the verge of hysteria and, after having got her to lie down on the living room sofa, Brown went back outside to ask the ambulance crew to do something for her when they arrived. Fortunately, the little girls did not seem to be at home.

The ambulance arrived quickly, but the crew had no time for Mrs Mitchell.

'This man is dying!' said the paramedic. 'His head's

been split wide open! It'll be a wonder if he's alive when we get him to the hospital.'

No wonder took place. The ambulance made a fast run, but Alan Mitchell was dead upon arrival.

The body was returned at once to the ambulance, which took it to the police morgue. It was virtually impossible for Mitchell to have received his head injury accidentally. The indications were that he had been murdered.

The matter, consequently, became the responsibility of the small and seldom needed homicide squad of the Paarl police.

Being seldom needed, none of the squad's members was on duty at that time of day, and it was past eight o'clock before Inspector William Dryer and Detective Sergeant Colin Marriner arrived at the house in Kirsten Avenue.

There, they found a large pool of blood on the path, and the Browns in the living room of the Mitchell's house, trying to calm and comfort their neighbour.

Their efforts had included several large brandies and Penelope was much comforted, but, if anything, in even less control of her emotions. She had not been told that Alan was dead, although the Browns had called the hospital and knew it.

She repeated what she had told Harley Brown and added that her daughters were spending the night with a school friend. She had no idea how the accident could have happened.

The inspector, a burly thick-shouldered man with a broad, open face and reddish-brown hair cut high at the sides, did not inform her that this had been no accident, but asked if her husband had been having any trouble with anyone recently.

Mrs Mitchell said that her husband never had trouble with anyone. He was a sober, hard-working man and his religious convictions did not permit him to frequent bars or other places where there might be trouble.

The inspector did not comment, but went back outside, where the sergeant was searching the hedges.

'Find it?' he asked.

The sergeant shook his head. He was a comparatively young man, muscular, compact and short of handsome only by reason of a somewhat too prominent jaw.

'Somebody has come through the hedge in two places,' he said, 'but that's all I've been able to determine.'

'May have been the Browns,' said the inspector. 'We'll have to check on that. You stay here and keep looking for the weapon. I'm going over to the morgue to see if I can find out what sort of weapon we're looking for.'

Dr Brian Cheevers, the criminal investigations department's medical officer, had been called in at the same time as the inspector and the sergeant, and the inspector found him at the morgue examining the body.

'Very violent blow to the back of the head with an axe or hatchet,' said the doctor. 'It split the skull wide open. It's astonishing that he lived until the arrival of the ambulance.'

Although in reality a kindly man and the father of two small children, his appearance corresponded closely to the popular conception of a dangerous criminal. His arms were too long. His hands were too large. His eyes were black and deep-set and his mouth was hidden by a thick, drooping moustache beneath a nose which looked broken but was not.

'Would a woman have had the strength to deliver the blow?' asked the inspector.

'If she was a very large, powerful woman, perhaps,' said the doctor. 'You suspect the wife?'

'Not any more,' said the inspector.

Penelope Mitchell was small and rather daintily built.

The inspector returned to Kirsten Avenue, where he found that the sergeant had been joined by most of the plainclothes officers of the criminal investigations department. They were searching the gardens of the nearby houses and the grass strips on either side of the road.

163

'I talked to the Browns,' said the sergeant. 'Only Brown went through the hedge. His wife came round the front.'

'So it was probably the murderer at the second break,' said the inspector. 'Seems fairly clear what took place. The murderer knew what time he came home and was waiting behind the hedge. As soon as Mitchell had passed, he jumped out, hit him over the head and ran for it.'

The sergeant nodded in silent agreement. Privately, he did not feel at all confident about the investigation which was now beginning. There had been other homicides in Paarl, but they had been impulsive, largely unintentional acts. This was the squad's first deliberate, planned murder, and he was wondering whether it might not be better to call for help from Cape Town.

'Not until we've had a shot at it ourselves,' said the inspector, reading his thoughts from his expression. 'It may be that, once we've gone into the backgrounds, the suspect will be obvious.'

'The wife's lover?' said the sergeant.

'That's what I'm thinking,' said the inspector. 'He certainly wasn't murdered for his money.'

It was an opinion that would soon be confirmed by the investigation into the history of the Mitchell family. Alan Mitchell had not had any money. He had had a good job and he had been able to support his family in comfort, but his total savings were hardly enough to bury him, and his life insurance was trifling.

As his wife had said, he was a sober, hard-working and devoutly religious man who had married for the first time at the age of thirty-four.

His bride, Penelope Bamford, had been just half his age and, presumably, ready to marry the devil himself to escape a home in which she, her mother and sisters were daily beaten half-unconscious by her drunken and brutal father.

The Mitchells were less than a month short of their tenth wedding anniversary at the time of Alan's death, and the marriage was regarded by their friends, neighbours and relatives as a happy one.

Disregarding the difference in ages, the Mitchells were a completely ordinary family except in one respect. Penelope was a hypnotist.

It was something mentioned by everyone who knew her as she was mildly famous for her hypnotic powers and held seances in her home twice a week.

She had been doing this for a long time. According to numerous sources of information, Penelope had first learned of her mysterious powers at the age of sixteen, when she was taken to see a professional stage hypnotist.

The performance had so impressed her that, immediately upon coming home, she tried it out on her sister.

The very first attempt had been a success and the subject fell into a deep sleep from which even Penelope's agonized screams, as her father beat her nearly senseless for hypnotizing her sister, failed to wake her.

After that, Penelope had conducted her experiments in hypnotism outside the home and kept a sharp eye out for anyone likely to marry her.

She had not needed to hypnotize Alan into asking her father's permission first to go out with her and then to marry her. She was seventeen and, when her face was not swollen or black and blue, pretty.

She had not needed to hypnotize her father either. As he had observed, there were far too many females in the house, and if Mitchell was willing to take one or more off his hands, he could only be grateful.

Penelope and Alan were married on 1 April 1971. That the wedding took place on April Fools' Day was, presumably, only a matter of convenience.

And that had, seemingly, been the part of the story which read, '. . . and they lived happily ever after. . . .'

Alan had bought the pleasant little house in Kirsten Avenue and Penelope had settled down to bearing children and amazing a select but surprisingly large circle with demonstrations of her strange powers.

Some said that the circle was so large because entertainment in Paarl was scarce and Penelope charged nothing, but this probably represented jealousy of her popularity.

Even the most critical had to admit, however, that Penelope put on a show worthy of any stage hypnotist. In trance, her subjects remembered where they had left mislaid objects, hopped about her living room in the belief that they were kangaroos and yelled with pain at the suggestion that their pants were on fire.

Alan took no part in the proceedings. To begin with, they took place in the afternoon when he was at work and, secondly, he was not at all certain that such goings-on were approved by the Church, although he could find no place in the Bible which expressly forbade them.

Even so, it had not been a point for dissension within the family. Alan was a mild-tempered man and even somewhat proud of his young wife's extrasensory abilities.

'I suppose it doesn't have anything to do with the murder,' conceded Sergeant Marriner, who had thought that it did. 'On the other hand, we haven't found any lover either, have we?'

'We have to look harder,' said the inspector. 'We know there has to be one. Otherwise, there's no rational motive for the murder at all. Mitchell didn't have an enemy in the world.'

'Maybe it wasn't rational,' suggested the sergeant. 'Maybe it was just a crazy person hiding behind the hedge who was ready to kill anybody who came along.'

'It's possible,' said the inspector doubtfully. 'We can run a check on the hospitals and psychiatric institutions, but, if it was a homicidal maniac, what was he doing in Kirsten Avenue and why hasn't he killed anybody else?'

The sergeant speculated that he might have killed somebody else and the body just hadn't been discovered yet, but he did not believe it himself and a check of the institutions with dangerous inmates showed none missing.

'No, it was the lover,' said the inspector. 'Absolutely

had to be. The situation was perfect for it. Here was Mrs Mitchell seventeen years younger than her husband and probably bored silly. Here was Mitchell, past forty and probably more interested in his dinner than his wife's body. Here was some young tom cat who . . .'

'. . . was invisible,' said the sergeant. 'Those houses in Kirsten Avenue are close together. None of the wives work and they all gossip. Nobody ever saw a male visitor at the Mitchells' house when Mitchell wasn't there.'

'Nobody admits it,' said the inspector.

'Why would they cover up for Mrs Mitchell?' asked the sergeant. 'Or did she hypnotize them into believing the young man they saw going into the house was Mrs Mitchell's aunt Nelly?'

The inspector looked at him thoughtfully.

'You know . . .' he said.

'Anyway,' continued the sergeant, 'Mrs Mitchell's afternoons were full. Twice a week, she had her seances. Two out of the other three days, at least, her children were at home. At weekends, her husband was. She couldn't have had more than a few minutes at a time. The lover would have had to sprint in, tear off her clothes, jump on her and – '

'All right. All right,' interposed the inspector hurriedly. 'No lover. And no homicidal maniac. So who murdered Alan Mitchell?'

'Somebody had a grudge against him,' said the sergeant.

'Nobody had a grudge against him,' argued the inspector.

'It's as likely as a lover,' said the sergeant.

The inspector sighed.

'Get out all the statements,' he said. 'We'll go over them once more together.'

The statements were, however, tape recorded and it was not possible for the officers to listen to different ones in the same office at the same time. The sergeant was, therefore, temporarily banished to the interrogation room.

Several hours passed.

'Why so much meat?' asked the inspector, opening the door to the interrogation room and putting his head in.

'What?' said the bewildered sergeant.

'Mrs Brown said that the Mitchells ate a lot of meat,' said the inspector. 'Why would she say that?'

'Because she's a vegetarian?' the sergeant guessed.

'No,' said the inspector. 'I don't think that's why she said it. What I want to know is, did the Mitchells really eat a lot of meat?'

'I could ask their butcher,' offered the sergeant, looking wonderingly at his superior.

'Do,' said the inspector.

The Mitchells, it seemed, ate no more meat than anyone else.

'Should I ask Mrs Brown why she said it?' asked the sergeant.

'I don't think she'd tell you,' said the inspector. 'Who's the Mitchells' butcher?'

'His name's Borken,' said the sergeant. His face suddenly brightened. 'It wasn't a hatchet or an axe! It was a butcher's cleaver and – '

'Young, athletic man?' interrupted the inspector.

'Who? Borken?' said the sergeant. 'He's past seventy. Around five foot four inches and he must weigh close to fifteen stone.'

'I take it he doesn't make his own deliveries then?' said the inspector.

'He has a butcher's boy by the name of Noel Hatting,' said the sergeant. 'Young fellow. Good-looking. . . . My God! You think . . . ?'

'I think that Mrs Brown suspects something, but she doesn't want to come right out with it,' explained the inspector. 'So she hinted.'

'She thinks that the butcher's boy was Mrs Mitchell's lover,' said the sergeant. 'God knows, she could be right. He would come mornings and nobody would find anything strange about him being in the neighbourhood.

The Mitchells wouldn't have been the only family where he delivered meat.'

'So now we have a potential suspect in the murder of Alan Mitchell,' said the inspector, looking remarkably complacent.

The sergeant looked thoughtful.

'I don't know,' he said. 'I only talked to Hatting briefly, but he strikes me as sort of a pipsqueak. Can't imagine him splitting anybody's head open with an axe. I think he'd faint.'

'Appearances are deceiving, Colin, my boy,' said the inspector expansively. 'You check Hatting out. I'll bet you'll find that he's one of the most feared barroom brawlers in Paarl. Butcher's boys always are.'

The sceptical sergeant checked. Noel Hatting was not a barroom brawler. He was twenty-six years old, slightly built and poetic-looking. Unmarried, he lived in a furnished room at number eleven Queen Street.

According to his reputation, he did not spend many nights there.

'Supposed to be a great Don Juan,' said the sergeant. 'The gossip is that, since he went to work for Borken, the business has doubled – and not because of the quality of the meat.'

'But that ties in perfectly!' cried the inspector. 'That's the mystery lover!'

'But not the mystery murderer,' said the sergeant. 'Hatting's a permanent delivery boy because he'll never be a butcher.'

The inspector looked at him, raising his eyebrows.

'Borken says he can't stand the sight of blood,' said the sergeant. 'Has a fit if he even sees an animal butchered.'

The inspector got up from his chair, walked twice around his desk, looked out the window, returned to the desk and sat down.

'Arrest him,' he said.

'Arrest him?' said the sergeant.

The inspector nodded.

'If he was Mrs Mitchell's lover, and we're nearly certain that he was, then he knows something about this,' he said. 'And, if he's the snivelling wretch you describe him, we should be able to scare the truth out of him.'

Noel Hatting, it turned out, scared easily. He had barely arrived in the inspector's office when he was already hard at work trying to pin the blame for the murder on his former mistress.

He admitted freely that he had been having sexual relations with Penelope Mitchell since the beginning of February of that year, but he denied that he had seduced her.

Rather, he said, she had seduced him. The very first time he delivered meat to the Mitchell's house, she received him nearly naked and the second time, more so. She told him that her husband was an old man who was no longer interested in sex, but that she was.

So was Hatting, and his morning encounters with Penelope so impressed him that he suggested she divorce Mitchell and marry him.

'It was a nuisance always having to do it in the morning,' he told the inspector, 'and it interfered with the meat deliveries.'

Penelope said that legalizing their love was impossible. Alan was too religious ever to consent to a divorce.

According to Hatting, he had accepted this obstacle to his happiness philosophically, but Penelope had not – hinting darkly at other ways of dissolving a marriage.

Hatting ignored these dangerous suggestions and Penelope said nothing more until the morning of March the twelfth, when she suggested that he come around that afternoon.

Her husband, she said, would not be home until seven and her daughters were spending the afternoon and night with a school friend. She had in mind a little experiment.

Hatting turned up at four o'clock and they spent two or three hours so enjoyably that he was temporarily unable to continue.

Penelope then announced that he had arrived at the condition necessary for her experiment.

Undoubtedly, she told the spellbound Hatting, he had seen demonstrations of hypnotism where the subject was rendered so rigid that he or she could be laid with heels and head on two chairs and remain in that position without further support. What she proposed was to hypnotize Hatting, but to render only a small part of him rigid. The experiment was to see how long it would remain that way.

Hatting was doubtful and protested that he was afraid of injuring himself and, anyway, if he were in a trance, he would gain no benefit from the experiment.

Penelope said that it was not a matter of benefit but one of scientific curiosity, and hypnotized him more or less against his will.

It was not the first time that she had done so and he was, apparently, a highly susceptible subject. But, when he recovered his senses this time, he was standing on the garden path with a hatchet in his hands and Alan Mitchell was lying on the ground covered with blood.

Penelope told him he had killed her husband, but she forgave him and would hide the hatchet while he went home, cleaned the blood off his hands, burned his clothes and took a bath. There was now, she pointed out, no further obstacle to their love.

Hatting thrust the hatchet into her hands and ran off in a state of near madness. He would have long since come to the police, but he had wanted to protect Penelope.

Taken into custody in her turn, Penelope Mitchell offered a somewhat different version of the events.

It was true, she said, that she and Hatting had been intimate, but he had practically raped her and she had wanted to terminate the affair.

Hatting tried to blackmail her into continuing by threatening to tell her husband. When she refused, he said that he would take care of the matter in his own way.

The account of the circumstances she had given to the police was true – she had heard Alan's car drive up and, a little later, a thump. When she went to investigate, however, she found Hatting standing over her husband's body with the hatchet in his hands.

She too had wanted to go to the police, but she was afraid that Hatting would incriminate her and she did not want to leave her children and go to jail.

She denied that she had hypnotized him.

The police were not inclined to believe either of these versions and, in January of the following year, neither was the court.

Experts on the subject of hypnotism testified that Noel Hatting was a person who could be easily hypnotized, but that no one in a hypnotic trance could be persuaded to do something to which they were morally opposed. Hatting might have been under hypnosis when he murdered Alan Mitchell, but all it had done was relieve him of his horror of blood. He had killed voluntarily.

Penelope's claim of complete ignorance before the deed was disproved by the fact that the murder weapon was the Mitchells' own hatchet. It had been kept in the kitchen and there was no way that Hatting could have obtained it without Penelope's knowledge.

Although there now appeared to be little affection between the accused, the court apparently came to the conclusion that they had been blinded by love at the time and, deeming this an extenuating circumstance, sentenced them on 8 January 1982 to a modest fifteen years' imprisonment each.

Unfortunately, as she denied it had ever taken place, there was no testimony concerning the results of Penelope's interesting hypnotic experiment.

14

THE HEART OF THE MATER

Although there is, exceptionally, no regulation governing the matter, West German clergymen tend to be large, bluff and red in the face. Protestant pastors are particularly so inclined, and the little town of Hofgeismar, fifteen miles to the north of the city of Kassel, is in a predominantly Protestant part of the country.

As in not a few other respects, Germany is divided religiously between north and south, the more austere schnapps drinkers of the north being Protestant and the merry beer tipplers of the south Catholic.

There are historical reasons for this, but they are tedious and of no interest even to Germans.

On the afternoon of 13 November 1983, an exceptionally fine example of Protestant clergymen name Rudolf Auerstein was proceeding in a dignified manner along Hofgeismar's Max Planck Strasse. It was a fine late-autumn day. The sun shone briskly in a rather watery blue sky and the soprano notes of an optimistic blackbird formed a chance near harmony with the baritone crunch of dead leaves under the clerical boots.

It was Pastor Auerstein's intention to pay a call on one of his parishioners, the eighty-one-year-old Mrs Elise Steckmann, who lived alone in her house at number two Max Planck Strasse. Mrs Steckmann had not been present at the morning services and the pastor was mildly concerned.

He was more concerned when his firm knock on the door caused it to swing slightly open. Not only had it not been locked, it had not even been latched.

This was an alarming – indeed, frightening – state of affairs. German ladies of Mrs Steckmann's generation generally believed, and with reason, that leaving the front door unlocked was roughly equivalent to suicide.

Such carelessness might have been explicable had Mrs Steckmann been more fuzzy in the head, but, as the pastor knew, she had her wits very much about her.

He therefore wasted no time but penetrated boldly into the house, calling out Mrs Steckmann's name. As he would later tell the police, what he feared was that she had been paid a visit by a member of the younger generation seeking financial support for an addiction.

In such encounters, which are tragically frequent, it is often found necessary to place the older person's feet in the oven as this stimulated recollection of where any savings might be hidden, and the pastor went straight to the kitchen.

Mrs Steckmann was seated near the table, her legs straight out in front of her, her arms hanging down on either side and her head tipped back. Her mouth was open and blood had run down her cheeks onto her neck. There was more blood on her face and forehead, and her white hair was soaked to a tapering brown cylinder which hung down behind the chair.

All this was bad enough, but the sight which turned Pastor Auerstein's ruddy cheeks pale and caused the hairs at the back of his neck to rise was the woman's chest.

It had been hacked roughly open and the severed ends of the ribs pried apart. Lying between them was the dead woman's heart, a tangle of arteries, some broken wires and a small metallic object.

The aghast pastor, having no experience in such matters, thought that, in some inexplicable manner, a bomb had exploded in Mrs Steckmann's chest.

So too did the police officers who responded to the pastor's near hysterical telephone call, but the police doctor, upon his arrival, recognized the machine for what it was.

'Someone has murdered this woman and cut the pace-maker out of her chest!' he exclaimed in a shocked voice. 'I think this should be turned over to Kassel immediately.'

The chief of police was in agreement. Hofgeismar has a population of fourteen thousand and a police force of corresponding size. Kassel is a city of close to a quarter of a million. Its department of criminal investigations is better equipped to handle such an unprecedented and horrible case.

Kassel has a special unit for dealing with such cases, but, it being Sunday, the unit was not on duty.

However, the report by the Hofgeismar police had left no doubt that a homicide, and a particularly barbaric one, had taken place. The key members of the rural homicide squad were hurriedly assembled and dispatched to Hofgeismar in succeeding groups.

The first of these consisted solely of the officer-in-charge of the squad, Inspector Karl Busch, and his second-in-command, Sergeant of Detectives Hans Bock, both short, stocky men with drooping, black moustaches. With the sergeant at the wheel, they covered the fifteen miles to Hofgeismar in something under fifteen minutes.

There, they found nearly the entire Hofgeismar police force surrounding the house and a badly shaken Pastor Auerstein sitting in one of the patrol cars.

He had already made a statement concerning the discovery of the body to the Hofgeismar police and he now repeated it into the sergeant's tape recorder while the inspector went in to take a look at the body.

It was quite bad as it had been described, but his conclusions differed from those of the local police and the pastor.

'It was a psycho,' he said to Sergeant Bock. 'An addict would have been after her savings. This fellow was after her pacemaker. I predict we'll find that he didn't even search the house.'

The prediction proved to be accurate. Nothing in the

house had been disturbed and Mrs Steckmann's savings, not very cleverly hidden, were intact.

Following the arrival of the inspector and his assistant, great number of technicians and specialists poured in from Kassel and a number of puzzling discoveries were made.

There had been, it seemed, three murder weapons – a rolling pin, a hammer and a large kitchen knife. All three were the property of Mrs Steckmann and all three were liberally smeared with blood – so liberally, in fact, that it was not possible to obtain fingerprints from any of them.

Mrs Steckmann had apparently been having breakfast shortly before she was murdered and she had not been having it alone. Still standing on the kitchen table were two cups containing the dregs of coffee, two bowls containing grapefruit rinds, a partially consumed loaf of bread, butter, and plates and cutlery for two people. Tests by the police laboratory showed that the breakfasts had been eaten on that same morning of November the thirteenth at approximately eight o'clock.

The last member of the squad to arrive at the scene was the official police medical officer, Dr Klaus-Martin Katzer, a stoop-shouldered, blunt-featured man with a very close-clipped sandy moustache, and pale blue eyes behind frameless glasses.

Not expecting to be called out on a Sunday, he had been visiting relatives in a nearby town and was located only with difficulty.

His report was, in any case, of no great significance to the investigation. Mrs Steckmann, he said, had been struck violently over the head from behind with the rolling pin and the hammer. Her skull was fractured in many places. She had been dead at the time that her chest was cut open, and the incision had been performed by a person who knew nothing about human anatomy.

'But he did know that she wore a pacemaker,' said the inspector.

'Not necessarily,' said the doctor. 'He could have been

after the heart and didn't take it when he discovered the machine in her chest.'

'What would anybody want with an old lady's heart?' asked the sergeant, looking nauseated.

'Magic, perhaps,' said the doctor. 'A human heart is used in certain occult rituals and concoctions.'

'You mean they eat it?' said the sergeant, looking more nauseated than ever.

'Well, in small quantities,' said the doctor. 'It's too hard to come by to gobble it down by the pound.'

The sergeant turned pale green and hurriedly left the room.

'Anything else?' inquired the inspector. He was not looking much at ease himself.

'Time of death was early today,' said the doctor. 'I'll be able to fix it exactly when I do an autopsy. No indications of a sexual motive. Underwear is in place.'

It was not an idle observation. Women as old as Mrs Steckmann and older were not infrequently raped.

'All right then,' said the inspector. 'I think that wraps it up here. Let's get the body back to the morgue, and I want the reports on what's been determined at the scene as soon as possible.'

As soon as possible was the following afternoon. The hunt for Elise Steckmann's murderer was not urgent as he had had ample time to clear out of the area before the body was discovered. It was more important that the maximum information be extracted from what clues were at hand.

'On the face of it,' said the inspector, 'it would appear that Mrs Steckmann knew the murderer, but I regard that as improbable.'

'Why?' said the sergeant. 'They had breakfast together.'

'She had breakfast with someone,' said the inspector. 'There's no proof that it was the murderer, and I doubt that it was. Can you imagine a woman of eighty sitting down to breakfast with someone who, after breakfast, beats out her brains and cuts the pacemaker out of her chest?'

'I can't imagine anybody doing such a thing at all, before breakfast or after,' said the sergeant, 'but it seems to me that, if she knew him well enough to invite him to breakfast, she'd know how crazy he was. The man must be a raving madman.'

'We don't know that it was a man,' said the inspector. 'Anyway, you can't always tell that people are insane by looking at them. Many psychopaths appear to be perfectly normal until they're carried away by some mad impulse like this. After all, it wasn't planned. The rolling pin, the hammer and the knife were all weapons of convenience.'

'Then why weren't there any fingerprints on the breakfast dishes?' demanded the sergeant. 'He or she must have wiped them off.'

The inspector thought this over for a few minutes.

'You're right,' he said finally. 'He wiped them off. There's no other explanation. And that means that the person who had breakfast with her was the murderer, after all. There'd be no point in wiping the fingerprints off the dishes and cutlery if it was only an innocent visitor.'

There was a silence of some considerable duration.

'A very puzzling case,' said the sergeant finally.

The inspector, who had been lost in thought, gave a start.

'Very,' he said, 'but not, I think, completely hopeless. There are some possible leads to follow. To begin with, we know now that she knew him or her well enough to ask them to breakfast. At her age, the number of people she knew that well should be limited.

'Secondly, we know the murderer is violently insane. It is highly likely that he or she has undergone psychiatric treatment or has even been released from an institution. Again, the number of such places in the area is limited.

'Combine the two known factors, and what we are

looking for is a fairly close friend or relative of the victim who has a history of mental illness.'

'Something else,' said the sergeant. 'A person with a perverted interest in hearts.'

As such a person might well be expected to have a criminal record, the first step in the investigation was a search of the police files, not only for the Kassel area, but for the entire country.

This was, of course, carried out by computer and did not therefore take very long.

The computer turned up a surprising number of cases in which the victims' hearts had been cut out, torn out, pierced with a stake and, in one instance, eaten by a starving rat strapped in a bottomless cage to the victim's chest. This last, however, had been an act of revenge and did not represent an interest in hearts as such. Most of the others had had an occult significance of one kind or another.

None of the cases had any significance for the investigation as every one of the perpetrators was either in jail or in a psychiatric institution.

'Four unsolved cases of hearts torn or cut out,' said the sergeant glumly, 'but none near here and none concerning elderly women. They were all children.'

'Black mass, no doubt,' said the inspector. 'There are more of these satanist cases cropping up all the time.'

'We look for satanists then?' asked the sergeant.

The inspector hesitated.

'I don't think so,' he said. 'I've never heard of that type of murder connected with such an old woman. Our murderer is, perhaps, a person with an interest in the occult, but I doubt there'd be an association with any formal group. We'll begin by assembling the list of her close friends and relatives.'

The decision was a logical one. The evidence was that Elise Steckmann had been murdered by someone she knew well enough to ask to breakfast. The murderer was, therefore, within her circle of close contacts.

Unfortunately for this theory, Mrs Steckmann had

had no close contacts and her only close relative was her son, Rolf Steckmann, who was forty-two years old and lived in Essen, a hundred and fifty mils to the east.

Like many older people, Elise Steckmann had lost most of her friends through death and, apart from Pastor Auerstein, she had had known few people in Hofgeismar. She had only moved to the town in February 1982, following the death of her husband, who had been a tax accountant in Berlin.

As next of kin, Rolf Steckmann was notified of his mother's death so that he could make arrangements for the funeral. Mrs Steckmann had not left a very large estate, but her son was a long distance technician with the state-owned telephone service and comfortably well-off. The telephone service in Germany being run by the post office, he was a civil servant.

'Well, now what?' said the sergeant. 'Apart from Pastor Auerstein, she didn't know anyone in Hofgeismar well enough to ask them to breakfast. Is Auerstein the murderer?'

'All right. I know it sounds crazy,' said the inspector, 'but we have to check him out for eight-ten on Sunday morning. That's when Katzer says she was killed. I'm sure you'll find that he was in church or at home, but we have to do it for the record.'

To the consternation of both sergeant and inspector, Pastor Auerstein had not been in church at the time in question. In fact, no one seemed to know where he had been during the hour from seven-thirty to eight-thirty on the morning of November the thirteenth.

'I haven't asked his wife,' said the sergeant. 'She'd realize immediately that he was being investigated. I can't believe this.'

'I don't believe it either,' said the inspector. 'There's some innocent explanation for his absence. You say that he would normally have been at the church at that time?'

The sergeant nodded.

'He inspects it with the housekeeper every morning to see that everything's in order for the services,' he said. 'He's very conscientious and fussy about the appearance of the church. The housekeeper expected him any time after seven-thirty, but he didn't show up until nine. She thought he seemed out of breath, as if he'd been hurrying.'

'I still don't believe it,' said the inspector, but there was uncertainty in his voice. 'You cautioned the house-keeper not to say anything about being questioned?'

'Of course,' said the sergeant, 'but I'm not sure she'll comply. You could see the *Schadenfreude* running out of her ears.'

Schadenfreude is the German term for joy over the misfortunes of others, an emotion not totally absent in countries having no name for it.

'Well, we have no choice,' said the inspector, drawing a deep breath. 'We have to press on. Do it as discreetly as you can, but find out everything there is to know about that pastor.'

It turned out that there was not a great deal to know, but some of it was, possibly, of significance.

Pastor Auerstein was thirty-six years old and came originally from Kassel, where he had attended the seminary and been ordained a minister in the Evangelical Church.

He had married in 1972 and was the father of two boys, aged seven and four. He had taken over Sankt Willibrord church in Hofgeismar at the beginning of 1980 and was regarded as sincere and hard-working, if not particularly inspired or inspiring, by his congregation.

It was the normal, tranquil life history of an almost typical Protestant pastor, but there was one detail which, in light of the circumstances, might be significant.

Six years earlier, in 1977, Pastor Auerstein had suffered a nervous breakdown and physically attacked one of his parishioners. The victim, an elderly woman, had not been hurt and she had refused to file charges. The pastor had been admitted to a psychiatric clinic, where he had remained under treatment for seven weeks.

'The records on this are not complete,' said the sergeant. 'As the woman refused to file charges, there's nothing in the police file except an account of the incident and the information that the pastor was sent for psychiatric therapy.'

'Have you talked to the woman?' asked the inspector.

'She died two years ago,' said the sergeant. 'She was eighty-six years old.'

'Not with the pastor at her bedside, I hope,' said the inspector.

'In the geriatric ward of the hospital,' said the sergeant. 'She'd been there for two months before she died. As far as I could determine, Auerstein never visited her at all.'

'What happened at the time of the attack, anyway?' the inspector wanted to know. 'Could you determine that?'

'Not precisely,' said the sergeant. 'Auerstein apparently tore open her dress and tried to get her breasts out. The hospital described his problem as a fixation on his mother. He apparently told the doctors that she'd breast-fed him until he was more than two years old.'

'Mrs Steckmann's breasts were exposed, of course,' said the inspector thoughtfully, 'but that's a long way from cutting out her pacemaker. Katzer said it was the pacemaker he was after. He didn't try to cut out her heart, just the machine.'

'But he didn't take it,' argued the sergeant. 'He left it there. What does that mean?'

'I don't know what any of this means, Hans,' said the inspector wearily. 'The only thing that seems certain is that it was somebody close to Mrs Steckmann, and that he or she is crazy.'

'Then it's either Auerstein or her son,' said the sergeant. 'They're the only two she knew that well. I'd swear to that.'

'Better check out the son, too, then,' said the inspector absently. 'We've not got very far with the pastor.'

Checking out the son meant mainly looking into his

background. As he lived in Essen and as considerable time had now passed, it was no longer possible to determine where he had been on the morning of November the thirteenth. It being a Sunday, he had not been at work.

Steckmann's history was unexceptional, although he had moved about a great deal. Having completed his training in telephone engineering at the technical school in Berlin, he had gone to Helmstedt, which is on the border with East Germany, where he had met and married a woman two years his junior.

The marriage had ended in divorce by mutual agreement the following year and Steckmann had not remarried.

In 1967, he had emigrated to Canada, but had returned to Germany in 1972. He had subsequently lived for shorter or longer periods in Paris, Berlin, Luxembourg and Yugoslavia before settling in Essen.

He was regarded by his colleagues and supervisors as professionally competant, but a social loner. As far as could be determined, he had no friends, either male or female.

'He's not a bad-looking chap,' said the sergeant. 'Doesn't seem to have anything wrong with him, but he just doesn't manage to make contact.'

'Any record of mental illness?' asked the inspector.

'None in this country,' said the sergeant. 'I'm checking out the other places now.'

The other places checked out. In so far as the police had been able to determine, Rolf Steckmann had no history of mental problems at all.

'And Auerstein has only a minor, unrelated incident six years ago,' said the inspector, discouraged. 'Those two must be the worst suspects ever turned up in a criminal investigation. The victim's pastor and her own son.'

'Could we canvass the residents of Max Planck Strasse?' suggested the sergeant. 'Show them pictures of

Steckmann and Auerstein. Ask if anyone saw either of them on the morning of November the thirteenth.'

'Try it,' said the inspector. 'I'm out of ideas.'

Having experienced nothing but failures so far, the sergeant was not optimistic concerning his own idea. With the cooperation of the Essen police, he obtained a photograph of Rolf Steckmann which the subject did not know existed. No photo of Pastor Auerstein was necessary. Everybody in Max Planck Strasse knew him by sight.

No one knew Steckmann by sight, but he had a heavy black moustache and the top of his head was largely bald, so that he was easily recognizable.

Two people, one of them a Sunday newspaper delivery boy, reported having seen him in Max Planck Strasse on that Sunday morning.

'Horrible!' said the inspector. 'Her own son!'

'Can we prove it?' asked the sergeant.

'Maybe,' said the inspector. 'We'll take him into custody and ask him where he was on the morning of the thirteenth. If he says Essen, we've got him.'

Rolf Steckmann did not say Essen. Apparently convinced that his arrest indicated positive police evidence of his guilt, he launched straight into an explanation of why he had found it necessary to cut out his mother's pacemaker.

'As long as that thing was in her chest, she couldn't die,' he said earnestly. 'The voices told me that the machine would keep her alive. I hit her on the head and I hit her on the head, but she didn't die, and the voices said it was the pacemaker.'

'But why did you want to kill your own mother?' said the shocked inspector. 'Was there bad feeling between you?'

'Of course not,' said Steckmann indignantly. 'She was my mother. We loved each other very much. It was just that the voices said it would be nice to be a murderer. They said it was better to be a double murderer, but

Dad died before I had a chance to do it. It wasn't my fault.'

Although ostensibly normal in all other respects, Rolf Steckmann was clearly insane in his attitude towards his parents. For what reason could not be determined. Perhaps there had been something in his childhood, but if so, it was buried too deep to be brought to the surface by psychological analysis.

Following testimony by state-appointed alienists on 21 September 1984, he was ordered confined for an indefinite length of time in the Psychiatric Clinic for the Criminally Insane at Hainer.

The mystery of the lack of fingerprints was solved by Steckmann's statement that he had put on kid gloves before sitting down to breakfast, although he was unable to explain why.

The mystery of Pastor Auerstein's whereabouts between seven- and eight-thirty on the morning of November the thirteenth was never solved.

Steckmann, who still appears completely normal, has stated that he is happy in the clinic and much prefers it to outside. He has taken up oil painting and is said to show considerable talent. His subject is always himself, and he titles his pictures *Mother Murderer*.

15

NEVER GET YOUR FORTUNE TOLD

There was something deep down in the glass, a dark gathering, a swirling, coagulating movement of half-seen, half-felt forms.

She had seen it before on the times it had really happened, often enough, but not always. A professional fortune-teller could not be expected to function like a machine. Sometimes there was something in the crystal ball, sometimes not.

If not, then experience and the skills of the trade had to serve. It was usually enough.

On a few occasions, she had had to dissimulate even though there was something in the ball. To reveal what was there would have been too painful for the client.

Painful, yes, but not like this horror that was taking form before her eyes. Blood! Blood! A sharp, heavy blade cleaving through black hair, through tender scalp, through brittle bone into the soft, vulnerable brain, the millions of neurons that had been the mind of a thinking being smashed, shattered, irrevocably destroyed!

Elisa Veronese raised her eyes from the ball to stare aghast into the face of the woman seated opposite her.

'I see bad omens!' she stammered. 'Bad luck! Blood! Death!'

The woman nodded calmly. She was not young, but she was very carefully groomed and expensively dressed. A woman with money.

'My husband,' she said. 'I know. What do you see in my future?'

Reluctantly, the fortune-teller lowered her eyes to the crystal ball on the round table with the purple cloth bearing the signs of the zodiac.

It was deathly silent in the dimly lit little room cut off from the world by the heavy crimson velvet curtains. She could hear the breathing of the woman on the other side of the table but not her own, and she realized that she had been holding her breath.

The truly psychic experiences always had a powerful emotional effect on her and, in her more than twenty years as a professional fortune-teller, she had had plenty of them.

But never like this. She could not bear to look deep into the ball. Instead, she focused her eyes on its surface.

'Good fortune,' she mumbled. 'You have had problems, but they are now over. You can look forward to a happy time surrounded by your family.'

The "family" was a slight risk. Although the woman had spoken of a husband, she might never have had children.

Whether she had a family or not, she appeared to be satisfied and, having paid the agreed fee, left.

Elisa sat for an instant, trying to collect herself and then, on a sudden impulse, leaped to her feet, stripped off her fortune-teller's gown and ran out into the street.

Her client was just turning the corner a few yards away. She was, Elisa noted with relief, on foot. Drawing a deep breath, she set out to follow her.

It was a little after three-thirty in the afternoon of 20 June 1986 – a Friday – and the weather was a delight of golden sunshine and the rich blue of the north Italian skies. There were masses of flowers everywhere, in the beds along the pavements, hanging from the balconies of the houses and on the windowsills. The little trees along the street were draped in the gentle green of early summer.

Although it was not near the centre of town, there were numbers of people in the street, many of them visitors. Verona is not a small city. Permanent residents number close to three hundred thousand, and during the tourist season the population is nearly double that.

So much the better, she thought. In the crowds, the woman would be less likely to spot her and realize that she was being followed.

She was not entirely certain why she was following her. It had been an impulse. In the crystal ball she had seen death – violent death, murder – and the woman had practically admitted knowledge of it.

Something had told her that she could not simply forget the matter. It had to be brought to the attention of the authorities.

The woman sauntered along, obviously in no hurry, and Elisa realized that she must be a visitor. The manner in which she looked at the buildings and sometimes hesitated before turning down a street indicated a person with a general knowledge of the town, but not the easy familiarity of the local resident.

When she finally got into the expensive Lancia sports car in the car park on via Luciano dal Caro near the Porta Nuova, Elisa was not surprised to see the licence plate number beginning with MI.

The woman was, it seemed, from Milan, and her car licence number was MI268–47. All that was necessary now was to inform the police and they could take care of the rest.

Elisa took two steps in the direction of the central police station and came to a halt.

It had just occurred to her that her report might not be very well received. She would have to identify herself as a professional fortune-teller and admit that all she knew of the matter was what she had seen in her crystal ball. Even if she knew that what she had seen was true, would the police think so?

Probably not, she decided. Police officers are not noted for trusting acceptance of such unconventional sources of information as crystal balls. They would say that they could not open an investigation simply because a fortune-teller came in and said she had seen a murder in her crystal ball.

They would send her packing and she might even have some trouble with her licence.

The truth was, she really knew nothing about the matter, not so much as the woman's name. Even if her husband had been murdered, it did not mean that she had had anything to do with it. He could have been murdered by anybody.

And yet, she was not convinced. There had been murder, bloody murder, and the woman was, in some way, involved.

In forty-seven-year-old Elisa Veronese's charmingly plump breast, there arose a curious itch, the nagging curiosity of the amateur detective.

Returning home, she changed her clothes, packed an overnight case, hung up the *No Consultations Today* sign and took the train for Milan.

The distance was not great, under a hundred miles, but she had got a late start and the offices were closed when she arrived at the main railway station.

She had never visited the city before and she was a little intimidated. Milan, with a population of over a million and a half, is one of the largest cities in the country.

There is, however, the usual Visitors' Assistance Office at the station and, through it, she obtained a room in a reasonably priced hotel, where she left her bag before going out for dinner in a rather good restaurant. She was not a skinny woman and, like many Italians, food was important to her.

After dinner, she strolled about the streets near the hotel, trying to plan what she should do the following day and eventually deciding to attempt an identification of the woman through the Automobile Club. The vehicle registration office would, of course, know to whom the car belonged, but she did not think that they would release the information to an unauthorized person.

The Automobile Club would be less demanding. She

could say that she had run into the car while it was parked and that she wanted to contact the owner in order to pay the damages. The only scratch was that the woman might not belong to the Automobile Club, although nearly everyone with that expensive a car did.

As it turned out, she obtained the information easily. Elisa was, after all, a very attractive woman and, without her fortune-teller's gown, highly respectable. The young male clerk at the Automobile Club did not hesitate for an instant and, having consulted the files, wrote down the name and address on a piece of paper and handed it with something of a flourish to Elisa.

Glancing at it with studied carelessness, she put it in her bag, tactfully warded off an invitation to lunch or dinner or, better still, breakfast, and went to the Giardini Pubblici, the nearby public park, where she sat on a bench and carefully read the name and address.

It was Mrs Lina Boseggia, 8 via Palmanova, but she had never heard the name and, as she did not know where the via Palmanova was, it made no impression on her. To judge by the car, it would probably be in an expensive residential district.

She took a cab, which cost her an alarming amount of money as the via Palmanova is in a suburb nearly five miles to the northeast of the city centre.

As she had expected, the district was expensive and the house was an elegant villa with extensive grounds. As if to confirm that she was on the right track, the Lancia stood parked in the drive.

Now that she had found the house and learned the woman's name, she was at a loss as to what to do next. She could hardly go up to the front door, ring the bell and say, "You have murdered your husband. Come with me to the police."

And for that matter, how did she know that it would not be the husband who opened the door? Perhaps her vision in Verona had been false.

But, in her heart, she knew that it had not been false. A dark-haired man, this woman's husband, had been murdered. His head had been split, like a cabbage, with an axe. Whether the woman was responsible or knew the identity of the murderer was something else, but she had known that it was murder and it had not upset her.

Whatever the case, there would be no peace for Elisa Veronese until she knew, and the first step was to learn whether Lina Boseggia's husband really had been murdered and, if so, under what circumstances.

The neighbours would presumably know, and Elisa, secure in her armour of respectable, well-dressed woman of a certain age, went boldly up to a house across and a little down the street from the Boseggias' villa. The next-door neighbours might be reluctant to talk about people living so close to them and, anyway, she liked the way the flowerbeds around the other house were tended.

Although it was a Saturday, the man of the house did not appear to be at home, but the wife was. She was about Elisa's age and she promptly invited her in, gave her a cup of tea and listened sympathetically to her account of an old friend who had lived at number eight Palmanova, but who now appeared to have moved away.

The woman's name was Emma Venturini and, when Elisa had finished explaining that she felt a little nervous about asking at a house occupied by such rich, important people, she said that she was quite right – Mrs Boseggia was a little taken with her own importance. As for her friend, she must be mistaken about the street number. The Boseggia family had owned the villa ever since it was built.

'Was that a long time ago?' asked Elisa.

'Nearly thirty years,' said Mrs Venturini. 'They'd only lived in it for four or five years when Mr Boseggia disappeared.'

'Twenty years ago?' exclaimed Elisa in astonishment. She had been assuming that the murder, if murder there had been, had taken place recently.

Was this a murder twenty years old? Now that she thought of it, she recalled that the man whose head she had seen split in the crystal ball looked much younger than Mrs Boseggia. His hair was black and he had a little black moustache.

'All of that,' said Emma Venturini. 'The police called it a disappearance, but the people in this street think it was something a little more permanent than that.'

'You mean . . . ?' whispered Elisa in pretended awe.

She had ideas of her own concerning the disappearance of Mr Boseggia, but she was not going to do anything to discourage the flow of gossip.

'Yes, indeed,' said Emma darkly. 'A very mysterious business. Everybody thought so at the time. Sante Boseggia was a very rich man and he had no reason in the world to disappear. He had a beautiful wife, even if she didn't come from the best social background in the world, and two fine sons. Damiano was seventeen at the time, as I remember it, and Dario – that's his brother – was sixteen. A lovely family. Of course, Sante was a little close, but then, so many rich people are, you know.'

'Aren't they?' agreed Elisa. 'And then?'

'Well, he just disappeared,' said Emma. 'One day he was there, the next day he was gone. Lina called in the police, of course, but they couldn't find him and nobody ever knew what happened to him. The newspapers said the police thought he might have fallen into a deep hole somewhere and couldn't get out.'

'Are there a lot of deep holes around here?' asked Elisa.

'None at all, that I know of,' said Emma. 'Of course, there's the river, the Lambro, but there's hardly a place in it deeper than your knees.'

'If he liked walking, he might have been a long way away on a hike,' suggested Elisa.

Emma gave a snorting laugh.

'The farthest he ever walked was to his car,' she said.

Elisa went back to her hotel, taking the bus this time to cut down on expenses, had a leisurely bath and lay down on the bed to think over the situation.

To begin with, everything she had learned seemed to confirm her suspicions. She had managed unobtrusively to extract a description of Sante Boseggia from Mrs Venturini, and it corresponded precisely to the man she had seen in the crystal ball: thirty-eight years old, handsome, dark-haired and with a small black moustache.

On the other hand, whatever had happened to Boseggia, it had happened a long time ago. Mrs Venturini said that it had been at the beginning of 1963.

Her resolve was starting to waver. Why dig into such an old affair? What could be proved now? And should anything be proved at all? What business was it of hers? She was a fortune-teller, not a detective.

A sudden thought struck her. If Mrs Boseggia really did not know what had happened to her husband twenty-four years earlier, why had she asked only about her own future? Why had she not asked what had happened to her husband?

It was not that she had simply forgotten him. She had known at once to whom Elisa was referring when she blurted out the words "blood" and "death".

The conclusion was unavoidable. There was no need for Mrs Boseggia to ask a fortune-teller what had happened to her husband. She knew. She had murdered him with an axe.

And disposed of the body so well that the police had never been able to find it? Alone?

She had not made the impression of a woman physically capable of smashing in a man's head with an axe, let alone lugging away his body to God knew what isolated hiding place.

A lover? Mrs Venturini had been emphatic about Lina's fidelity to her missing husband's memory.

'Except for servants, there's never been a man in that house since the boys left,' she had said. 'They're men in their forties now, of course. Both married, I think. Neither one lives in Milan. She's lived alone in the villa for over fifteen years. If she'd had a lover, everybody in the street would know it.'

And so, reflected Elisa, would the servants. Of course, there might not be any now, but Lina Boseggia had not looked to her like a woman to do her own cooking or her own laundry or her own anything else. Unless she was mistaken, hers were hands that had never touched dishwater.

A shrewd judge of character, like all fortune-tellers, she also suspected that Mrs Boseggia might not be the most pleasant person in the world to work for. It could be that the servants would be happy enough to gossip about their mistress.

They were, all four of them. The following day she went to the servants' entrance, where she inquired about her mythical old friend who had, perhaps, worked as a servant there.

The cook had replied that if she had, she must have been hard up for work. She herself had been there three months and she was leaving next week.

The housemaid, the footman and the gardener were equally sour and all had a great deal to say about their mistress. None of it was good, but it was of no use to Elisa as none of them had been there longer than a year.

The only new information of any significance at all was that Mrs Boseggia had had her husband declared legally dead in January 1981. The estate, which she had, up until then, administered in her husband's name, was now hers.

Elisa had gone as far as she could go. She had reached the end of her investigation, unless the crystal ball could show her where Boseggia's body was buried, and she did not think it was going to do that.

There remained two alternatives. She could forget about the whole thing and go home. Or she could go to the police and risk being taken for a crank or a mental case.

It was a difficult decision. She did not mind being taken for a charlatan. She was accustomed to that. What troubled her was whether she was doing the right thing.

Even if Mrs Boseggia had murdered her husband, perhaps there had been every justification for it. Boseggia might have been a torturing monster who threatened his wife's and sons' lives. The murder could have been an act of self-defence.

In the end, she decided for the police. She could not judge Mrs Boseggia's motives. That was something for the competent authorities. She was merely a citizen who had come into possession of certain information which it was her duty to report.

The following morning, she went to police headquarters and, not having prepared any speech, experienced some difficulty in making the sergeant on the charge desk understand what she wanted.

Eventually, she was taken upstairs and turned over to an olive-skinned, round-faced and fiercely moustached sergeant of detectives named Rocco Scorcese, who listened gravely and silently to her account of the matter, beginning with the fortune-telling session in Verona.

She did not think that she had presented the matter very well, but, when she had finished, the sergeant said that the matter would be investigated and that she could now go back to Verona. If there was any further need of her services, she would be contacted.

Elisa went back to Verona. Even without her crystal ball, she had a clear vision of the sergeant dropping the tape recording of her statement into the waste basket.

This time, however, her vision was wrong. The sergeant, a sober, prosaic civil servant, had simply passed the tape on to his superior, Inspector Lino Mantinelli.

The inspector's nature was different to that of his assistant. A small man with the hair and skin coloration of a German, but with the nervous, quick character of the peoples of the Mediterranean, he was very modern in his attitudes, well-informed and fully aware that parapsychological phenomena such as fortune-telling had now gained respectability and were, indeed, under study in many parts of the world.

He therefore took Elisa's statement quite matter-of-factly and instructed the sergeant to call for the file on the disappearance of Sante Boseggia.

It was duly located in the "Investigations Terminated"

section and proved to contain little information other than the bare facts that Sante Boseggia had disappeared on 31 December 1962 and that the police had been unable to find any trace of him.

They had tried. Boseggia was a wealthy man and his disappearance had not been taken lightly. That had been one of the problems. He had been so wealthy that he could have disappeared voluntarily and gone almost anywhere in the world.

There was some support for this theory. Mrs Boseggia reported that some of her husband's clothing and a suitcase were missing as well as an undetermined amount of money. Like all wealthy Italians, Boseggia had been, to say the least, circumspect in financial matters. No one knew precisely what he had or where he kept it.

Not surprisingly, foul play had been considered, but the investigation had determined that neither Mr nor Mrs Boseggia had had any extramarital interests and, in any case, the boys had been on holiday from school, so no crime could have taken place in the house without their knowledge.

The official theory of Boseggia's having fallen into a deep hole was out of respect for Mrs Boseggia, who did not want it thought that her husband had left voluntarily, and the police had not believed it themselves.

'A voluntary disappearance doesn't seem very likely,' mused the inspector. 'The man had the money to buy himself a divorce if he was sick of his family.'

'Are you reopening the investigation?' asked the sergeant. 'If they couldn't solve it over twenty years ago, what makes you think we can now?'

'The brilliance of the people working for me,' said the inspector. 'Go and see if you can find out how Mr Boseggia felt about his family.'

The sergeant, to whom it made little difference which case he was investigating, dutifully went off, talked to neighbours and other people who had known the family and returned with the report that, however Boseggia had felt about his family, they had thoroughly disliked him.

'Very close with money, it seems,' he said. 'Not with himself, but with his wife and children. Their father was rich, but they had the pocket money of a greengrocer's sons.'

'Interesting,' said the inspector. 'Could have been a quarrel over money ending in a more or less accidental homicide. Small man, Boseggia? It doesn't say here.'

'Big,' said the sergeant, 'and, according to the family doctor, in good physical condition, although he never took any exercise. The doctor's in his seventies now, but he remembers Boseggia well.'

'Fine,' said the inspector. 'Now see if you can find out who was handling Boseggia's financial matters. He must have had somebody. A fortune of that size needs professional management.'

This assignment was more difficult. As Italians dislike paying taxes, they often tend to secrecy over their financial arrangements, and the more money they have, the more secretive they become. Sante Boseggia had had a great deal of money.

'And he apparently didn't take it with him,' said the sergeant. 'The financial advisor refuses to be identified or even to make a formal statement, but, privately, he says that there was no substantial sum missing after Boseggia disappeared. He would have had to leave with what he had in his pockets.'

'And what does this suggest to you, Rocco?' asked the inspector, resting his elbows on the desk and making a little tent with the joined fingers of his two hands.

'Fell in a deep hole?' said the sergeant, who was not as humourless as he appeared to be.

'Probably not deeper than four feet,' said the inspector. 'Graves dug by amateurs seldom are.'

'The boys would have had to be in on it,' mused the sergeant.

'I think they did it,' said the inspector. 'Pick up a warrant and get some parties searching the grounds of the villa. You can tell the judge the case has been reopened because of the receipt of new information.'

'You can't find a grave nearly twenty-five years old,' objected the sergeant.

'You can with a metal detector,' said the inspector. 'We'll just have to hope they buried him with his rings or his wristwatch.'

In fact, they had buried him with the axe that had split his skull, and the metal detector went off like a burglar alarm.

It was barely in time, as the Boseggias' attorney had just obtained writs of habeas corpus and the inspector had not had sufficient evidence to bring his suspects before the examining magistrates.

Although nothing remained of Sante Boseggia other than his bones, he was identified by his clothing, his jewellery and his dental work.

The cause of death was easily determined as the skull had been shattered by at least three blows of the axe.

These represented the individual contributions of the three murderers, Lina, Damiano and Dario Boseggia. They had, they said, wanted to assume equal guilt in the murder.

It had taken place on the night of 31 December 1962, when Boseggia had partaken a little too freely of the wine in celebrating the New Year.

Otherwise, the murderers were vague. Although all three insisted that the murder had been an impulsive act and not planned, they could neither say who had struck the first blow nor offer any motive other than that Sante had been too close with money.

Mother and sons were brought to trial in the spring of 1987 and, on May the fifteenth, found guilty of unpremeditated homicide and sentenced to twenty years' imprisonment each.

16

BLACK MAGIC

The scene was classic. Despite her fifty-two years, the victim was lovely and her figure was as slender and firm as a woman in her twenties.

She lay sprawled on the floor, her stockings down around her ankles, naked except for the brassiere twisted to expose one breast, and her thighs were parted as if the rapist had just risen from her body.

There was not a great deal of blood. A little had run from the narrow slits of the knife wounds in abdomen and belly and had dried to red-brown stripes across the pale flanks, but most of the bleeding had been internal.

Lying on the bed next to her was a pornographic magazine, the pages opened to a centrefold featuring a couple engaged in mutual oral sex.

A textbook illustration of a sex-murder scene.

Apart from one minor detail.

The look of utter, unbelieving astonishment on the woman's face.

'Well, seven deep stab wounds, to begin with,' said Dr Jerome Lasalle, bending his narrow, aristocratic face over the corpse and probing at the wounds with long, slender, rubber-gloved fingers. 'Now we'll take a look at the sex organs. . . .'

He inserted the twin polished blades of the speculum into the dead woman's genitals, dilated and took a series of samples with cotton swabs which he placed in test tubes and corked.

'I could be wrong,' he said, 'but I see no signs of semen or even of penetration.'

'What I thought,' said Inspector Maurice Tessy. 'It's too perfect to be real. What about the time?'

'Yesterday evening at around ten o'clock,' said the doctor. 'Give you a closer reading when I've done the autopsy.'

"Yesterday" was Wednesday 25 September 1980 and a fine later-summer day in Toulouse in the southwest corner of France and only ninety miles from the Mediterranean.

On the afternoon of that day, forty-six-year-old Isabelle Dupres had gone to the block of flats at 6 rue du Soleil-Levant to pick up her friend, Maria Mognot. Isabelle was divorced; Maria was separated from her husband, and the two women had fallen into the habit of passing the afternoons together, usually at a café.

Isabelle had found the door to Maria's flat unlocked and slightly ajar.

That had immediately terrified her. Toulouse, with a population approaching half a million, was hardly such a safe place that a single woman would leave her door unlocked, whether she was in the flat or not.

The logical thing to have done was call the police, but Isabelle, too concerned to take the time to run to the nearest telephone, had courageously gone in, crying out her friend's name between chattering teeth, and found her dead and as she thought, raped in the bedroom.

Although the blood on the body was dry, she had not grasped that the murder had taken place some considerable time earlier and she had panicked at the thought that the murderer might still be in the flat.

She had become so hysterical that she would later have no recollection of having run home to telephone the police, but she had, for it was in her own flat that the officers from the patrol car found her.

Although they were in uniform, she would not let them in at first and, when she did, she was in such a state that she could not remember Maria's address and had to guide them to the building.

While she waited in the car, the patrolmen went up

to the two-roomed flat on the third floor and one of them quickly came back down to summon the homicide squad while the other remained guarding the door of the flat.

Twenty minutes later, the inspector, the doctor and the inspector's assistant, Detective Sergeant Jules Sabotier, arrived at the scene.

The inspector and the doctor had gone up to examine the corpse while the sergeant, a mild-mannered man with close-cropped black hair and a black moustache running like a bar across his upper lip, took a statement from Isabelle Dupres.

Isabelle had now regained a degree of calm, but she was unable to offer much information of value to the investigation other than the victim's name, age and something of her background. Concerning the murder itself, she knew nothing.

The background was a little unusual. At the age of twenty-two, Maria had married a man named Odo Mognot, one year older than herself, and, for the next thirty years, both had worked like dogs, but with success.

Although he had begun as a simple stonemason, Odo had become a prosperous building contractor, and for many years he and Maria had been rich.

They owned a large estate at Foubeauzar – an exclusive suburb of Toulouse – a villa on the Riviera, several luxury cars and fine furniture. Maria had furs, jewels and designer clothes from the great French couturiers.

There was, however, no time to enjoy any of these things. Having worked like a dog for thirty years, Odo could not stop, and he would not let his wife stop either. Millionaires, they continued to put in ten- and twelve-hour days, seven days a week.

There had been increasingly violent quarrels, which had ended on 4 January, 1980, when Maria moved out of the villa into the little flat in the rue du Soleil-Levant, filed a divorce action and claimed a share of the joint property.

Odo had been amazed at his wife's action and, when

he learned that she stood a very good chance of obtaining fifty per cent of the property and the business, terrified.

He had pleaded with Maria, threatened her, offered her anything in the world that she wanted except for one thing.

Free time.

'Appears to be a faked sex crime,' said the inspector, coming out of the house, followed by the doctor. 'We'll need the full squad.'

A short man, but strongly built and broad in the shoulders, he had a curious way of walking, his body held very erect and almost rigid like a soldier on parade.

'Good possibility that it was the husband then,' said the sergeant. 'She'd filed for a divorce and a property settlement.'

'Let's hope that he didn't get somebody else to do it for him,' said the inspector. 'If he did it himself, we may be able to clear this up in a day or two.'

Odo Mognot was contacted at his home, but not arrested as he had a completely unassailable alibi. On the evening of September the twenty-fifth, he had been host to a party of some twenty people at his villa in Foubeauzar. Every one of them was prepared to swear that he had not left the party once during the time from seven in the evening until midnight.

'Which proves that he's guilty,' said the inspector. 'That was apparently the first and only party he's ever thrown in his life. That it should take place on the evening his wife was murdered is no coincidence.'

'With his money, he should have been able to afford a better assassin,' said the sergeant. 'The man was negligent. If he'd actually raped her, it would have been more realistic.'

It was now definitely known that he had not. The body of Maria Mognot had been transferred to the police morgue and Dr Lasalle had already completed most of the postmortem. Maria, he reported, had not been raped nor had there been any attempt to rape her. The indications were that she had not been sexually active for some time.

The report by the police laboratory supported the doctor's statement. No semen or other sexual indications had been found on the bedclothes or anywhere in the flat, they said.

They were still attempting to analyse and evaluate such potential clues as had been found at the scene, the most promising being the pornographic magazine, which had certainly not belonged to Mrs Mognot and had, therefore, presumably belonged to her murderer.

It had not belonged to him very long, not long enough for him to read it – or, rather, look at it, for the contents were largely pictorial – because some of the pages were still stuck together, indicating that it had never been thumbed through, even.

'A prop for the stage setting,' said the inspector. 'You can buy these things at any newsstand. There's no hope of tracing it.'

'And there wasn't a fingerprint on it,' added the sergeant. 'He must have been wearing gloves. A carefully planned operation.'

The specialists were, in the end, able to deduce only a few things. The murderer had apparently entered the flat during Mrs Mognot's absence and had hidden in the clothes closet in the bedroom. Some shoe boxes on which he had sat were crushed and there was still an odour of perspiration in the closet, which had been hot and airless.

He had used either a duplicate or a skeleton key to get into the flat and he had left no fingerprints on the door handle. The door had been open because the lock was old and the spring had failed to function.

In so far as could be determined, the man had entered the flat and hidden himself in the closet early in the evening while Mrs Mognot was having dinner at a restaurant.

Upon her arrival home shortly before ten o'clock, he had waited until she had undressed almost completely before bursting out of the closet and stabbing her to death. The clothing she had been wearing was found neatly hung or folded, and not crumpled in a heap as it would have been had it been torn from her body by a sex criminal.

Nor had she been forced to strip under duress, for the autopsy provided evidence that the murder had happened very quickly. Although Mrs Mognot had had time to look astonished, her glands had not had time to react and the level of adrenaline in the blood was only slightly above normal.

Despite these meagre findings, the investigation had made substantial progress and excellent descriptions of a promising suspect had been obtained.

The descriptions were by residents at 6 rue du Soleil-Levant who said they had seen an enormous black man, described by some as handsome, in the building on several occasions during the two weeks preceding the murder.

He had been either visiting or looking for Maria Mognot, for every other occupant of the building had been questioned and no one knew or had contact with any large black men.

On the other hand, Isabelle Dupres was absolutely certain that Maria had not had contacts with any black men either.

'She didn't like anything African,' said Isabelle. 'The idea of her having a black lover is grotesque.'

The sergeant had suggested that Mrs Mognot, being quasi-unattached, might have become lonely for male company. He was not as convinced as the inspector that Odo Mognot was responsible for his wife's death.

Mognot had either lied deliberately to the police or he had been monumentally mistaken, for he had told the inspector that his wife had had dozens of lovers. It was, no doubt, one of them who had murdered her, he said.

The inspector knew, however, that Maria Mognot had had no lovers. As she had spent a good deal of time with Isabelle Dupres and as the other tenants in her building were as nosy as most, it had been possible to trace her movements and whereabouts for days on end. There had been no time for a lover in her schedule.

The same had been done for Odo Mognot with even greater ease. He too had had no time for a mistress. In fact, he had done nothing but work.

Nor was there any evidence of contacts between him and a conspicuously large Negro, although he had, at times, employed Africans on his construction jobs.

'Maybe it wasn't Mognot,' said the sergeant. 'Maybe the killer's one of those sex psychopaths who're incapable of intercourse. He locked onto Mrs Mognot and just kept following her until he found the right opportunity. That's typical behaviour for a sex killer.'

'No,' said the inspector. 'He was in the building casing the place. All the sightings by the tenants were in the afternoon when Mrs Mognot was out. He wasn't following her. He was waiting for her.'

The sergeant said nothing and continued to look mildly sceptical.

'It had to be Mognot,' insisted the inspector. 'He had the motive. He went to great lengths to establish an alibi. He probably picked a black killer deliberately because he knew his wife didn't like Africans.'

'We can't indict him, with that alibi,' said the sergeant.

'We can once we find the black monster,' said the inspector. 'That was Mognot's mistake. If he'd hired somebody less conspicuous, we couldn't have traced him. As it is . . .'

'. . . we can't trace him anyway,' concluded the sergeant.

But he was wrong. Even in a city the size of Toulouse, there are not great numbers of very black men over six feet four inches tall and weighing an estimated two hundred and sixty pounds.

Although it was probable that wanted posters stuck up at strategic points in the city would produce results, particularly if a reward for the information was promised, the inspector was unwilling to resort to this. Not only informers would see the posters. So would the fugitive, and leave Toulouse as expeditiously as possible. The inspector did not want to be hunting all over the country for him.

To lull suspicion, he made a statement to the press that a suspect in the murder of Maria Mognot had been arrested, put pressure on the network of police informers within the African community and, having charged Odo Mognot with making false statements to the police in connection with the investigation of a felony, obtained a warrant for a search of the villa in Foubeauzar.

Results were forthcoming from both initiatives. The informers reported that the largest and blackest man in Toulouse was Mr Goutrand, a professional sorcerer who ran advertisements in the local press offering to solve by occult means all problems, whether marital, emotional, professional or financial, for a modest fee.

And the search of the villa produced a periodical from which an advertisement had been cut out. When compared with the magazine's file copy, the advertisement proved to be one of Mr Goutrand's.

This was quite enough for the inspector, and Mognot's charge was changed to conspiring to commit homicide.

At the same time, Mr Goutrand was taken into custody at his place of business and charged with homicide.

Mognot denied that he had ever laid eyes on Mr Goutrand or that he had cut the advertisement out of the magazine and Mr Goutrand, whose name was really Hildebert Yatou and who came from the French Caribbean island of Guadaloupe, denied that he had ever heard the name of Odo Mognot.

Unfortunately for both, they had been all too business-like in their dealings and a search of Yatou's flat uncovered a promissory note signed by Odo Mognot.

Undoubtedly one of the most compromising documents ever to turn up in a criminal investigation, it read:

I promise to pay to Hildebert Yatou the sum of 300,000 French francs for the elimination of my wife, Maria Mognot.

Signed: Odo Mognot

Confronted with this document, both Mognot and Yatou broke down and confessed, but to rather different things.

Yatou, who had come to France in 1970 and worked for two years as a house painter before going into the magic business, said that Odo Mognot had first visited him in response to his advertisement on February the seventeenth. He had said that his wife had left him and that he wanted Mr Goutrand to cast a spell that would bring her back.

Yatou, whose only qualifications as a magician were a sharp business sense and a casual knowledge of occult jargon gleaned from reading the advertisements of other magicians, had pointed out that this might prove difficult and expensive. He had noted Mognot's suit, jewelry and the car he was driving.

Mognot, who was normally a good businessman but astoundingly naive in occult matters, replied frankly that the alternative would be a lot more expensive as it could cost him half of everything he owned.

Yatou had then extracted a deposit of twelve thousand francs (about twelve hundred pounds) and done a little boning-up on magic at the public library.

Although he believed in his incantations himself, they had had no effect on Mrs Mognot, who remained as adamant as ever in her resolve to strip her husband of half his fortune.

However, at the end of May, following the casting of such dreadful spells that he succeeded in frightening himself, Mr Goutrand finally appeared to have achieved a measure of success. Maria agreed to meet her husband and discuss matters.

Odo was jubilant, but it turned out that what Maria wanted to discuss was the manner in which her share of the property and business was to be handed over. Was Odo interested in buying her out?

Odo was not, and, in bitter disillusionment, he turned on his magician, calling him a charlatan and charging him with obtaining money under false pretences. He was, he said, going to the police.

Yatou, who saw his lucrative business going down the drain, retorted that the fault lay not with his spells, but with his client's niggling nature. He had brought Maria to the negotiating table, but Odo had muffed it. Now there was nothing left but a radical treatment which would so fill Maria with love for her husband that she would either return to him or perish.

Odo had said simply, 'How much?'

Yatou, who was beginning to find the French climate rather too warm for his taste and was seriously considering a return to Guadaloupe, picked the sum of three hundred thousand francs as adequate to set himself up in business there, but Odo had become cautious. First results and then money, he said.

As Yatou was unwilling to work on credit, the idea of the promissory note was conceived.

Curiously, both parties had thought that they could put pressure on the other with it, not realizing that its exposure would implicate them as well.

Up to this point, there was reasonable agreement in the two statements, but on the subject of the murder itself, the stories diverged.

According to Mognot, he had never authorized Yatou to murder his wife and would have prevented him had he known that he was planning such a thing.

According to Yatou, Mognot had quite simply hired him to kill Maria and had signed a promissory note to that effect.

He complained that the note had not been honoured and that he had only realized after the murder that he could not use it to force payment without facing a murder charge himself.

As for the details of the murder itself, they corresponded closely to what had been surmised by the police.

Yatou, who was no more a professional murderer than

he was a magician, had experienced great difficulty in finding the victim at home. He had gone four times in all to the building in the rue du Soleil-Levant, intending simply to ring the bell and murder Mrs Mognot when she opened the door, but she had been out every time. Finally, in desperation, he had gone back to Mognot, who had provided him with a key to the flat and told him to wait inside until Maria returned.

This version was contested by Odo Mognot, who said that he had no idea how Yatou had got into the flat, as he had never furnished him with any key.

The question of the key was important. If Mognot had supplied it to the magician, it was evidence that he had had knowledge of Yatou's intention of killing Maria – which he steadfastly denied.

Whatever the case, the key was not recovered and Yatou said he did not know what he had done with it.

Maria, he said, had never seen him before and he thought that she had been very surprised when he came out of the closet.

'I think she was too,' remarked the inspector. 'Imagine what she must have felt. There she was, undressed and ready to get into her nightgown in her own bedroom, and, all of a sudden, a six-foot five-inch Black she's never seen in her life comes charging out of the clothes closet with a butcher's knife in his hand.'

'The surprise alone could have killed her, if she'd had a weak heart,' agreed the sergeant. 'I wonder if she ever realized that her husband was behind it.'

Her husband continued to insist that he had not been behind it, but he was not believed, largely because of the terms of the promissory note he had signed, and on 3 April 1981 both he and Hildebert Yatou were found guilty of murder and conspiracy to commit murder and sentenced to life imprisonment.

17

DR HYDE, I PRESUME

It was not a suitable sight for a fifteen-year-old girl.
Muguette Boucher had been wearing only a dressing
gown and it had fallen open, fanned out on either side
of her battered nude body.

There was, however, nothing erotic about the scene.
Rather, it was horrifying, the throat marked with the
purple-blue bruises of strangulation and the cheeks
nearly black with suffused blood. In a last, agonized
gasp, the mouth gaped vainly for the air which the stran-
gling hands were denying the lungs, and the tongue
protruded. Filled with a mute appeal for help or mercy,
the violet-blue eyes stared at the ceiling.

'Mama!' screamed Claudine, falling to her knees
beside the corpse.

It was five o'clock in the afternoon of Tuesday 10
December 1985, and Claudine Boucher had just come
home from school to find her mother murdered in their
flat at 10 rue Dulong, in Rouen.

There are, in this world, teenage girls who know how
to cope with such situations, but Claudine was not one
of them. In her home town, she might have managed
better, but she and her mother had only moved to Rouen
the preceding year and she still looked upon it as a big
city.

It had, in fact, a population of only a little over
110,000, but her home town of Neufchâtel, twenty-five
miles to the northeast, numbered less than five thousand
residents.

Claudine had many relatives in Neufchâtel – uncles,

aunts, cousins. The only relative lacking was a father. Muguette had never told her who he was and she suspected that she herself was far from certain.

Struggling with hysteria and in a state of profound shock, Claudine ran to the telephone with the intention of calling her uncle in Neufchâtel. Uncle Charles was big, strong and reassuring. Whatever needed to be done, he would do.

There was, however, no sound from the instrument and, following the cord with her eyes, she saw that the wires had been ripped out of the wall.

The mute sign of violence tipped her over the edge into full-blown uncontrolled panic. Thus far, grief and horror had blocked out any feeling for herself, but now the thought that the murderer might still be in the flat sent her running pell-mell out of the door and down the stairs into the chill, clean air of the winter day.

For a moment, she did now know where she was and the nearly deserted street seemed surrealistic as if she had been transported to some alien world.

It was less than two weeks to the solstice and a dull, red glow on the horizon marked where the sun had just set. Overhead, the sky was completely clear, a deep, rich, imperial blue, but, strangely, a little snow was falling.

The cold air calmed her and, recovering her orientation, Claudine sprinted to the café on the corner, where she telephoned her uncle, speaking in a low voice so that the drinkers at the bar would not learn what had happened.

Charles Boucher did not question her story for an instant. Her distress was only too evident in her voice.

'Wait for me at the café,' he ordered. 'Don't go home. I'll be there in half an hour.'

In fact, he arrived in Rouen in something under half an hour, but, as he went first to his sister's flat, it was another ten minutes before he came to collect Claudine.

She was sitting at a table in the corner, her face buried

in her hands, and crying bitterly. She and her mother had been very close.

Boucher had determined that his sister was beyond help and he telephoned the police from the café, gave his name and address and took Claudine with him back to Neufchâtel. He too was badly shaken.

'It must have been Michel!' wept Claudine. 'He was always so rough with her.'

Charles Boucher knew who she meant. Michel Labbé had sometimes been very rough indeed with Muguette and, during the six years they had lived together, she had had to call on her brother more than once for protection.

Charles had invariably responded by coming to the flat Michel and Muguette occupied in Neufchâtel and leaving lumps all over Michel's head.

Michel had not resisted or even resented the correction. In the first place, when he was in his "good" phase, he was too opposed to violence to defend himself and, secondly, he was too feeble, even in his "bad" phase, for anything more than punching women in the face or scalding animals.

It was because of the dog that Muguette had left him and eventually moved to Rouen.

In one of his periodic "bad" phases, he had drenched the animal, a small mixed-breed named Molly, with boiling water and thrown it out into the freezing temperature of the January day.

Muguette and Claudine had rushed to the rescue and the dog had not died, although it had suffered terribly. The vet who treated it had notified the Society for the Prevention of Cruelty to Animals, and Michel had been fined.

He had paid the fine gladly. By now his gentle, non-violent, "good" self again, he loved animals, children, flowers, anything alive. He was a man who avoided stepping on ants.

The dog was not the first incident. Nine months before that, he had killed Muguette's cat by smashing it against a wall. He had then boiled the carcass and, when

Muguette returned home, flung it in her face. The point was, he said, to demonstrate that he could kill.

Muguette found the demonstration convincing and, in the end – although Michel was a delight when he was "good" and had even adopted Claudine, with whom he got on famously – she had decided to move out.

Michel had not taken this badly. He had simply ignored it, passing in and out of Muguette's new flat as freely as if they were still living together.

He had, in some manner, obtained a key to the flat, and Muguette suspected that Claudine had allowed him to copy hers. The girl was very attached to her stepfather.

In the end, Muguette had decided to move to Rouen. She would find work there, start afresh. At thirty-five, it was still not too late.

Now, however, it was too late for everything except the Rouen homicide squad, which arrived shortly after confirmation of Charles Boucher's report by the patrol car sent to the scene.

Detective Sergeant Paul Montreuil, a burly, good-natured man with short-cut sandy hair and an enormous moustache of the same colour, was immediately sent to Neufchâtel to take statements from Charles Boucher and Claudine, while his chief, Inspector Jean-Marie Ville-main, waited impatiently for the police photographer to complete the pictorial record of body and scene as found.

Until this had been done, the corpse could not be examined by the squad's medical expert, Dr Serge Sava-rin, and the six detection specialists from the police laboratory could not begin their work.

'Dead approximately two hours,' said the doctor, once the photographer had finished. 'Cause was manual strangulation. No indications of sexual abuse. She fought with him. There are bruises on many parts of the body, particularly the forearms and hands, and two of the fingernails are broken.'

He recited the details in an emotionless, almost sing-song manner, as if he were reading off an inventory of unimportant objects. A man in his late fifties, grey-haired, stoop-shouldered, his face heavily lined, he had seen a great number of murder victims, many of them in far worse condition than this one.

'Anything under the nails?' asked the inspector.

He was a lean, sallow man, a chain-smoker, who looked as if he did not get enough sleep and, indeed, did not.

'If there is, we'll find it at the autopsy,' said the doctor, sliding plastic sacks over the dead woman's hands and fastening them at the wrists with rubber bands. 'I don't want to risk losing something here.'

The inspector nodded and turned his attention to the specialists going over the flat.

'Anything significant?' he said.

'We don't know,' said the technician in charge. 'We've recovered a few items, textile fibres, cigarette ash and one cigarette end, a button – could be a trouser button – but nothing specifically associated with the murder. Lots of latent prints, but again, none that are demonstrably connected to the crime.'

The inspector nodded a second time. His was an old, practised team; every member knew his job and not much discussion was necessary.

In the meantime, the sergeant had arrived in Neufchâtel, where he found Claudine making hysterical accusations against Michel Labbé and her uncle expressing doubts that he would have had the strength to strangle Muguette.

'The man has tuberculosis and he's partly crippled,' he told the sergeant. 'His left leg's two inches shorter than the right. Muguette was a strong, healthy woman. He's tried to strangle her before and he never managed it.'

'If he's tried to strangle her before, he's a suspect,' said the sergeant. 'Where can I find him?'

'At home, I expect,' said Boucher. 'He runs his business from the same place.'

'Business?' said the sergeant.

'He's a mesmerizer and dowser,' explained Boucher. 'Locates water underground and hypnotizes people to stop smoking. That sort of thing.'

'My chief will be interested in meeting him,' said the sergeant. 'He's been trying to stop smoking for years.'

He drove to the address given him, took a cheerfully cooperative Michel Labbé into custody and returned with him to Rouen.

He had made tape recordings of the statements by Claudine and Charles Boucher, but they were hardly necessary as Labbé was prepared to tell the inspector everything he wanted to know about himself, his background and his relationship to Muguette Boucher.

This was obviously going to take some time, and the inspector sent a junior detective down to the police canteen to bring up beer and sandwiches for himself, the sergeant and the suspect.

Thus encouraged, Labbé launched into a detailed history of his life and what he knew of the dead woman's.

His mother, he said without embarrassment, was a clerk in the mayor's office in Neufchâtel and so astonishingly promiscuous that he had three half-brothers and one half-sister, none of whom could boast the same father. He was in his teens before he knew who his own father probably was.

Perhaps because of this uncertain parentage, Labbé was sickly and developed tuberculosis at an early age. He was also unlucky and, at the age of five, was involved in a car accident which broke both his legs and shattered his pelvis. Between the ages of five and nine, he was almost permanently in the hospital.

Despite his handicaps, Labbé was industrious and from 1961 to 1964 he served an apprenticeship as a cook in the renowned Neufchâtel hotel, the Lion d'Or. His mother then took him to Paris, where he found work as a cook in the Barthélémy Centre, a psychiatric institution at Etampes.

One of the inmates of the centre was a woman named Gisele, and Michel married her on 6 June 1969.

Although they had four children, one every year from 1969 to 1972, the magic soon went out of the marriage. Gisele had been under treatment for nymphomania in the psychiatric centre and the treatment was not successful. She was not unfaithful to Michel, but, as he said, it might have been better if she was. With his frail constitution and poor health, her sexual demands exhausted and nearly killed him.

Unfulfilled although almost permanently pregnant, Gisele steadily worsened, and in September 1972 she was committed at her own request to her old institution for an indefinite period.

Labbé had, by this time, despite the great demands on his fragile health, managed to get himself romantically involved with a woman named Françoise Mallet, by whom he eventually fathered two more children, Sylvaine in 1974 and Pricilla in 1976.

None of this was particularly confidential information. Michel and Gisele having settled in Neufchâtel following their marriage, the details of his life were very well known there and, indeed, formed one of the little town's main topics of conversation.

At about the time that Labbé set up housekeeping with Françoise Mallet, he gave up cooking for dowsing and hypnosis.

Although he had no formal training in the field, he evidently possessed a natural talent, for he was immediately successful, servicing as many as a dozen clients a day.

There were, therefore, no financial problems. But, following the shift in professions, Labbé's personality underwent a strange change. Up until then the mildest of men, he began to experience periods when he became violent and aggressive, his behaviour contrasting almost comically with his feeble physique.

In February and March of 1978, he made unsuccessful attempts to strangle Françoise, who then departed, taking the children with her.

Labbé who, although sickly, far from handsome and

distinctly strange, was remarkably popular with women, responded by setting up house with Muguette, despite the violent objections of all her relatives.

There were many of these relatives. As in the case of Labbé, Muguette's mother had been an active and rather absent-minded woman, so that Muguette had numerous half-brothers and half-sisters, all of whom were uncertain of the identity of their fathers, as, indeed, was their mother.

Needless to say, in such a small community, the unconventional domestic arrangements of the Bouchers and the Labbés aroused great interest, and even Charles Boucher, in his statement, termed the conduct of all concerned scandalous, although he maintained a discreet silence over his own affairs.

The inspector, who had had no idea that such things were going on in Neufchâtel, ran Boucher's tape through twice, making an occasional note.

Although he was careful about his language, it was obvious that he thought Labbé as mad as all the March hares in France, but equally obvious that he did not think him physically capable of the murder.

Assuming that the stories were true, the inspector did not think so either. If Labbé had tried to strangle his other mistresses without success, why should he have succeeded with Muguette, who was at least as strong as her predecessors?

Boucher had said that Labbé had been given a two-month suspended sentence for trying to strangle Françoise, and the inspector called the records section to ask if they had a file on it.

They did. Although the crime had taken place in Neufchâtel, the trial had been in Rouen and, in any case, the records section computer had access to all files in the region.

It tended to corroborate Boucher's statement, and the inspector lit a fresh cigarette, leaned back, closed his eyes and tried to form a picture of the players in this strange little tragedy.

He could recall very well how Muguette Boucher had looked sprawled on the floor. She had been a relatively big woman, blonde, not fat but solidly built. She did not impress him as a woman whom a weakling such as Michel Labbé could have bested in a hand-to-hand struggle.

However, it was possible that she had been knocked unconscious or had been under the influence of alcohol or drugs.

The inspector telephoned the morgue. Dr Savarin would not be performing the complete autopsy till that night, but he would be carrying out a detailed examination of the corpse. As he had not reported, he had not yet finished it.

Were there any indications of a blow to the head which might have rendered the woman unconscious before she was strangled? the inspector wanted to know.

The doctor said there were none. Muguette had simply been strangled until she lost consciousness and ultimately died.

'What about drugs or alcohol?' asked the inspector. 'Our only suspect so far is supposed to be as weak as a kitten.'

'No alcohol and I doubt drugs,' said the doctor. 'If you have the right man, your suspect is more of a Bengal tiger than a kitten.'

'You'll test for narcotics, chloroform and so on, though?' persisted the inspector.

'Of course,' said the doctor, 'but I should be very surprised if we got a positive on anything like that.'

The inspector hung up the telephone, considerably puzzled. Like any investigations officer in a city the size of Rouen, he had his share of homicides, one or two a year on average.

Ninety per cent of these were domestic. Husband murdered wife or vice versa, whether legally married or otherwise. In a good half of these cases, the murder was reported by the repentant murderer him or herself. In most of the rest, the identity of the perpetrator was immediately obvious. Very few required extensive investigation.

This case was different, not in the relationship of murderer and victim, but in the sheer physical capacity to commit the crime.

Unless, of course, the reports of Michel Labbé's weakness were greatly exaggerated.

On the basis of appearance, they were not. Labbé was a little man, a scant five foot four inches tall, scrawny, obviously sickly, and he limped badly. His hands were hardly larger than those of a girl.

He had been in his "good" phase when the inspector saw him, and had nearly wept over his inability to gratify him with a confession.

'After all the trouble the sergeant went to coming all the way up to Neufchâtel,' he said. 'I feel terrible that I can't be of more help. Poor Muguette!'

'Poor Muguette,' said the inspector. 'Where were you at four-thirty this afternoon?'

'I had an appointment,' said Labbé. 'A Mr Leon Bretcher. I was helping him give up smoking.'

'Did you check that?' asked the inspector, looking at the sergeant.

The sergeant nodded.

'Bretcher confirms it,' he said. 'Mr Labbé had him under hypnosis in Neufchâtel at around the time the murder took place here.'

The inspector questioned Labbé a little more concerning any enemies that Muguette might have had, and he swore that she had not had any. She had been, he said, such a wonderful, warm, caring person that no one could have wanted to harm her.

The inspector refrained from pointing out that some one manifestly had and a junior detective drove Labbé back to Neufchâtel.

'I had a feeling from the beginning that he was too obvious a suspect,' said the inspector. 'The man has the physique of a sick fieldmouse.'

'It doesn't matter, I suppose, because he's got a solid

alibi,' said the sergeant, 'But I have the feeling that he's not as nice a Nelly as he makes out. I keep thinking of the dog and the cat.'

The sergeant was fond of animals.

'Different phases of his character, I suppose,' said the inspector. 'He's pretty obviously bonkers, but he's not the only one in this part of the world. Anyway, he didn't do it, so what we have to think about is who did.'

'It has occurred to me that the daughter is very attractive, and fifteen is an age where there are often differences of opinion between the generations,' suggested the sergeant cautiously.

'You'll have to check whether the girl really was at school at the time,' said the inspector. 'She wouldn't be the first matricide we've had. You recall that case two years ago? The girl was younger, though – only fourteen.'

'I was thinking more of a boy friend,' said the sergeant. 'The girl's considerably smaller than her mother was. I doubt she'd have the strength.'

'Seem to be nothing but weaklings in this case,' remarked the inspector. 'Look into it tomorrow.'

The reports from the morgue and the laboratory proved to contain nothing of interest to the investigation, so the inspector and the sergeant went home.

The following day, the sergeant sent a team of handsome young detectives to the secondary school which Claudine attended.

They were quickly able to determine that Claudine had been at the school at the time of the murder, but they were unable to learn where her boy friend had been.

He was twenty-year-old Yves Garuelles, who had never been arrested or charged, but was believed by the police to be involved in drug dealing and, possibly, teenage prostitution.

'Not precisely the sort of young man that most mothers would like to be seeing their daughters,' said the sergeant. 'If Miss Boucher knew about her daughter's friend, she might have raised strong objections.'

'It's a weak motive,' said the inspector, 'but we're dealing with weak-minded people. See if you can get a set of Garuelles' prints and we'll check them against the ones recovered from the Bouchers' flat.'

'Any motive would be weak,' remarked the sergeant. 'The woman didn't have any money or any enemies. It was an emotional thing.'

'Or a crazy thing,' said the inspector, 'but that brings us back to Labbé, and we know he didn't do it.'

The fingerprints were obtained, perhaps not by entirely orthodox means, and proved negative. If Yves Garuelles had ever been in the Bouchers' flat, he had not left any prints there.

'Some of the prints in the girl's room are Labbé's,' said the sergeant.

The inspector gave him a thoughtful look.

'Neither he nor she mentioned his coming to visit them in Rouen,' he said. 'Where in the girl's room?'

'Head of the bed, night table,' said the sergeant noncommittally.

'Damn!' swore the inspector. 'This gets stickier all the time. The girl's a minor. If her mother caught her having it off with Daddy. . . .'

'He has a confirmed alibi,' said the sergeant. 'And he's not strong enough.'

'That we don't know,' said the inspector. 'Maybe in his "bad" phase. . . . Did you check out the fellow who furnished him with the alibi? Maybe he's Labbé's cousin or something.'

'I doubt it, but I'll look into it,' said the sergeant.

Leon Bretcher was not related to Michel Labbé in any way and his first meeting with him had been the hypnotic session to cure him of smoking in Neufchâtel at the exact time Muguette was being murdered in Rouen.

'But the thing is that the appointment wasn't on Tuesday,' said the sergeant. 'When I talked to Bretcher's wife and his boss, they both said that he'd gone for his treatment on Monday. He still swears it was on Tuesday.'

'Labbé must have planted the wrong day in his mind while he was under hypnosis!' exclaimed the inspector in astonishment. 'My God! Do you know what this means?'

The sergeant nodded.

'Premeditation,' he said.

'Bring him in and we'll see what he has to say,' said the inspector, shaking his head in disbelief.

What Michel Labbé had to say was that he had murdered Muguette, but that it had been in his "bad" phase and therefore he could not be held responsible for the act.

As a demonstration of how lacking in responsibility he was, he immediately went into a "bad" phase and proved to be so strong that it took the combined efforts of three hefty detectives to subdue him.

So much time went into the psychiatric study of Michel Labbé that it was over two years before he came to trial. Even then, opinions were divided. Some psychologists thought that Labbé suffered from a split personality. Others pointed out that he was obviously capable of planning "bad" acts when in his "good" personality and that the motive for the murder had been the banal one of the discarded suitor. All agreed that his hypnotic and dowsing powers were genuine and that they had some connection with his personality changes. What it was, they could not say, but, in the end, they decided that he was competent to stand trial.

At the trial, which took place on 21 and 22 March 1988, the defence entered a plea of not guilty by reason of temporary insanity.

The prosecution countered with the evidence of premeditation, but accepted that he was not entirely responsible for his actions.

The jury thought he was, found him guilty of intentional homicide and sentenced him to twenty years' imprisonment.

18

SAVIOUR

It was noon on the Sunday two days before Christmas of 1979.

Five miles to the east of the city of Amiens, the little village of Corbie lay isolated and lost amidst the snow-covered plains of Picardy.

For many in Corbie, it would not be a merry Christmas. In this once prosperous steel and mining district in the north of France, many mines and steel mills were now closed and there was widespread poverty.

For some, there would be no Christmas, not this year or ever again.

The bell in the church tower had just hammered out the final stroke of twelve when the shutters of the dilapidated little house at 47 rue Tessier were thrust open and a tiny, haggard woman leaned head and shoulders out of the window.

She was bleeding from a wound in the forehead and the blood was running down over her cheeks to drip from the point of her chin.

'My husband and children are dead!' she cried in a high, thin voice and fell backwards out of sight.

Corbie is not a large place. The startled passers-by in the street knew very well who lived in the house, and they supposed that the woman was Mrs Francine Sauveur, twenty-six-year-old mother of two and wife of Georges Sauveur, who worked in an Amiens steel mill.

For many of them, however, it was their first glimpse of the woman. Mrs Sauveur rarely went out, the shutters of the house were always drawn and, unheard of in such a small community, she had not exchanged so much as five words with her neighbours in as many years.

Georges was better known. It was a rare evening when he did not drop into the neighbourhood tavern. A giant of a man, he was a moderate drinker, by local standards, and generally good-natured although rather taciturn. His surname means "saviour".

As Georges was only thirty years old and strong as a bull, it seemed unlikely that he would have died of natural causes, or the children either. Three men and women charged into the house while a fourth man ran for the village doctor.

Mrs Sauveur was lying unconscious on the floor in front of the living room window. There was no sign of Georges, but the children, Alexandre, three, and Alexia, ten months, were on a mattress in the middle of the floor, limp and lifeless as dead kittens, with small pools of fresh blood surrounding their heads.

The woman neighbour, a mother herself, fell to her knees and searched desperately for signs of life.

'They're dead!' she said in a shocked voice.

Mrs Sauveur was not, and the men picked her up and carried her out into the street. It was an unthinking act intended to take her away from the sight of her dead children and, when they got her outside, they did not know what to do with her.

Fortunately, the doctor, a comparatively young man with a neat beard and steel-rimmed glasses, came running up at that moment and ordered them to carry her back in. The temperature was below freezing and, whatever her injuries, exposure to the weather would scarcely be of benefit.

As far as the doctor could immediately determine, she was merely suffering from a small head wound. He was unable to decide what had made it, so he sent one of the men to telephone for the emergency ambulance in Amiens.

He then went to examine the children, but was only able to come to the same conclusion as the woman neighbour. They were dead, and of wounds in the head similar to their mother's.

The news that something terrible had transpired in the rue Tessier had passed like a chill wind through the village, and most of the population were now assembled in front of the house, alarmed and frightened.

The wildest rumours were being whispered behind cupped hand. Mrs Sauveur had been dressed in a long scarlet velvet gown. The children had been wearing brand-new clothes. Bizarre signs and diagrams had been drawn on the walls and floor with some sticky black substance. Strange books with exotic bindings and objects, the use of which no one knew, had been found arranged in purposeful and ominous patterns.

For a highly superstitious village such as Corbie, this signified only on thing.

Witchcraft!

The Amiens ambulance arrived quickly. The secondary road to Corbie was narrow and winding, but there was little traffic on it to slow the ambulance's progress.

Francine Sauveur was taken away to the hospital, still wearing her scarlet gown, the upper part now marked with a darker red.

Not so very surprisingly, no one in Corbie had called the police, but the ambulance crew did. They had little choice. They had seen the injuries to the heads of mother and children and they knew gunshot wounds when they saw them.

Although Corbie does not have a police force, it does have a village constable and, when the Amiens homicide squad arrived, they found him standing guard in the doorway of the living room of the Sauveur's home, eyeing the bodies of the children sorrowfully and the strange signs and objects apprehensively.

He had been one of the last to arrive at the scene and had immediately telephoned the Amiens police, only to be told that the homicide squad was already on the way.

'Do you know these people personally?' asked Inspector Louis Prevost, the elderly, greying chief of the rural homicide unit. 'Were they known sorcerers?'

It was a legitimate question. The French are strong believers in the supernatural and not a few villages around Amiens have their resident sorcerers or witches who earn a modest income through fortune-telling, dowsing, love potions and, something a little more sinister.

'Not to my knowledge,' said the constable. 'They're not from here. Only been here about five years, and they've kept pretty much to themselves, the woman more than the man.'

'Who found the bodies?' asked the inspector. 'Do you know?'

'I can find out,' said the constable.

'Tell them to report to me,' said the inspector. 'I want to talk to them.'

The constable left and the inspector went over to where Dr Leon Jacquin, the department's medical expert, was examining the bodies of the children.

'Small-calibre gunshot wounds in the head in both cases,' said the doctor, looking up. 'Two each at point-blank range. No other indications. It happened within the past hour.'

He stood up and began wiping his hands nervously. A small, thin man with a receding chin, he looked deceptively worried and upset even when he did not feel it.

'No indications of abuse?' said the inspector.

'None,' said the doctor, looking more concerned than ever.

Like many highly civilized countries, France was experiencing a rapid and enormous increase in sexual abuse of children, not infrequently by their own relatives.

'This is occult stuff here,' said Sergeant of Detectives Charles Grigny. 'Devil worship, maybe.'

A handsome, elegantly dressed young man with a fine black moustache, he had been examining the objects scattered about the room.

The inspector nodded.

'Ritual killing,' he said, 'but the use of a gun is unusual. Normally, they'd have been killed with a sword or a knife. This is more like an execution.'

'If there's nothing else . . . ?' said the doctor diffidently.

'Not now, Leon,' said the inspector. 'Why don't you go back to Amiens and see what condition the woman is in? Take the tape recorder. If the hospital will let you talk to her and she can make a statement, tape it.'

He turned to the sergeant.

'Go and talk to the neighbours and anybody else you can find who knows these people,' he directed. 'They'll probably know everything about them in a place like this. I'm calling Amiens to send out the full squad. I'm not quite sure what we're dealing with here.'

The sergeant was quite sure. For him, it was a clear-cut case of sorcery, or possibly devil worship, and his opinion was soon confirmed by the villagers.

Strange things had been going on in Corbie since the arrival of Sauveurs, they whispered in the low, guarded tones reserved for speaking of the dark powers. Cows had gone dry. Chickens had stopped laying. A pig had died.

The sergeant listened without comment, aware that he could have obtained similar statements from the residents of almost any village in the region, but not entirely sceptical. He too came from the country around Amiens. The stories were not totally without foundation. Things did happen.

However, in Corbie it seemed that there were things that could not be heard in almost any village. Knocks on the door late at night and, when the door was opened, no one there and no footprints in the new-fallen snow. Stealthy little sounds as if something were prowling about the locked and barred houses, trying to get in and, again, no tracks in the snow.

The sergeant's expression did not change, but inwardly he shuddered. He knew only too well the eerie

227

atmosphere that sometimes hung, thick and ghostly as the winter fog, over the impoverished little communities whose cows and pigs and chickens were not the livestock of prosperous farmers, but the desperate attempts of family fathers to supplement the inadequate income of unemployment compensation.

'Well?' said the inspector as the sergeant appeared at the kitchen door of the Sauveurs' house.

'Not much,' reported the sergeant. 'The people here think there was something loose in the village, and some of them thought it was the Sauveurs. Now, all of them do. Nothing concrete, of course. Very few of the people ever laid eyes on Mrs Sauveur.'

'I talked to the people who found the bodies,' said the inspector. 'They say that she called out that her children and her husband were dead, but he's not in the house or anywhere close to it. Maybe somewhere else in the village, but I doubt it.'

'He's the main suspect, I suppose?' asked the sergeant.

The inspector shrugged.

'Who else?' he said. 'It sure as hell wasn't robbery. These people are miserably poor.'

'Sauveur is supposed to be working,' said the sergeant.

'They had an expensive hobby,' said the inspector.

'The occult stuff?' guessed the sergeant.

'The occult stuff,' confirmed the inspector.

But, according to the specialists from the technical section of the Amiens police, the Sauveurs had not spent so very much on their hobby. Most of the equipment was home-made and many of the books had been stolen from the public library in Amiens. A great number of perhaps magic potions, consisting of infusions of plants which the Sauveurs had presumably gathered themselves in the fields and forests around the village, were stored in empty jam jars scavenged from the dump.

'Poor man's occult operation,' said the inspector. 'More dirt than devil.'

It was the following day and the police party was

back in Amiens, operations at the scene having been concluded.

The little bodies of the Sauveur children were spending Christmas Eve in the police morgue, the tops of their skulls sawn off so that Dr Jacquin could recover the bullets that had killed them.

Their mother was in hospital, partially paralysed, incapable of speech and mentally confused. The single twenty-two-calibre, long-rifle bullet which had ploughed through her brain had destroyed her as a functioning human being, but had cruelly left her alive. Dr Jacquin had been unable to obtain a statement.

The bullet in her head was assumed to be identical to those that had killed her children, but the doctors had decided that it would be too dangerous to try to remove it.

Otherwise, very little progress had been made in the investigation. The house was filthy dirty and there was neither heat nor anything to eat in it. Nine pictures of the children had been found carefully torn into tiny pieces. Five twenty-two-calibre, long-rifle empty cartridge cases had been recovered from the living room floor. Georges Sauveur was still the first and only suspect.

'It seems,' said the inspector, 'that they moved down to Corbie from somewhere up near Arras. Go up there and see if you can locate any relatives. Sauveur may have simply gone home. Here's an address they found in the house, but the name isn't Sauveur. Friend, maybe.'

The sergeant went to Arras. It was not a long trip, but it was an unpleasant one. A winter fog had drifted in from the English Channel and visibility was down to thirty feet. There was a good deal of ice on the road.

The address turned out to be that of Mrs Sauveur's parents, who expressed horror and astonishment at learning that Francine was seriously injured and her children dead. They had, they said, no idea who might be responsible.

The Montilets were a large family. Francine was the

seventh child out of twelve and, as her parents freely admitted, had always been strange.

She had dropped out of school while still in her teens, had severed relations with her family, refusing even to greet them in the street, and had supported herself by working as a cleaning woman.

'I don't think she hated us,' said her mother sorrowfully. 'It was more like she was afraid of her family.'

Her husband had not been. Although Francine had not invited any of her relatives to the wedding on 12 July 1975, they were on excellent terms with Georges, whom they described as hard-working and good-natured, although not intellectually outstanding.

He came from the same sort of lower middle-class family as Francine and had originally hoped to become a cook. He had, however, failed his examinations several times and, after his compulsory military service, had lived on unemployment compensation for three years before finding the job in Amiens and moving to Corbie.

The sergeant did not mention that Sauveur was the leading suspect in the murders of his children and the idea apparently did not occur to the Montilets. They were, in fact, concerned that something might have happened to him.

Having determined that they had no notion where he might be, the sergeant went to call on Sauveur's parents, who also expressed bewilderment and concern. They had not seen Georges in months, they said.

'Has he always been interested in the occult?' asked the sergeant. 'Even before he was married?'

The Sauveurs said that, to the best of their knowledge, Georges had never been interested in the occult, mainly because it required a good deal of reading and Georges was not strong on reading.

'That crazy woman he married may have been,' said Mrs Sauveur. 'They lived with us for two years while Georges was looking for work, but we never got to know her as well as we know the postman. Stayed locked in her room the entire time she was here. He had to take her meals up on a tray.'

'You didn't notice any strange markings on the floor or the walls after they left?' asked the sergeant.

'You couldn't see the floor or the walls,' said Mrs Sauveur. 'They were that dirty.'

The sergeant returned to Amiens no wiser than he had left.

'We've had a telephone call from the Veau d'Or in Boulogne-sur-Mer,' the inspector told him. 'They read about the murders in the newspaper and they wanted to know if the Sauveurs' reservation for Christmas Eve was cancelled.'

'The Sauveurs had a reservation at the Veau d'Or for Christmas Eve?' said the sergeant incredulously. 'That's a very expensive restaurant. I thought they were nearly starving to death.'

'The power company cut off the electricity at the beginning of November for nonpayment and Leon says the children were seriously undernourished,' said the inspector. 'There was no heat in the house, no means of cooking, and they were using candles for light, but Sauveur was still going to the tavern every night. I don't know what to make of it. You better run over there and see who made the reservation and under what circumstances.'

The sergeant, having just returned from Arras, was not enthusiastic about a trip to Boulogne-sur-Mer, which was on the coast south of Calais and over forty miles from Amiens. As it turned out, the information obtained was not worth the trip. The reservation had been made by Sauveur personally on December the seventh, for himself, his wife and the two children.

The Sauveurs had eaten at the restaurant before, although not often, and the owner knew them casually. He was aware that they had little money, but had not found it surprising that they should eat in an expensive restaurant.

In France, where a third of the family's income goes

on food and dining out is the most popular form of entertainment, it is not unusual for working-class people to save up for an entire year in order to have one magnificent dinner in a first-class restaurant, often at Christmas or New Year.

While the sergeant was in Boulogne-sur-Mer, the inspector had been having wanted posters printed, and police units throughout the area were alerted to keep an eye out for Georges Sauveur.

'I've ordered that all reports of suicides of adult males be sent to this office,' he said. 'While you were gone, we held a conference on the case and the consensus of opinion was that the Sauveurs were mixed up in some kind of occult business and decided to commit mass suicide. Sauveur lost his nerve when it came to himself, but, once he realizes the situation he's in, he may go through with it.'

'He wasn't contemplating suicide when he made the reservations at the Veau d'Or,' said the sergeant. 'Something must have happened to change his mind during those two weeks.'

'Maybe he was going to lose his job,' suggested the inspector, 'so they decided to have one big, last splurge and then end it all, but they ran out of money and had to give up the idea.'

'Could have spent what they had on the new clothes,' said the sergeant, 'but, if they were going to kill themselves anyway, why not have dinner first? They wouldn't need to worry about paying.'

The inspector shrugged.

'Lower-middle-class mentality,' he said. 'The people are basically honest. They're capable of murdering their children or each other, but they wouldn't dream of swindling a restaurant out of a free meal. It's a pity that these suicide-pact people always want to take the kids with them.'

'They don't want them left orphans,' said the sergeant.

'Would you rather be an orphan or dead?' asked the inspector.

232

'I'll have to think that over,' said the sergeant.

A check with the company for which Sauveur had worked showed that he had been in no danger of losing his job, and the sergeant prepared, a little nervously, to celebrate Christmas himself.

His apprehensions were promptly justified, for he had barely sat down to dinner with his family when the telephone rang and the duty officer informed him that he was wanted immediately at headquarters.

Georges Sauveur had been arrested by the railway police while trying to clamber over the guard rail of an overpass, with the apparent intention of flinging himself onto the tracks below.

Brought to the inspector's office, he immediately confessed to the shooting of his wife and children, and the twenty-two-calibre revolver found in his pocket at the time of the arrest was determined by the ballistics department to be the murder weapon.

Although Sauveur confirmed that the intention had been mass suicide of the entire family, he denied that there was any connection with the occult and placed the blame squarely on the injustices of French society.

'Other people were driving around in cars, living in fine homes,' he whined. 'Our electricity was cut off. It was cold in the house. We didn't have anything to eat. Society isn't fair.'

'But you had a good job,' said the inspector. 'Half the families in Corbie are worse off than you. What did you do with the money.'

'I spent some of it at the tavern,' said Sauveur.

The inspector sighed.

'And you had no interest in the occult?' he probed, changing the subject.

'I don't know much about it,' said Sauveur. 'Francine had a lot of books and things, but I don't read so good. She only got interested this last year when she saw a programme about witchcraft and devil worship on television. She thought we could get a lot of money that way, but all we ever got was messages from her grandma who's been dead since nineteen-sixty and ain't too right in the head any more.

'Francine had funny ideas. Said she was out of her body sometimes and she was afraid she wouldn't be able to get back in. Wanted us all to sleep on the floor so the earth currents would protect us.'

'But you didn't believe in those things yourself,' said the inspector.

Sauveur hesitated.

'There was something,' he admitted finally. 'Something was casting spells on us. That's why we didn't have any money. At night, you could hear it going around the house and sometimes it would scratch on the door, but, if you opened it, there wouldn't be nothing there.'

'Did you know that other people in Corbie had similar experiences?' said the inspector.

Sauveur nodded.

'They talked about it in the tavern,' he said. 'Corbie's an evil place. Francine hated it, and she said it hated her. She was afraid to go outdoors. She thought people would give her the evil eye.'

'Whose idea was it to kill yourselves?' asked the inspector, offering Sauveur the possibility to place the blame for the killings on his wife, who stood little chance of being brought to trail.

He did not find the man and his media-inspired whining about the inequalities of society sympathetic, but he did recognize that his mental level was too low for him to be held completely responsible for his actions.

Sauveur did not, however, take advantage of the opening.

'We worked it out together,' he said. 'I borrowed what money I could and we bought all new clothes so we'd look beautiful after we were dead, and the gun, but then we didn't have enough left to pay for the restaurant.

'We'd wanted to do it after dinner, but there wasn't going to be no dinner so Francine said, "Why wait?"

'We put on our new clothes then and Francine laid down on the mattress with one of the kids on each side of her. I was supposed to shoot her first, then Alexia, then Alexandre and then me.

'But Alexandre kept trying to get away and play, so I shot Alexia first. That scared Alexandre and he came to put his face against Francine's chest so I shot him in the back of the head.'

The detail was final confirmation of the accuracy of Sauveur's account. Only the police and the murderer knew Alexia and Francine had been shot in the forehead, but that the frightened little boy had died with his face pressed against his mother's breast.

Following the shooting, Francine lost consciousness and Sauveur thought that she was dead. Finding that he lacked the courage to shoot himself, he had fled and had been trying to throw himself under trains ever since.

Sauveur was indicted on two counts of premeditated murder, but Francine, permanently crippled mentally and physically, was found incompetent to stand trial.

Reading her husband's confession, she nodded to indicate that it was true and, in the only intelligible words she would ever bring out, croaked, 'Don't bury children in consecrated ground!'

The reason, according to her husband, was that she had come to believe that evil was stronger than good.

'She said, in a world like this, the devil has more mercy than God,' he said.

There was some question among the state psychologists as whether Sauveur was competent to stand trial, but it was eventually decided that, although of below normal intelligence, he understood that his acts were wrong and realized the consequences of them.

He was, therefore, brought to trial, with the prosecution calling for a sentence of twelve years. The Sauveurs, the prosecutor charged, were neither crazy nor underprivileged, but merely drunk, dirty and careless with money.

The jury not only agreed, but found the prosecution too lenient and, on 25 April, 1983, sentenced Georges to sixteen years' imprisonment.

Francine will remain for the rest of her life in an institution, and her final wishes concerning her children were not honoured.

Even though their lives and deaths were something of a confirmation of their mother's beliefs, Alexandre and Alexia were given Christian burials.

19

THE DEMONS DID IT

To the west of Rouen, where the Seine loops like some great, reluctant serpent across the eastern plains of France to the Atlantic, lies the little community of Le Trait, once a village, but now a suburb of that city of over a hundred thousand inhabitants.

Like many residential suburbs in France, it is not the most charming place in the world to live, being largely given over to endless rows of remarkably similar high-rise blocks of flats.

The shoddy housing did not, however, trouble Marielle Chesny. She had been born in Le Trait a scant ten years earlier and, for her, it was normal and home.

Or, rather the flat on the ninth floor of the building at 76 rue Clemenceau was home and, on Wednesday 10, December 1986, she was in a hurry to get there. Christmas was barely two weeks away, and Marielle had big plans for it.

At approximately five minutes before noon, she scampered up the steps to the front entrance, ran down the hall towards the lifts and was seized from behind by a man in jeans and anorak who pulled her so tightly against his body that she could neither breathe not cry out, clapped a hand over her mouth and bundled her down the dark stairs leading to the basement.

There, in the semidarkness, he stripped her, not tearing the garment away but removing them slowly with relished anticipation, wrapped her stockings around her head to muffle her screams and raped her.

He was a normally built adult male and Marielle was a little girl. The pain was so intense that she fainted.

When Marielle recovered her senses, she was lying on top of her clothing on the floor of the basement and bleeding heavily from her torn sex organs.

It hurt terribly to move, but she was so terrified of bleeding to death that she ignored the pain, crept to the foot of the stairs, dragged herself up the cold, gritty concrete steps and into the entrance hall.

It was empty. The time was now half-past twelve and the occupants of the buildings were having their lunch.

Naked, in shock and shaking so badly that she could hardly press the buttons, Marielle crept into the lift, took it to her floor and staggered down the hall to her parents' flat.

It was only when she reached the door that she began to whimper and cry out.

Marielle did not know it, but she had just become the first victim of what would later be known, in some quarters, as the Demons of Rouen.

Even if she had, she would not have been able to tell her parents what had happened to her, but it was not necessary. When her mother opened the door to find her daughter naked and with the blood running down her thighs, she knew at once.

Nearly as traumatized as her daughter, she screamed for her husband, who hurriedly wrapped Marielle in a blanket and carried her down to the car.

Mrs Chesny held her in her arms all the way to the hospital in Rouen, where she was taken immediately to the operating room as the damage to her genitals required minor surgery.

It was only after the Chesnys had been assured that her life was not in danger that it occurred to them to telephone the police.

Crimes against children being sadly common in progressive Western Europe, the Rouen police had a special unit for dealing with them.

The Chesnys' call was, therefore, transferred directly

to the Offences Involving Minors Investigation Section, generally known as OIMIS, where a sergeant of detectives called Yves Juscarde listened to the report and said that someone would be out immediately.

The someone was Sergeant Juscarde himself. A small, compactly built man with a grave, round, olive-skinned face and very correct manners, he came to the hospital, where the Chesnys were waiting for their daughter to come round from the anaesthetic, and drove with Chesny to Le Trait.

Although Marielle had been too hysterical to tell her parents where the attack had taken place, the sergeant could guess. He went directly to the basement, where he found Marielle's clothing and her school bag, both smeared with her blood.

While Chesny remained at the scene to prevent anyone from disturbing it, the sergeant returned to his car, called his office and requested a detection unit from the police laboratory to examine the basement for possible clues to the identity of the rapist. He then left Chesny to wait for the arrival of the technicians and drove back to the hospital in Rouen.

Marielle had not recovered consciousness, and the doctor told him that it would not be possible to question her for a long time, and possibly never. The extent of the emotional damage was not known, but it was severe.

This was what the sergeant had expected and, having left word that he was to be informed if there was any change in the situation, he returned to headquarters and reported to his section chief.

Inspector Jean-Marie Leboeuf listened to his report in silence. The case was more or less routine. Little girls were frequently raped in the great blocks of flats and, statistically, the rapist would be an adolescent youth living in the same building or a relative of the victim. The sergeant was experienced in such cases. There was no need to instruct him.

However, neither he nor the sergeant knew about the demons.

Two hours later, the technicians returned from Le Trait, bringing with them Marielle's clothing and school bag. It was all they had found.

That evening, the sergeant put half a dozen detectives on to questioning the occupants of the building. The evening was the best time as the maximum number of people would then be home.

The detectives were especially looking for information on two counts. Who had been in the building at noon that day, and who among the male residents had shown an unusual interest in female children.

The time of the attack indicated an adolescent. Most of the working men had been at lunch with their families or did not come home during the day at all.

All the adolescents came home for lunch. Either in school or unemployed, they ate at home because it was free.

The sergeant was not surprised when all the potential suspects turned out to be teenagers, nor when all of them denied any connection with the crime.

Two were detained briefly, but, there being no physical evidence against them, they were released.

'At least it wasn't a relative,' said the sergeant. 'Her parents are her only relatives in Le Trait.'

'And no reports of strangers in the building?' asked the inspector.

The sergeant shook his head.

'None,' he said, 'but that doesn't mean anything. The place is wide open. He could have followed her in from the street and grabbed her as soon as he saw there was nobody in the entrance hall. It wouldn't have taken him more than two minutes to get her down the stairs to the basement.'

The inspector scowled. He was a big man, not exceptionally tall but very thick-limbed and broad in the chest. His hair was straight, the colour of iron, and he wore it combed straight back.

'That would be worse than a teenager,' he observed.

'If it was an adult deviate, it could be the beginning of a series.'

'The computer's tagged to send up any similar reports,' said the sergeant. 'We'll have to hope there aren't any.'

There would be, though, and only two days later after the rape of Marielle Chesny. This time the scene was Canteleu, also a suberb of Rouen and also to the west of the city.

Ominously, the circumstances were nearly identical.

Eleven-year-old Annie Poiret had entered the block of flats where she lived with her parents at approximately four o'clock in the afternoon and had been seized by a man who carried her, struggling, to the basement.

He had removed her clothing without tearing it, but rather more quickly than had been the case with Marielle Chesny, and had raped her, holding a hand over her mouth to stifle her screams.

As Annie did not have the good fortune to pass out, the man strangled her until she did, but he did not kill her and fled as soon as she lost consciousness.

Once again, a naked, bleeding, hysterical little girl dragged herself out of the basement, but this time there were people in the entrance hall who came to her aid.

In a state of shock, Annie was unable to pronounce her parents' names, but some of the other tenants recognized her and she was soon on her way to the hospital.

In the excitement, no one thought to call the police or look for the attacker so that, by the time the computer switched the hospital report to the inspector's office, the rapist had had ample time to make good his escape.

Even so, the sergeant raced to Canteleu with a detachment, but all that was found was Annie's clothing with her blood on it.

In one respect, the Annie Poiret case was more favourable. She was not as profoundly traumatized as Marielle Chesny and, although the doctors would not let the police near her, she did describe the rapist to her mother.

It was, understandably, not a very exact description,

but it was useful. The man, she said was small and thin and wore jeans and an anorak. He had said nothing at all, but had made a sort of grunting noise while he was raping her.

Marielle Chesny would later confirm this description and add the detail that the rapist had a black moustache, but she was now still in hospital and had not yet made a statement to anyone.

The inspector was convinced by the similarity of the crimes that a series had begun.

'This is no adolescent kid,' he told the sergeant. 'He's an adult psychopath, and we're going to have to move fast if we want to prevent him from killing someone. A little more pressure on the Poiret girl's throat and we'd be investigating a homicide now.'

'This wasn't a copy of the first case either,' said the sergeant. 'We released nothing to the press except the flat statement that a minor had been raped in Le Trait.'

'No, it wasn't imitation,' said the inspector. 'And it wasn't an adolescent or a relative or friend of the family or anyone she knew and these are, probably, the only two such cases so far – in this area, at least.'

The sergeant nodded in understanding. Rape cases are often not reported, but the victims here were so young and had been so seriously injured that, had there been previous cases, there would be reports in the files – and there were none.

'I'll continue to work on the residents,' he said, 'but after that, I'm afraid . . .'

'. . . we'll have to wait for the next one,' said the inspector grimly, finishing the sentence.

None of the residents answered to the description furnished by Annie Poiret, and none could recall seeing a stranger in the building who did.

In the meantime, however, Marielle had recovered sufficiently to describe the rapist to her mother, and it was known that he was small, adult and had a moustache. It was enough for a sketch by the police artist, and wanted posters were printed and distributed.

The inspector had also arranged for extensive coverage in the local press. The near certainty that it had been the same man in both cases made the theory of a series highly probable, and it was important that parents and children be alerted to the danger.

'He's probably picking them out in the street and following them home,' said the inspector, 'but, in a lot of cases, the circumstances would not be favourable. Too many people around or the girl too far from the basement door.'

'He must look over the buildings in advance,' said the sergeant. 'Otherwise, how would he know where the basement door was?'

'Those low-rent buildings in the suburbs are all pretty similar,' said the inspector, frowning, 'but you're right. He'd have to know. If he made a mistake like dragging the girl into somebody's flat, it could be fatal.'

'If he looks over the buildings in advance, someone might notice him,' said the sergeant. 'We could run an appeal to the public for information on anything suspicious.'

'Not a public one,' said the inspector, 'because that would warn him. We might distribute handbills in the sort of block of flats he favours. No need to bother with Le Trait and Canteleu. Lightning may strike twice in the same place, but not child molesters.'

Five days later, on December the seventeenth, the rapist struck for the third time.

It was in Canteleu.

'Raving mad or wily as a fox,' said the inspector. 'This one's exceptional.'

The handbills were distributed. They produced no witnesses, but did result in a letter to the chief of police. In it, the writer said that demons were driving him to rape little girls and he wished the police would hurry up and catch him. He felt that what he was doing was dangerous.

It was an accurate impression. The latest little victim had barely survived.

243

Hugette Arnold was only eight years old and a delicately built child with long blonde hair and large china-blue eyes. Theoretically, she should have had nothing to fear from the rapist. Both the previous victims were dark-haired with brown eyes, and sex deviates normally show strong preferences for a specific type and colouration.

For that reason, the police were uncertain as to whether it was the same man. There were no witnesses and a statement from the victim was out of the question.

The doctors thought it would be years, at least, before she could confront what had happened to her. The experience had seriously affected her mind, and her physical injuries had been nearly fatal as there had been extensive loss of blood due to a rupture in the lower bowel. Major surgery had been required and the child was still in the intensive care unit.

As in the other cases, however, the attack had taken place in the basement of block of flats, and it was there that Hugette had been found. Smaller and weaker than Marielle and Annie, she had regained consciousness, but had lacked the strength to drag herself up the stairs.

It was only because a teenage boy who lived in the building had been passing the basement door and had heard her sobbing in the darkness below that she was discovered in time to save her life.

This hair's-breadth rescue caused the inspector to alter his policy on the case.

So far, only bare reports of the rapes had been furnished to the press. This was standard procedure for sex crimes involving minors. There were far too many disturbed persons at liberty who might be inspired to copy them.

Now, however, it had become obvious that parents would have to make frequent checks of basements in blocks of flats, particularly if a female child was unaccounted for.

All printable details of the three cases, with the exception of the names and addresses, were therefore released to the press, and an appeal was made to the public to come forward with any permanent information – such as reports by children of being followed or approached by strangers.

'He couldn't succeed every time,' said the inspector, 'but some parents are so stupid that they wouldn't report an incident to the police if the child was injured. We have to scare them.'

Apparently a good many were scared, for there was a flood of telephone calls, mostly anonymous, some well-intentioned, and not a few from mentally disturbed persons who, in some cases, sincerely believed themselves guilty of the crimes.

'We're checking them out as well as we can,' said the sergeant, 'but, so far, there's nothing promising. Maybe, when he strikes again. . . .'

But the rapist did not strike again. The year ended without reports of further incidents and, by the end of January 1987, the inspector was beginning to think that the series had ended.

'It was the publicity,' he said. 'It scared him more than the parents. We should have done that sooner.'

'Valoir says it's impossible to scare off a compulsive sex psychopath,' said the sergeant. 'Says they have no control over their actions.'

Valoir was Dr Simon Valoir, the senior medical expert attached to the Rouen Department of Criminal Investigations.

'Then he wasn't a psychopath,' said the inspector. 'He hasn't just gone somewhere else. The profile is with every police force in the country, and there've been no reports.'

'He could have been run over by a truck,' observed the sergeant optimistically.

The optimism was unwarrented. The rapist had not left the area, nor was he dead or disabled. It was merely that he was active only when the demons were active, and they had not been for some time.

Back in December, the demons had been raging so

that the human in which they nested could scarcely recognize himself. He was a pious man, a practising member of a strict Christian sect, and the father of two girls himself. They were now sixteen and eighteen, older than any of his victims.

He had not been frightened off by the publicity, as the inspector had surmised. When the demons were active, he was afraid of nothing, although, at other times, he was anything but brave. He was not a big man nor, under normal circumstances, very strong. Most people who knew him thought him something of a weakling.

But a hard-working, good-natured weakling who paid his round at the tavern and who was about as inclined to violence as a butterfly.

True, he had been a little quieter since his wife left him, and his experiments with the unwed mother of three, who had moved in briefly, and the eighteen-year-old swinger, whose stay had been even briefer, had left him jumpy and irritable.

Elizabeth was, it seemed, irreplaceable. They had grown up together, gone to school together, lived together for eighteen years. At the age of forty, he was too old to make the adjustment.

He had not given up entirely, however, and continued to read the classified ads for partners or, at least, he did when the demons were silent.

The demons were confusing, an improbable mixture of shame, fear, nausea, sorrow, lust and heart-splitting ecstasy. He could not remember clearly what had happened when they were there and, when they were not, he hoped and prayed that they would never return.

And yet, somewhere deep down in the most private inner depths of his being where he dared not look, he could feel them stirring, hot, red, wet as the blood from between the parted thighs of a girl child. One day, they would awake again.

On February the third they awoke.

Yvetot, a town of some eleven thousand inhabitants, lies nearly nine miles to the west of Rouen and, although the mothers of little girls there read the Rouen news-papers and were aware of the danger, they did not feel directly menaced. So far, all the attacks had taken place on the outskirts of Rouen.

On that cold, overcast Tuesday afternoon, thirty-one-year-old Paulette Fourgere was even less concerned about her little daughter than usual. Odette, eight years old and within the high-risk group, was absent, but she was not alone.

She had spent Monday night with her cousin, Denise Troisgros, who was a year younger and her favourite playmate. Now, after school, Denise was coming to the Fourgeres' to spend the night with Odette.

Paulette knew that everything was all right. When she had telephoned, her sister had said that the girls were just leaving.

That had been four o'clock, however, and now it was past five. Even allowing for the nonsense and running about of two lively little girls, Odette and Denise should have arrived.

For the tenth time, Paulette went to look out the fifth-floor living room window at the street below.

There were very few people about and, although the street lamps had come on, visibility was poor. A freezing winter fog had come creeping in from the English Channel, a scant twenty miles to the northwest, and was pouring through the streets like a sinister grey river.

Paulette gave an involuntary shudder and, although the flat was well heated, hugged herself as if to shut out the cold.

Suddenly, without warning, the newspaper reports of the raped children rose in her mind, clear as if they were engraved on the glass in front of her face.

Beneath them, in capital letters, were the warnings of the police.

IF THE CHILD IS MISSING, DO NOT WAIT. LOOK FOR HER IMMEDIATELY. ABOVE ALL, THE BASEMENTS OF BLOCKS OF FLATS . . .

With no knowledge of how she had got there, Paulette Fourgere found herself in the lift going down with what seemed agonizing slowness and a painfully beating heart.

She had just time to think, "I'm panicking!" when the lift door stopped, the door slid open and she was in the basement.

A dim white ceiling lamp was on, and what Paulette Fourgere saw by its diffused light was something that a great deal of psychiatric therapy would only allow her to live with but not to forget.

Fifteen feet away, a man wearing jeans and an anorak was kneeling between the grotesquely spread legs of a naked little girl; his hips jerking in the convulsive movements of orgasm.

At the sound of the lift door, he turned his head to look over his shoulder and, for an eternal moment, the gaze of rapist and mother met.

Then Paulette was on him, clawed fingers searching hungrily for his eyes, feet kicking at his genitals.

She had not seen the face of the child on the floor, but she knew. It was her child Odette.

The man, stumbled backwards, throwing up his arms to protect his face, but not before the raging mother's nails had drawn four parallel bloody grooves down his cheek.

He was not a large man, and she might well have killed him had Odette not began to wail in pain and terror.

Paulette turned to her wounded child and the man ran off up the stairs and disappeared.

But not from Paulette's mind. Every detail of his appearance was so burned into her memory that she would never be able to forget it for the rest of her life, although she would have given a great deal to do so.

'He was a small man,' she told inspector Leboeuf. 'Only an inch or two taller than I am. Scrawny build. He looked unhealthy and had frown lines on his forehead and between his eyes. He hadn't shaved that day. There was a pimple on the right side of his jaw. He was wearing . . .'

There was a great deal more. Odette was in the hospital and so was Denise, although only Odette had been raped. Trussed like a turkey with her own clothing, Denise had been forced to watch her cousin's torment, and it had been necessary to place her under sedation.

The children safely in the hospital, Paulette had gone at once to the police in Rouen and had done such a good job of describing the rapist that the police computer was able to produce the file of a potential suspect, although he had but a single charge on his record.

On 7, January 1984, Alain Toutain, a forty-year-old pipefitter, had been charged with indecently exposing himself to a nine-year-old girl in Barentin, his home town, which was five miles east of Yvetot. He had admitted the offence but claimed he had been drunk, and the charges had been dropped.

Taken into custody, Toutain, who had four fresh deep scratches on his left cheek, at once admitted to the rapes of Odette, Hugette, Annie and Marielle.

It was not he who had done these things, he told the inspector earnestly. It was the demons. They had taken control of his body and he could not rid himself of them. The only solution was to lock him up. The demons would be unable to do anything then.

The inspector found this an excellent idea and, after Toutain had been under psychiatric observation for some time, so did the doctors.

Whether it was demons or dementia that made Alain Toutain dangerous, the effect was the same and on 11, September 1987, he was committed to an institution for the criminally insane, where his chances of recovery are deemed to be slight.

20

TAILOR TO TART

March the sixteenth was a little early for wild asparagus, but it was a Sunday and a beautiful sunny day. Even if there was no asparagus, it was worth a stroll in the country.

Actually, there was nothing exceptional about the weather. Spring in Florence, is normally warm and sunny, and 1986 was no exception.

Luigi Capelli therefore set off shortly after lunch in his elderly Fiat, which was parked beside the Via Bolognese to the northwest of the city and, by two o'clock, was strolling leisurely over the fields in a not very sincere search for asparagus.

He did not find any, but, to his indignation, he did come upon a number of bright blue municipal rubbish sacks scattered over an area of several hundred yards. Obviously, one of the slum barbarians to be found in any city of nearly half a million had decided it was too much trouble to take his refuse to the dump.

The sight and smell enraged Capelli, who like many Florentines, was a man with a strong sense of civic pride. He ran forward and gave the nearest sack a violent kick.

His impulsive action only made the pollution worse. The mouth of the sack was tied with thin string, which promptly snapped and allowed the contents to spill out.

Something like rotting cabbage rolled away and, suddenly, Capelli's nostrils were assaulted by the most vile stench he had ever encountered in his entire life.

Choking and retching, he turned and ran off for a short distance, but then stopped.

250

What kind of rubbish could this be that stank so frightfully?

Holding his breath and walking on tiptoe as if he were afraid of stirring up whatever was in the sacks, he circled back to where the cabbage lay, a yard and a half from the open sack, and bent over to look at it more closely.

Peering up at him from sockets swimming with the yellow-greenish fluids of putrefaction were two dull brown eyes. The withered layers peeling away from the cabbage were not dead leaves. They were strips of rotting skin and flesh.

Capelli turned around, bent over double and vomited so violently that he nearly strangled.

Feeling weak, sick and on the verge of fainting, he staggered off in the direction of his car.

Forty minutes later, the Florence homicide squad arrived at the scene.

It consisted of a large number of specialists, technicians and detectives, a photographer, a medical expert and the officer in charge, Chief Inspector Luciano Matteoli, a short, dark, intense sort of man with tightly curled blue-black hair.

Although the inspector looked as if he should be impatient and talkative, he was neither, and he waited in patient silence while Dr Giuseppe Recco, a big, handsome man with smooth pink cheeks and rimless glasses, supervised the removal of the rotting chunks of human body from the sacks to a sheet of heavy plastic.

'Well, it's human and it's been dead for over a month,' said the doctor finally. 'Can't say with certainty whether it was a man or a woman. I'll have to get it to the autopsy room before I can determine anything definite.'

'Will you be able to then?' asked the inspector. 'The condition looks terrible to me.'

'Oh I think so,' said the doctor. 'It's not as bad as it looks, at least for my purposes. Seems to be all there.'

'Some clothing too,' remarked Sergeant of Detectives Mario Antonelli. 'Must have been a woman. Those look like frilly underpants. A man wouldn't wear such things.'

'Some would,' said the doctor.

The inspector and the sergeant looked at him questioningly, but he did not seem prepared to expand on his statement.

The twenty-nine pieces of the corpse, none of them larger than the head, were wrapped up in the plastic sheet, lifted into a metal coffin and taken away to the morgue. The rubbish sacks which had contained them were wrapped in another sheet and taken to the laboratory.

In the meantime, the detectives and technicians had formed a line and were passing slowly, heads bent, across the field, putting any artificial objects found into little plastic boxes tagged with the coordinates of their location as shown on a grid map of the area.

Sergeant Antonelli, a slender, wiry man with a long drooping black moustache, was directing the operation with a rather mournful expression which was, however, his normal one.

The inspector and the doctor returned to police headquarters with the corpse, and the doctor immediately began the autopsy while the inspector went to wait in his office. Until he had more information, there was nothing he could do.

He had expected a quick autopsy report, as he did not think much could be done with the pieces of rotting flesh, but he had still heard nothing from the doctor by the time the others returned from the scene at seven o'clock.

'Great many things found,' said the sergeant, dropping wearily into the chair behind his desk and tucking a cigarette into the corner of his mouth, 'But I doubt that any of it has a connection to the murder. We all think that the sacks were just brought there and dumped.'

'Probably were,' agreed the inspector, 'But we have to go over the area anyway. You can never tell. Recco still hasn't reported.'

'Want me to check on him?' asked the sergeant.

'No,' said the inspector. Go home and have your dinner. I'll look in on him myself.'

The sergeant was, however, curious and went with the inspector to the morgue. There was something disturbing about the corpse which both he and the inspector had sensed, even though they were unable to define clearly what it was.

'Some interesting aspects,' commented the doctor, washing his hands at the sink. 'I was just about to come over to your office.'

'Your finished then?' said the inspector, looking askance at the body, which had been reassembled like some ghastly three-dimensional jigsaw puzzle on the marble slab. It still did not look very human.

'For today,' said the doctor. 'I have a few tests to run tomorrow.'

'And?' said the inspector.

'Date of death was around February the fifteenth,' said the doctor, 'and the cause was a fractured skull. Murder weapon was a heavy, smooth, cylindrical object approximately one and a half inches in diameter. Probably a walking cane. The corpse was cut up with a handsaw, bones, flesh and all.'

'Was she sexually abused?' asked the sergeant. 'Could you tell that?'

'Was she she?' said the doctor. 'This was a person of indeterminate sex, neither man nor woman – or, if you prefer, both.'

'A true hermaphrodite?' said the inspector. 'Isn't that terribly rare?'

'It's not common,' conceded the doctor. 'Fortunately. This one was artificial, however. She'd had a sex-change operation.'

'Male to female, I take it?' said the inspector. 'That could make her easier to identify. Anything else?'

'Not tonight,' said the doctor. 'I'll check for traces of narcotics tomorrow. You'll have the full report by noon.

253

I've sent what was left of her underwear to the laboratory.'

The doctor left the morgue and the investigations officers followed him. Instead of going directly home, however, they walked in unspoken agreement the short distance to the small taverna where many of the headquarters police took their meals and drinks.

'Well?' said the sergeant after the waiter had brought a pitcher of Brunello and left. 'What do you think?'

'Not too tough,' said the inspector. 'Kinky, but not difficult. The motive was almost surely unrequited love, jealousy, something personal. That means once we identify her, the suspect or suspects will become obvious. All we have to do is prove it.'

'And identify her,' the sergeant pointed out. 'It certainly won't be by sight, and those fingers didn't look to me as if they'd yield prints.'

'Perhaps not,' said the inspector, 'but don't forget, she's unusual. There can't be that many people who've switched from man to woman in Florence.'

There were, according to the best estimates available nearly a hundred, most of whom were working either as female impersonators in the nightclubs and bars which featured such entertainment, or as prostitutes.

'That's not such a terribly big group,' said the inspector bravely. 'You should run through that in no time.'

The sergeant looked more mournful than ever, but said nothing.

'Start with the underwear,' suggested the inspector. 'The lab got a label out of it. It's from an exclusive sort of boutique in the Viale Marrini. They may know of some customer who's not been around for a while.'

The sergeant left the office, still without speaking. He already knew about the underwear, which was the only clue that had resulted from the investigation so far. Dr Recco had been able to detect traces of what he thought were sleeping pills in the corpse, but this yielded no clue to the victim's identity. Efforts to obtain fingerprints had failed.

As the murderer had sawed through it and as it had been subjected to the corrosive liquids resulting from the decomposition of the body, the underwear was in such a state that the sergeant had little hope of the boutique's salesgirls even recognizing it as underwear, but, to his surprise, they not only identified it as having come from their shop, but were able to provide him with the names of several customers who bought such underwear.

'All show-business people,' said the manageress.

'Not whores?' asked the sergeant, gazing expressionlessly at a split-crotch model in scarlet lace.

'Well, that too, I suppose,' said the manageress. 'It's sort of the entertainment field too, isn't it?'

'How many of these people have been in here during the past month?' asked the sergeant.

There was a consultation among the salesgirls and it was eventually decided that nearly all the customers for the type of underwear in question had been in – with the exception of two.

Once he was told their stage names and the names of some of the places where they performed, the sergeant had little difficulty in tracing them and, contrary to all expectations, obtained his identification easily.

One of the transsexuals was alive and well. The other had not been seen since the middle of February, when she had mysteriously failed to turn up for her performance in a local nightclub, although she had money coming to her.

'Not a real girl,' said the nightclub owner, 'but a very, very reasonable facsimile thereof. Even the people who knew Jackie was Alfredo didn't care.'

The victim's name had been Alfredo Tolaba originally, but she had become Alfreda, the feminine form of the name, after the sex-change operation. Jackie was her professional name.

She was thirty-four years old at the time of her disappearance and had earned her living as a striptease artist

and prostitute. Before that, she had been an assistant to
a stage magician.

The sex business had paid well. Alfreda had been
unusually pretty and the operation had been such a success that only a doctor could be certain that she had not
been born a girl.

'It wasn't all business,' said the sergeant. 'We found
a couple of pounds of love letters, photos, all sorts of
things that a girl involved in a series of love affairs might
have.'

He had just returned from Alfreda Tolaba's rather
plush flat at 13 via delle Oche, where a detachment
from the police laboratory was still carrying out a careful
examination of the contents.

'We have confirmation of identification,' said the
inspector. 'The dentist recognized her bridgework.'

One of the most important results of the search of
Alfreda Tolaba's flat was the name of her dentist. He
was brought to the police morgue, where he managed to
identify his dental work in the rotting jaws before being
overcome by nausea and going off to vomit.

'There are going to be a lot of suspects,' said the
sergeant. 'She was not a girl to settle down with a husband or a single boy friend. She played the field, and
there'll be a good many jealous lovers, rejected lovers,
disappointed lovers and, probably, just plain crazy
lovers. A man who would take up with a person like
that would be pretty weird himself.'

'It's possible it was someone who thought that she
really a girl and lost his head when he found out she was
female only by the grace of surgery and silicone,' said
the inspector. 'That could be quite a shock to a lot of
men.'

'It would be to me,' assented the sergeant. 'Anyway,
we're checking all the names we found in the flat. Incidentally, she seems to have been pretty much into the
occult. Sizeable library on the subject and a bunch of
trick stuff that the lab is still trying to work out.'

Over from her days as assistant to the stage magician,

no doubt,' said the inspector. 'Might not be a bad idea to have a talk with him too.'

Alfreda's former employer, The Great Gorbanzo, was, in private life, forty-four-year-old Aldo Prodini. A distressingly clumsy stage magician, he supplemented his income through the sale of good-luck charms, love philtres and, according to some, less benign forms of occult intervention.

'Supposed to be in Sicily at the moment,' said the sergeant, 'but I don't think we'll ever be able to prove where he was at the time that Tolaba was murdered. He's slippery enough even when he isn't trying to cover up anything.'

'We might find witnesses who saw him with her at the time,' said the inspector, 'but that would still leave the question of motive. Were he and Alfreda anything more than associates in show business?'

'Everyone assumes they were,' answered the sergeant, 'but there's no evidence. Some say that he's homosexual, but I suppose that wouldn't matter with Miss Tolaba. Or would it? The sex relations in this case confuse me.'

'No more so than the participants,' said the inspector. 'What else do we have?'

'Three men known to have had recent affairs on a noncommercial basis with the deceased,' said the sergeant. 'We're trying to trace their movements and whereabouts around the middle of February. Don't think we'll have much luck. The most promising is the most recent. Bernardo Leocci, aged thirty, bisexual. He was still going with her when she disappeared. Didn't report her missing, though.'

'You were able to trace all the men whose names you got from the flat?' asked the inspector.

'All the men, yes,' said the sergeant. 'We have one mystery woman or, maybe, man. It's a recent photo of a pretty ugly person in women's clothing. She's made up like a tart, but somebody wrote on the back "Cornuto", which would indicate it was a man.'

Cornuto means "horned", and is the Italian term for

a man whose wife is deceiving him with others. It is a common insult.

'No name or address for Cornuto,' said the sergeant, 'but a lot of others, including one for a Mrs Maria Ponessa in Argentina. Probably of no significance to the investigation, but we've asked the Argentine police to help us out. Could be a relative of the victim.'

The response from the Argentine police was not immediately forthcoming and, in the meantime, a number of potential suspects were eliminated.

The Great Gorbanzo was found to be not only in Sicily, but in jail there. He had been in jail since the first of the year for selling a woman a potion to put in her husband's coffee.

This was supposed to render him less susceptible to the charms of other women, and its effects were not misrepresented for it contained such a high proportion of a common insecticide that, had the husband drunk much of it, his interest in women and everything else would have ceased. However, as it did not taste very good, he had drunk only a little and had survived.

Not long after the disappearance of The Great Gorbanzo from the suspect list, a letter was received directly from Mrs Maria Ponessa in Argentina.

She wrote that she did not know anyone named Alfreda Tolaba, but that she wanted the police to look for her husband, Domingo Ponessa.

She and her daughters were starving, she complained, and Domingo had not sent them a cent since the beginning of February.

There is something very funny going on with Domingo [wrote Mrs Ponessa]. On February the tenth, I received a photograph of him in the mail and he was dressed up as a woman. Our daughters thought this very funny, but I do not.'

This case gets more weird all the time,' said the inspector. 'See if you can locate this Domingo Ponessa, and I'll try to contact the wife over the telephone. Maybe she can give us an address.'

Mrs Ponessa could not, and what she had to say concerning her husband left the inspector more puzzled than ever.

Domingo Ponessa was a not-very-good men's tailor who had been born in Palermo, Sicily, but who had spent thirty of his forty-nine years in Florence.

In the hope that the Argentinos might be less demanding in their tailoring requirements, he had emigrated with his wife and their two daughters, aged fifteen and sixteen, to Buenos Aires in August 1984.

As it turned out, the Argentinos had been even more particular than the Florentines and, in September 1985, Ponessa had returned to Italy alone, as he lacked the fares for the rest of the family.

At first, things had gone no better in Florence, but, at the end of October, he had written to say that he had found well-paid work and would be able to send the return fares for Mrs Ponessa and the girls within a few months. He included money.

The optimistic letters and money had continued to arrive up until February the tenth, when she received the envelope containing no letter, but a picture of her husband wearing women's clothes and make-up. There was no return address and the writing on the envelope was not Domingo's.

Since then, she had heard nothing.

The inspector told Mrs Ponessa to go to the Italian consulate, which would arrange for her and her daughters passage back to Florence.

'Notify the foreign office that they're wanted as material witnesses in a homicide case,' he told the sergeant. 'The prosecuting attorney's office will pick up the cost of the return fares.'

'You consider Ponessa a suspect?' said the sergeant.

'I think he must know something about this business,' said the inspector. 'His wife's name and address was found in the victim's flat and, in the photo, he was a man dressed like a woman. So was the victim.'

'Well, a little more than dressed,' the sergeant pointed out.

'Whatever,' said the inspector.

The arrangements for the return of Mrs Ponessa and her daughters were made and the search for the husband and father began.

It was unsuccessful, and the police soon determined that Ponessa was not in Florence. He would have to be earning his living either as a tailor or as a transvestite entertainer, and those possibilities were soon exhausted.

However, it was known that Ponessa came from Palermo, and the police in Sicily requested to help in the search. Fugitives often return to their home towns.

Ponessa had, and as the Palermo police having excellent facilities for locating such exotic individuals as a tailor making a living as a striptease artist, he was soon in custody. At the time of his arrest, he was performing a not very seductive strip routine in a club catering to sexually confused people.

Brought back to Florence, Ponessa said he had murdered Alfreda and he was glad.

It was she, he said, who was responsible for his becoming a woman part of the time. Granted, he had made money at it, but then she had disgraced him with his wife and daughters. She was a witch who deserved to die.

Ponessa apparently believed in all sincerity that his transsexual friend had cast a magic spell over him which turned him into a woman whenever he dressed like one.

He had first met Alfreda in October 1985 when she approached him on the street with an offer of sexual services.

Ponessa had replied that he did not have even the price of a good meal, and Alfreda, who had apparently taken a liking to him, said that this time would be on the house with dinner thrown in.

The dinner was an offer that Ponessa could not refuse, particularly as he did not realize that Alfreda had started out life as a man.

She had told him later, and assured him that he could earn enough in the same manner to support his family and bring them back to Italy.

Ponessa had replied that he was prepared to do anything to discharge his duties as a husband and father, but he could hardly afford a sex-change operation.

Alfreda had said that this would not be necessary. She was a practitioner of the black arts and could perform a little ceremony which would make a woman out of him when required, but leave him a man when off duty.

The tailor, a simple man with little education and a firm belief in the occult, had agreed, and there had been a ceremony in Alfreda's flat involving chanting, clouds of coloured smoke, fresh blood bought from the local pig butcher and a great deal of sex.

'It worked just the way she said it would,' he told the inspector earnestly. 'All I had to do was put on make-up and get into women's clothing and I was a woman. There was all kinds of money in it.

Alfreda shouldn't have sent that picture to my wife. How would you like your wife and daughters to see you wearing make-up and a satin mini-skirt with black net stockings and high heels?'

The inspector made no reply. He could think of none that was appropriate.

Ponessa and Alfreda had quarrelled over the division of a payment for an act they had performed together, and Alfreda, who was inclined to be bitchy, had sent Maria the picture. She showed Ponessa a copy and told him what she had done the following day.

Ponessa had pretended forgiveness and invited her to a reconciliation dinner at his studio in the via Ariosto.

He had laced her soup with sleeping pills and, once she had lost consciousness, had beaten her to death with a walking stick.

For no reason that he could explain, he had left the corpse in a tub of warm water until it became stiff, and only then had cut it up with a handsaw, put the pieces into the rubbish sacks and taken them to the tip for disposal.

Understandably, Domingo Ponessa was the subject of a lengthy psychological study. This resulted in the opinion that, although he was sane and realized the consequences of his actions, he was also sincerely convinced of the magic powers of the victim.

Although he had earned a comparatively large amount of money not only as a striptease artist but also as a prostitute, he was not homosexual and had found the work disgusting. He had done it quite simply to support his family.

This was taken into consideration by the court, as was the extreme provocation to which Ponessa had been subjected and on 20 March 1987, he was sentenced to the modest term of four years imprisonment.

His wife and daughters were present at the trial and promised that they would wait for him to get out of prison.

After the trial had ended, the inspector and the sergeant repaired to the taverna to share another pitcher of Brunello in thoughtful silence.

'That tailor was nearly fifty years old and skinny as a goat,' said the sergeant, after a long interval. 'He looked no more like a woman than I do. How in the name of God could he make a living as a prostitute?'

'It was magic,' said the inspector.